THE
BLACK
FOLDER

Personal
Communications
on the
Mastery of Hoodoo

edited by
catherine yronwode

Missionary Independent
Spiritual Church

→ 2013 ←

The Black Folder:
Personal Communications on the Mastery of Hoodoo
Edited by catherine yronwode

Texts used by permission of the following authors,
who retain co-copyright to their individual contributions and have granted
Missionary Independent Spiritual Church (MISC) the right to print and reprint their contributions:

Pages 4-7, 15-16 © 2013 catherine yronwode and MISC; pages 8-9, 10-11, 17-18, 19-20, 39-40, 43-45,
63-64, 82-83, 90-91 92-93, 101-102, 103-104, 105-107, 113-114, 115-116, 119-120, 121, 122-123, 126-
127 © 1995, 2002, 2013 catherine yronwode, Lucky Mojo Curio Company, and MISC; pages 21-23 ©
2011, 2013 catherine yronwode and MISC; pages 29-30 © 1995, 2008, 2013 catherine yronwode and
MISC; pages 53-56, 109 © 2012, 2013 catherine yronwode and MISC; pages 65-67 © 2008, 2010, 2013
catherine yronwode and MISC; pages 68-70 © 2009, 2013 catherine yronwode and MISC; pages 71-73 ©
2011, 2012, 2013 catherine yronwode and MISC; pages 110-112 © 1995, 2011, 2013 catherine yronwode
and MISC; pages 12-14 © 2009, 2013 Dr. James Dotson and MISC; pages 24-26 © 2009, 2013 Prof.
Charles Porterfield and MISC; pages 27-28 © 2013 Dr. E. and MISC.; pages 31-33 © 2012, 2013 Dr. E.
and MISC.; pages 36-38 © 2011, 2013 Dr. E. and MISC.; pages 34-35 © 2013 Lou Florez and MISC;
pages 128-130 © 2012, 2013, Lou Florez and MISC; pages 41-42 © 2009, 2013 Lara Rivera and MISC;
pages 46-48 © 2012, 2013 ConjureMan Ali and MISC; pages 49-50 © 2013 ConjureMan Ali and MISC;
pages 51-52 @ 2010, 2013 Sister Robin Petersen and MISC; pages 57-62, 133-134 © 2013 Dr. Johannes
Gårdbäck and MISC; pages 74-76 © 2013 Michele Jackson and MISC; pages 77-79 © 2011, 2013
Valentina Burton and MISC; pages 80-81 © 2012, 2013 Marin Graves and MISC; pages 84-85 © 2008,
2013 Tanisia Mooney-Greer and MISC; pages 86-87, 108 © 2012, 2013 Sindy Todo and Susan Diamond
and MISC; pages 88-89 © 2013 Khi Armand and MISC; pages 94-97 © 2010, 2013 Miss Bri Saussy and
MISC; pages 98-100 © 2013 Deacon Millett and MISC; pages 117-118 © 2009, 2013 Ms. Robin York and
MISC; pages 124-125 © 2011 Missionary Independent Spiritual Church; pages 131-132 © 2013 Elvyra
Curcuruto-Love and MISC; pages 135-136 © 2013 Kast Excelsior and MISC.

artwork:
charlie wylie, catherine yronwode, Dr. E., Dr. Lea Goode-Harris

typesetting and production:
catherine yronwode, nagasiva yronwode

First Printing 2013, Second Printing 2014, Third Printing 2016

Published by
Missionary Independent Spiritual Church
6632 Covey Road
Forestville, California 95436
MissionaryIndependent.org

ISBN: 0-9836483-7-9
ISBN13: 978-0-9836483-7-6

Printed in Canada.

THE BLACK FOLDER
Table of Contents

INTRODUCTION
catherine yronwode

This book has been a long time in the making. The earliest portions of it were written about 20 years ago for publication in a now almost forgotten region of the internet known as the Usenet (yes, with the definite article and capital "U"). I joined the Usenet in the mid 1990s, after a couple of years in the transient arena of private bbs and listserv communication. My second marriage had ended, my daughter was grown up, and i had lots of time to write, because none of my boyfriends lived with me.

The Usenet was a strange free-for-all virtual space where people could discuss whatever interested them in neatly threaded and mostly unmoderated forums called newsgroups. There were newsgroups for everything from the practice of magic (alt.magick) to the worship of the goddesses Kali, Astarte, and Inanna (alt.fan.kali.astarte.inanna). My "own" newsgroup — and the very idea of "owning" a newsgroup was part of the ridiculous fun of being there — was alt.lucky.w, which was bestowed upon me by one Carlos "Froggy" May, who also hosted proto-steampunk flash-mobs in the weirdly obscure alt.current-events.blizzard-of-93 newsgroup. In alt.lucky.w i began to write about my lifelong collection of folkloric good luck charms.

Most of the writers in the Usenet were educated, erudite, and only slightly socially maladjusted. I met many interesting people there — including, i am happy to say, my future husband nagasiva — and i began to use the place as a venue to reply to my email in public, in an attempt to discourage people from sending me email. Since many of the emails i received contained queries about folk-magic, i became a fairly prolific poster in magical usenet newsgroups.

Back in 1987 i had become interested in Apple's then brand-new Hypercard application. This cool little object-oriented forerunner to hypertext (and hence to the world wide web and wikis) set me on the path of attempting to externalize and interlink all the data in my mind (an as-yet-incomplete project). In 1994, while seeking out more robust forms of interlinkage, i was taught how to write web pages in hand-coded html by my long-time collaborator Fred Burke. My first web pages were hosted by a kindly helper at a university in North Carolina, secreted away inside a folder reserved for material on sustainable agriculture. (I was a staff editor at *Organic Gardening* magazine at the time.)

In 1995, i set forth to migrate all of my texts from the Usenet and private listservs to the nascent world wide web, starting with the alt.lucky.w material on folk-magic, which i decided to call the Lucky W Amulet Archive. A batch of material from alt.sex.magick became the Sacred Sex Archive. From an elist on sacred geometry, i retrieved my texts for a web site titled Sacred Landscape. And so it went.

It's difficult to believe now, in the days of cheap bandwidth, but i was paying $250.00 per month for internet connection on a dial-up modem. In 1996 i took the plunge, bought my own web domain, and "/~yronwode" became LuckyMojo.com. There were no secure shopping carts and no Google search results, but people found the Lucky Mojo Curio Company and ordered my hand-made herbal oils, imported amulets, and incense powders. Those LMCCo. sales kept me in Macintosh upgrades and my dear colleague and co-worker Susie Bosselmann in paychecks.

My internic handle was cy182 and my husband-to-be's was tn86. When we actually met in meat-space in 1998, it was a marriage made in tech-sex-heaven. We were wed as the Great Odometer tripped over from 1999 to 2000. Nagasiva's generous attention to our online activities, plus the fact that he has always seen to it that i am well-fed and warm, has allowed me to write thousands of web pages and several books, to teach, and to answer the call to pastor at Missionary Independent Spiritual Church. A co-founder of YIPPIE (the Yronwode Institution for the Preservation and Popularization of Indigenous Ethnomagicology) and AIRR (the Association of Independent Readers and Rootworkers), nagasiva is my shining star.

Meanwhile, Lucky Mojo customers wanted product information. Not all of them had internet access, so i designed printed paper catalogues, and filled them with tech-hopeful pointers to my sprawling online free book "Hoodoo in Theory and Practice." Verbally conveying these URLs to customers over the phone was daunting, and the web pages were unwieldy for Susie to print on demand, so in 2002 i condensed the most-often requested pages and set them in tiny type in order to fit them onto nine hand-out sheets. For more than ten years, those flyers have gone into every package we have mailed out and into every shopping bag handed across the counter in the shop.

In 2005, i began giving informal workshops to my new employees and interested customers, mostly around the time of my birthday in May, when the roses were in bloom. These workshops were mini-extensions of my ongoing apprenticeship program, broken down into individual topics and geared toward people who were new to the subject matter. At these workshops in 2005, 2006, and 2007, i either gave out shop flyers or Susie would print out copies of relevant pages from "Hoodoo in Theory and Practice" to distribute as documentation.

In 2008 my friend Robin York set forth to restructure our informal get-togethers, creating out of my hippie chaos MISC's current Hoodoo Workshop program. It was she who planned the first formal MISC workshop at which there would be additional teachers beyond myself. This program was held at the Home of Truth Spiritual Center in Alameda, California, and while Robin prepared the venue and catered the dinner, i hit on the idea of giving printed hand-outs and goody-bags to class attendees. My teaching colleagues were taken off-guard by this — and, on their behalf, i will admit that it had not occurred to me that not all teachers are writers, much less typesetters.

The result of my impulsive plan was that good old Shop Hand-Out No. 1 and 2 was pressed into service at a "Candle Magic" class taught by Dara Anzlowar, while material i had previously written about mojo bags was quickly re-cast into a new flyer for Dr. Kioni to present. Christopher Warnock, who was scheduled to co-teach (and write a book) with me on astrology and hoodoo, cancelled his appearance at the last moment, and so i wrote my own text, "Astrology for Conjure Doctors" and gave the lecture as a solo act. A fourth workshop, Robin York's "Gambling Spells," was delivered impromptu over the fabulous dinner she had prepared, and there was no flyer for it at all.

We only taught five workshops that year, and the big hit was "Spiritual Foot Washing," ably brought forth by Tanisia Mooney, with her own well-written hand-out to accompany it. Having been in the publishing business for years, i knew the value of copyrights, and Tanisia's flyer was the first that MISC published under a joint-copyright agreement whereby either party can reprint the text, with royalties paid for commercial distribution only. All of the texts in this volume, therefore, are co-owned by MISC and the authors, with the authors sharing in royalties from the sale of this book on a pro-rated per-page basis.

The 2009 May Workshops program was sad, because Susie was in hospice and would not be with us anymore, but we had a wonderful get-together, back in Forestville, adeptly aided and abetted by the Texas Trio of Lara Rivera, Starr Casas, and Professor Charles Porterfield. We taught nine classes, one of which, the Jack Ball Master Class, was limited to my Hoodoo Rootwork Correspondence Course graduates only, and counted as part of their Apprenticeship training.

Lara contributed a flyer on "Container and Bottle Spells" and Charles wrote about "Oil Lamps," Robin York gave a "Cursing With Doll-Babies" class, and Dr. James Dotson introduced us to "Hoodoo Perfumes and Incenses." Starr taught her own "Practical Money Spells," but for text she distributed my old Shop Hand-Out No. 7 and 8, drawn from 1995 web pages. Lara and Starr collaborated on "Spiritual Foot Washing," at which the hand-out was Tanisia's flyer from the previous year. I wrote my own flyer for a "Tea Leaf Reading" class at which each attendee was given a porcelain fortune telling cup and a 96 page book on how to read the leaves. The only undocumented classes were Carin Huber's workshop on "Portable Altars" (dozens of bright and beautiful things to assemble, all crafts, all the time), and "Drink Your Sins, Drink Your Prayers," a hoodoo healing by Lukianos.

The 2010 May Workshops marked the beginning of two new traditions. With the visionary help of the Lucky Mojo shop manager, Sister Robin Petersen, we expanded my Apprenticeship Program into a robust community study venue, and Sister Robin presented her first annual Conjure Cook Off and Recipe Round-Up, on the topic of "Herb Use Methods for Kitchen Witchery." In addition to the hand-out and a banquet of wondrous foods to taste and judge, participants also received copies of the 2010 edition of the annual MISC "Hoodoo Food" cook book, featuring recipes from magical cooks all over the country.

Miss Bri brought us "Love Conjure" and Robin York reprised her undocumented 2008 talk on "Gambling Magic Charms," this time with text drawn from my "Hoodoo in Theory and Practice" web site. I expanded on the "Astrology for Rootworkers" class i had taught in 2008, with a revised flyer and illustrations. Lara was again called into service for "Spiritual Foot Washing," the most-often requested course in our repertoire. Deacon Millett presented his first "Sweetening Spells" class, using my shop hand-out No. 5 on "Honey Jars" as his text. And i gave a candle workshop, with the same shop flyer we had used in 2008.

At the 2010 event, the first one held after Susie's passing, people began to ask about workshops they had missed, and events that had taken place before they had found out about our teaching programs. Acting on their requests, we collected all of the undistributed and left-over shop hand-outs and workshop flyers from past years, three-hole punched them, and bound them together in black school report folders. To our surprise, "The Black Folder" became an instant best-seller in our shop. The original edition sold for $9.00, with all of the proceeds going to the church, to fund the printing of the next year's hand-outs.

2011 was the year that we moved from teaching at picnic tables and in a rented tent to establishing a permanent tent set-up on the grounds. We held nine wonderful workshops that year, and we began to advertise what had already become a bit of a side-event — readings by professional diviners — and, of course, we added all of the year's new flyers to The Black Folder, upping the price to $10.00. We also formalized the idea of an opening service to set the tone for the MISC workshop weekends. We had first done this in 2008, but not in the following years, and restoring it gave us a chance to present, in yearly succession, the rituals of the world's religions. The 2008 convocation had been led by Dr. Kioni, a former Assemblies of God minister; by 2011 he had become a tata in the African Diasporic religion of Palo, and he brought that way of working with him, adeptly assisted by Dr. E., another Palo tata, in a road opening ceremony during which we were brushed down by Dr. E. with bunches of fresh herbs.

The Conjure Cook-Off led the workshop line-up, with the "Kitchen Witchery" flyer from the previous year, plus a new 2011 "Hoodoo Food" cookbook, and prizes for the best entries. Dr. Kioni held a "Palo Protection Packet" class; however, the hand-out he distributed came from a copyright-protected book, so we can't reprint it here. I gave a workshop on "Divination From Candles," for which i used Shop Hand-Out No. 1 and 2, plus a new flyer, "Some Thoughts About Candles." "Professional Reading and Root Doctoring" was Valentina Burton's class and she sure upped the ante on the whole "hand-out" concept by presenting a hand-made 96-page book to each workshop participant. This was later published in a mass-market edition as "The Fortune Teller's Guide to Success," which we sell in our shop. We have included a small taste of it here as well. If you like it — and i predict that you will — you can order it from the Lucky Mojo Curio Company.

Dr. E. taught an inspirational course in "Making Doll-Babies for Ritual Use," at which he showed his students the vast array of forms and fabrication methods used in the creation of magical dolls and led them in crafting doll-babies for themselves. Sister Robin brought us her wonderful, well-planned "Making and Working With Mirror Boxes," at which each attendee actually assembled a complete box in which to confine an enemy, using mirror-glass pieces pre-cut by crafty Robin. At "Introducing the Crystal Silence League" Deacon Millett, Rev. John Michael Hilford, and i spoke about the resurrection of a world-wide prayer chain founded in 1919 by C. Alexander. A 32 page book, "Personal Codes, Lessons, and Instructions for Members of the Crystal Silence League," plus a crystal ball, were the hand-outs, and Rev. Hilford led a blessing service for Miss Bri's new baby, Jasper, in front of a lovely crystal altar. We can't print the book here, but, again, an excerpt will give you the flavour of the thing, and if you like it, you may purchase it at your convenience. Rev. Hilford then presented a class on "Throwing the Bones" for which i wrote the hand-out, a text that became the basis for my own 2012 book "Throwing the Bones: How to Foretell the Future with Bones, Shells, and Nuts." Everyone who attended was given a starter-set of bones.

In 2012 we got a jump on the creation of the workshop flyers by requesting presenters to turn their texts in ahead of time for typesetting. The collation of all of 2012 flyers with the previous years' flyers and binding them into Black Folder report covers took several people more than an entire day, and i swore that we would never do this again. The 2012 Black Folder was priced at $12.00, and it became obvious that the economics of scale would push us into actual book production the next year.

The 2012 workshops began with "Sarayeye, A Santeria Blessing and Road Opening Ceremony," a group ritual led by Dr. E. of the Santeria Church of the Orishas, with the support of others in the African Diasporic Religions, including Vicky Sirgo Gutierrez and ConjureMan Ali. We were again cleansed with herb bundles, but this time we circled as we sang a harmonious chant in the Yoruba language. Sister Robin Petersen's annual Conjure Cook-Off topic was "Grocery Store Magic" and in addition to some great tasting edible magic, the attendees also received her new 2012 "Hoodoo Food!" compilation of culinary sorcery for all occasions, and prizes were awarded to those whose recipes gained the most acclaim on the old applause-o-meter.

"Prosperity Spells: Money Drawing in the Conjure Tradition" was a class led by Susan Diamond and Sindy Todo. "Supernatural Protection and Spirit Traps" followed, with ConjureMan Ali taking attendees on a brief world-tour of spirit traps from many cultures, followed by an intensive hands-on class in blue-glass spell bottles. The publication of my new book, "Throwing the Bones: How to Foretell the Future with Bones, Shells, and Nuts," was celebrated with a new bone-reading workshop, this time led by me. Participants received a bone throwing starter-set and a copy of the 96-page book. "Working With Santisima Muerte" was Lou Florez's class, and against a spectacular Santa Muerte altar, he passed out sugar skulls and candles and led attendees in loading and preparing them.

Dr. E. took his turn as a presenter with the deceptively-basic sounding "Mojo Making" class, but his body-mind-spirit theory of trick bags and tobies added new dimension to this classic topic. "Fortune Telling by Telephone: How YOU Can Be a Psychic Reader" was a workshop for professionals led by Marin Graves, outlining everything needed to work on "the psychic lines." Marin's flyer, a bottle of her own Psychic Parlour spray, and a copy of Valentina Burton's book were the take-aways for attendees. "The Cursing Colloquium" was the first of our new panel discussion workshops. This event featured Ms. Robin York, ConjureMan Ali, nagasiva yronwode, Dr. E., Deacon Millett, and myself in a fast-paced in-your-face presentation of our favourite methods for spiritually messing people up. We gave out spiritual supplies used in cursing spells, plus flyers about cursing from previous years' workshops. And after all of that negative energy was released, our program concluded with "Egg Cleansing and the Meditation of Saint Michael," led by Susan Diamond and Sindy Todo.

The May 2013 Workshops are a couple of months away as i write this, but the hand-outs are already in-house, because i am including them in this complete Black Folder collection.

This year we will be hosting a total of twelve workshops, presented over two days. Our weekend opens with "Walking the Labyrinth," a Goddess-centered convocational ceremony led by Elvyra Curcuruto-Love, with assistance from Dr. Johannes Gårdbäck, featuring our brand-new permanent landscape feature, The Red Brick Labyrinth, built under the direction of Dr. Lea Goode-Harris of the Santa Rosa Labyrinth Foundation.

This year's Conjure Cook-Off spotlights Swedish trolldom, as Dr. Johannes Gårdbäck and Sister Robin Petersen present "Bread Bewitchery," a collection of Nordic bread spells, plus the 2013 "Hoodoo Food! cook book. In "Contact Conjure: Hands-On Rites and Techniques" Khi Armand shares the most shamanic forms of spiritual work. "Skull Sorcery" by ConjureMan Ali is a unique combination of world culture survey and down-and-dirty spell-casting. "Candle Magic and Candle Ministries: Hands-On Training" introduces my new 96-page book, the "Art of Hoodoo Candle Magic in Rootwork, Conjure, and Spiritual Church Services." Copies of the book, which includes material on "How to Conduct a Candle Light Service" by the late Mikhail Strabo, will be given to all attendees and then go on sale in the shop; a couple of pages are sampled here as well. "Hoodoo One-on-One With Ms. Robin" is a private teaching session for beginners that covers the making of a mojo bag, an anointing oil, a doll-baby, and a coffin spell. Flyers from previous years by Ms. Robin and others are the supporting texts.

"Catholic Saint Packets" brings teacher Lou Florez's background in Texas curandismo to the fore. "Rustic Oil Lamps in the Conjure Tradition" is Dr. E.'s workshop on the "other" side of candle magic, namely working with lamps. "Secrets of Hoodoo Honey and Sugar Spells" is the title of Deacon Millett's workshop and his brand new 96-page book, which will be given out to all attendees of his class and then go on sale in the shop; a short sample of the book is included in this collection. "Queer Conjure and Love Workings: Attracting LGBTQ Relationships" is this year's panel discussion, and it includes Khi Armand, Dr. E., Miss Michaele, Lou Florez, Robin Petersen, Lisa Warrick, and Deacon Millett. "The Art of Tarot: Design Your Own Divination Deck" is the latest in our series of "crafty" classes, with hands-on lessons from renowned tarot card designer Michele Jackson. The weekend concludes with "High-Tech Hoodoo: Conjuring Through Current Technologies" by Kast Excelsior, aided and abetted by Professor Ames and members of the AIRR Tech Team. Each participant will receive a 2-CD set of audio and graphic files to empower a whole new style of 21st century hoodoo.

And there you have it, the secret origin of The Black Folder, an omnium-gatherum for the ages.

— catherine yronwode

P.S. As always in my books, the capitalization of the species-names of animals and plants is intentional, and is offered out of respect for their alliance.

HOW TO USE SPIRITUAL OILS AND SACHET POWDERS
catherine yronwode

ANOINTING AND DRESSING OILS

Touching a drop of oil to your finger and then placing it on yourself or another person is called "anointing." Drizzling oil, rubbing it, or touching a drop of it onto an inanimate object is called "dressing." (Synonyms for dressing are "preparing" and "fixing.") When a man rubs John the Conqueror Root Oil on his penis, he is anointing himself; when he rubs it on a red penis-shaped candle or a John the Conqueror Root, he is dressing or fixing the it.

ANOINTING WITH OILS

Methods of anointing and dressing the body with oils vary from one practitioner to another, and certain forms are only used with certain named types of oil. Here are just a few of the methods i know — but please understand that none of these are hard and fast rules; rather they merely reflect instructions given to me over the years by various root workers with whom i have conversed:

When using an anointing oil for Uncrossing or jinx-breaking, rub the body downward from head to feet. Expel bad tricks put on the person by rubbing them down the legs and out the feet and toes. The same is done when bathing someone for Uncrossing.

When anointing oneself in love spells or money spells to draw luck, rub the entire body upward from soles of feet to armpits, then from palms of hands to armpits, then up over the head to the mould of the head. This may be administered to the self but is more often a treatment given by a root worker.

When using King Solomon Wisdom or Crown of Success oils, anoint the head only: place oil on thumb, index, and middle fingers of dominant hand. Starting at the bridge of the nose, brush outward, above and parallel to the eyebrows, with thumb and middle finger, then brush upward from the bridge of the nose along midline of scalp with index finger. End with a squeeze to the head and a prayer.

Anoint the mould of the head (the under-side of the back of the head) with Blessing Oil for healing, power-enhancing, and life-changing; use your palm and make a massage-like squeezing-rubbing motion, end with an upward brush of the palm.

When dressing the genitals with an oil such as Come to Me, Follow Me Boy, Love Me, Stay With Me to draw, keep, or enforce faithfulness in a lover, anoint the penis from tip to root, or anoint the vulva from perineum to clitoris; this draws the person closer.

When dressing the genitals with oil such as Cast Off Evil, Break-Up, Run Devil Run, or any other formula intended to break up with a lover, anoint the penis from root to tip, or anoint the vulva from clitoris to perineum; this sends the person away.

Anoint the palms of both hands right before you go to play at games of chance, using money-drawing or gambling oils such as Lady Luck, Fast Luck, Money Drawing Three Jacks and a King, or Special Dice Oil.

DRESSING OBJECTS WITH OILS

Oils to attract good fortune are used for dressing objects. For instance, among gamblers, the money set aside to play is dressed with Money Drawing, Money Stay With Me, Three Jacks and a King, Lady Luck, or Fast Luck Oil prior to betting. People who are working love-drawing spells burn candles dressed with Come To Me, Love Me, Attraction, or Follow Me Boy oil. Van Van Oil and Special Oil No. 20 are the most popular all-purpose dressing oils. Van Van is especially linked in folkloric practice with the lucky rabbit foot charm. And, of course, mojo bags and their contents are usually dressed with a condition oil or with alcohol, or both.

Most oils are used both for anointing the person and for dressing charms, candles, or mojo bags. Since many have pleasant scents, they can be treated as a form of perfume. Thus, a person who feels under slanderous attack from an enemy may dress his doorstep with Fiery Wall of Protection and also wear the oil as a personal scent if he has to meet the enemy in a social situation. Oils used for dressing as well as anointing include Crown of Success, King Solomon Wisdom, Psychic Vision, Cast Off Evil, Stop Gossip, John the Conqueror, Come To Me, Kiss Me Now!, and Lavender Love Drops, Money Drawing and Lucky Hand Oil.

Read more at our informative web page on oils: **LuckyMojo.com/oils.html**

SACHET POWDERS

SPRINKLING SACHET POWDERS

Mix sachet powders with some local dirt (so it won't be so easily seen) and sprinkle it out while walking backwards, taking an odd number of steps, like 7 or 9 or 21. Say a prayer (or a curse, if doing evil) while sprinkling. To protect a house, sprinkle the door steps or go all the way round the building. To draw wealth to a place of business, sprinkle Money Drawing mixed with sugar (to sweeten the customers) across the doorstep every Friday. Love powders are used to draw a lover to your home; bad luck powders can be used to cross or jinx someone or stir up trouble in an enemy's home. To create problems for someone, some folks take an evil powder, such as Crossing, Goofer Dust, or Hot Foot Powder and sprinkle it across the enemy's door step or simply throw it into his yard so that he must walk through the mess. Throwing for someone is also called "poisoning through the feet."

LAYING DOWN TRICKS WITH POWDERS

Conjures who perform candle spells and rituals often lay out and appropriate sachet powder on their altar in a design such as a star or cross and place their candles at the vertices of the design. In the down-home tradition, powders are usually put down in four inconspicuous little piles in the corners of a room, with a fifth small pile in the center, under the rug, in a five-spot pattern. If used for love-drawing or marital fidelity, the fifth pile is placed under the bed instead of at the center of the room. Cross-marks, crosses in circles, and "wavy snake lines" intended to hurt an enemy can be drawn with destructive or get-away type powders on a sidewalk or street. They are placed in the footpath where the victim will walk and activated by spitting into them while cursing enemy's name. This is a form of poisoning through the feet or foot-track magic. Such a mark only affects the one for whom it was called, but most people never walk across such a mess if they see one, because "you never know who it was called for."

DRESSING ALTAR CANDLES WITH POWDERS

In some families the dedication to sachet powders is such that all candles are "double-dressed," first with oil, then with a powder. In my experience, the practice of double-dressing candles is more commonly found among women than among men, for what its worth.

BLOWING SACHET POWDERS

Powders can be blown to the four quarters of the compass to rid an area of evil spirits. This has become especially popular with the good luck powders like Blessing and Peaceful Home. You just put a little bit of powder in the palm of your hand and blow to the East, South, West, and then North, saying your prayer while you do so. This brings a pleasant fragrance to the room and settles out bad conditions. You may also blow powders toward a person, either present or absent. This practice is used by Spiritual Church members more than other root workers. If the person being blown toward is not present, blow in the direction you believe them to be located, or toward their home, if you know where it is.

DRESSING MONEY AND OTHER PAPERS

To dress money, applications, business cards, letters, or test papers, sprinkle a pinch of powder on the back. Drag your four fingers down through the powder, top to bottom, in "wavy snake lines." To further empower the work, light an appropriate incense powder and waft the pages in the fumes before sending them out. This is called "smoking" the letter or papers. This same technique can used for money drawing, court cases, love drawing, or any condition, just by choosing the right powder and incense.

WEARING AND CARRYING POWDERS

Dust yourself or your clothing with good luck and love sachet powders, to keep the feeling of good luck and romantic allure with you all day long. A small sachet bag worn in the brassiere — a "bosom sachet" — will produce as similar result.

SNEAKY TRICKS WITH POWDERS

Sneaky tricks are accomplished by blending spiritual condition powders into a target's personal body dusting powders, particularly foot powders, and praying over them for your intention.

Read more at our informative page on powders:
LuckyMojo.com/powders.html

"Anointing Oils and Sachet Powders" was Lucky Mojo Shop Hand-Out No. 17 in 2002. The text is adapted from my 1995 book "Hoodoo in Theory and Practice," found in fuller form at the URLs cited above. I am a member of the Association of Readers and Rootworkers (AIRR) and Hoodoo Psychics, and i can be reached for readings and magical coaching at my Yronwode.com/misscat web page.

HOW TO USE INCENSE, BATH CRYSTALS, AND WASHES
catherine yronwode

HOW TO USE INCENSE

INCENSE IN MAGICAL RITES

The practice of burning incense to accompany invocations or prayers is particularly favoured by Christian root workers who follow the kabbalist-inspired practice of reciting certain Psalms for magical effect. In addition, if a job of work involves a person far away, incense may be burned to "carry" the wish or desire to him or her. On a more practical level, some workers "smoke" themselves and their clothes, while many also smoke talismanic charms, candles and mojo bags in incense after dressing them with oil. Also, in a pinch, loose powdered incense can be sprinkled on the ground after the manner of sachet powders.

NATURAL RESIN, WOOD, AND HERB INCENSES

The oldest and most original incenses used by mankind have been tree resins and herbs or woods that burn with a fragrant smoke. Typical herbal incenses include Sage and Tobacco, much favoured by North American Indians and those who follow their traditions. Sage is typically utilized in the form of wrapped and tied smudge sticks, while Tobacco is burned in a ceremonial pipe. The best-known wood chip incense is the rare and expensive Sandalwood, which is made of finely shaved chips of the tree of the same name. Resin incenses, which are granular lumps of dried tree sap, include the Biblical Frankincense and Myrrh as well as Benzoin and Copal, the latter a holy incense of the Mayan Indians of Central America. Resins are often burned in mixtures, the light scent of golden Frankincense combining beautifully with richly musky Myrrh and sharply aromatic Benzoin. Another favourite mixture is cleansing Camphor and purifying Pine Resin.

COMPOUNDED INCENSES

Compounded incenses are made by blending fragrances such as the essential oils of herbs and flowers into a base of finely shaved wood. Hoodoo incense makers use the same herbal and floral essences that go into their condition oils, and often add colouring as well, according to the same colour-symbolism by which offertory candles are coloured.

A small amount of saltpeter is added to compounded incenses to improve ease of lighting. Once an incense has been compounded, it can be sold in a number of forms, including: Stick, (Agarbatti, Agarbathi, Joss Stick), Cones Or Logs (Dhoop), Coils, and Self-Lighting Powders.

AGARBATTI INCENSE STICKS, DHOOP CONES, AND COIL INCENSE

The Indian name for incense sticks that have been hand-rolled onto slivers of bamboo is agarbatti, sometimes spelled agarbathi. When the incense is formed into cones or logs, it is called dhoop. In Vietnam and China, similar incense compounds are formed into long coils which are suspended from a hanger and will burn for many hours. Following the symbolism of the herbs and flowers used to scent them, they have many uses in magic. Those made with Rose fragrance tend to be used for love spells, those scented with Jasmine for psychic and spiritual work, and those that bear a Musk aroma are favoured in rites of sex magic or sacred sexuality.

SELF-LIGHTING POWDER INCENSE

In the African-American tradition, loose powder "condition" incense has always been the norm because many root workers like to blend appropriate herbs, minerals, or root chips into the finished product. To use self-lighting incense powders, you take a small scrap of paper and twirl it into a little cone about an inch or two tall — or use a candle-snuffer cone. Pack it very tightly with powdered incense, carefully set the cone upright in a brazier or on a non-flammable surface and tap it. The powder will come out in perfect a cone shape. Light the tip. You can also scatter incense powder on burning charcoal. Although incense formulas for luck, love, money, and personal power are pleasant smelling and can be used to perfume a room, formulas used to do tricks or evil work may contain ingredients which should not be inhaled by the practitioner. The usual way to use these powerful materials is to ignite an entire package in the enemy's front yard at once and quickly leave the area.

Read more at our free web page on incense: **LuckyMojo.com/incense.html**

HOW TO USE BATHS AND FLOOR WASHES

SPIRITUAL BATHING AS A MAGICAL RITE

When bathing to draw in good luck, rub the body in an upward direction after pouring the bath. If the bath is for the removal of evil conditions, rub in a downward direction. Air dry after spiritual bathing.

Used bath water, enhanced by the essence of the bather, may become an ingredient in further spell work, used to wipe away enemy tricks, or added to floor wash. The used wash-water may be thrown into the front yard or the washing-out may continue down the house-path toward the road and conclude by throwing the water at the border of the property while saying a short prayer. This is followed by an inward wash from the sidewalk to the front door to draw good things and to protect the premises.

HERB BATHS

Ritual bathing may utilize special herbs for love-getting, money-drawing, protection from evil, or the removal of curses. Steep the herbs in boiling water, strain the mixture, let the liquid cool, and pour it over the body while standing in a wash tub.

The most well-known bath-herb in the African-American Christian community is Hyssop, mentioned in Psalms 51 of the Bible as the herb to use for purification from sin. Other herbs used in ritual baths include Damiana for love, Rue for protection, Agrimony to reverse a jinx, and Cinnamon Chips or Chamomile flowers to draw money. Special mixtures like 7 Herb Bath, 9 Herb Bath, and 13 Herb Bath are used to draw luck in love and money, to increase personal spiritual power, and to remove jinxes, respectively.

HERBAL HAND WASHES

The same money-drawing herbs used for ritual bathing are also made up into lucky hand washes used by gamblers for cleaning and empowering the hands when going out to play at games of chance.

To use herbal hand washes, the practitioner makes up a batch as a strong "tea," strains out the herbs, and stores the liquid in the refrigerator, using just enough every time to thoroughly wash the hands and prepare them for their work.

PERFUMED BODY WASHES

Floral-scented Colognes and Toilet Waters are employed to rid an area of bad spirits, attract or pay homage to good spirits, and refresh those who are suffering from psychic distress. Colognes may be added to floor washes, mixed with water and placed in a bowl on an altar, sprinkled or wiped on the body. or used as an alcohol medium to extract herbal essences, such as protective Devil's Shoe Strings and empowering High John the Conqueror root. The most popular products for these purposes are Florida Water, Hoyt's Cologne, Rose Water, Orange Water, and Kananga Water.

HOW TO USE MINERAL-BASED BATH CRYSTALS AND BLUEING

The simplest mineral baths contain three ingredients, such as salt, saltpeter, and epsom salts or salt, epsom salts, and laundry blueing. Modern mineral baths are scented with essential oils or "condition" oils, from which they then take their names. Mineral baths can be taken by the pouring method, or by dissolving the crystals in a bathtub of hot water and scooping up the ritual number of handfuls of water to pour over the head.

If you are laying a trick for someone, you can add a large pinch of the crystals to the rinse water of their laundry. This will dress them without their becoming suspicious. Similarly, to help yourself when going for a job interview or out on a date, add the appropriate mineral crystals (e.g. Steady Work or Love Me) to your own laundry rinse water and dress yourself.

FLOOR WASHES

Ritual floor-washing is first done outward to remove evil and then inward to draw in good luck. The same mineral crystals used for bathing can be mixed up as floor washes, but the most famous of all the home cleaners, Chinese Wash, is never used for personal bathing. The old slogan says it best: "Clear away that evil mess with Chinese Wash!"

Read more at our free page on baths and washes: **LuckyMojo.com/baths.html**

"How to Use Incense, Bath Crystals, and Washes" was Lucky Mojo Shop Hand-Out No. 18. It was also given out at MISC workshops on Incense and Foot Washing. The text is from my online book "Hoodoo in Theory and Practice," at the URLs cited above. I teach a one-year course in hoodoo; read about it at LuckyMojo.com/mojocourse.html.

HOODOO PERFUMES AND INCENSES
Dr. James Dotson

HOODOO PERFUMES

Perfumes are simply fragrant materials in a solvent, though they have been more astutely defined as "halfway between a thing and an idea." In nature, scents are used by both plants and animals to transmit information which can be used to attract and repel. Occult perfumes do the same; they are airy, semi-material substances that communicate with the spiritual world. Just as a flower can attract a pollinator, the perfume of Rose or Jasmine can attract spirits, people and circumstances.

The earliest historical evidence for perfume manufacturing was on the island of Cyprus (the birthplace of Venus) about 4,000 years ago. These first fragrances were resins, spices, herbs, and flowers infused into oil or fat. Ancient Egypt, Mesopotamia, and Rome all had highly developed trades in perfumes and unguents, but it wasn't until the 8th or 9th century, when Persian alchemists made the process of distillation widely known, that alcohol based scents became available. Hundreds of years later, perfumes were sold by the apothecaries of religious orders in Renaissance Italy, while in France perfumery developed into a secular art. By the 19th century, Paris was the center of haute parfumerie but scents were also made in the U.S., and the increasing use of synthetics and modern manufacturing techniques made perfumes more affordable and available.

MATERIALS

The most common scent materials are woods, resins, herbs, roots, spices, fruits, and flowers. Animal ingredients like Musk and Civet are also used, but are now almost always synthetic. Synthetics are used to overcome the expense of naturals, or the difficulty of reliable sourcing, or because there are no ways to extract a scent from a material (i.e. Strawberry, Pineapple, Wistaria).

Though petrochemicals are used in the synthesis of fragrances, many synthetics are derived from plants. For instance, vanillin, which has an intense candyfloss Vanilla scent, occurs naturally in Vanilla bean and Benzoin but can be made from Pine sap or cellulose fiber. Rosy odorants, like geraniol, can be obtained from more affordable Palmarosa or Rose Geranium.

Historical methods of isolating frangrances include:

TINCTURES

A hundred years ago, many perfume components were derived from macerating chopped up plants in alcohol, a process called tincturing. This method are now virtually obsolete.

ENFLEURAGE

Because flowers release very little fragrance in alcohol, they often had to go through the labour-intensive process of enfleurage which involved placing them in fat, and then later washing the fat with solvents. This method is now virtually obsolete.

Nowadays, most perfume components consist of the following ingredients:

DISTILLED ESSENTIAL OILS

These are steam-distilled, and in addition to their use in sacred and secular perfumery, they are also the basis of aromatherapy.

ABSOLUTES

These are solvent-extracted fragrances derived from natural botanicals.

CO2 AND OTHER HIGH-TECH EXTRACTIONS

These recently-developed forms of extraction have allowed perfumers to work with previously difficult to extract botanical ingredients, but if one wishes to reproduce antique perfumes, they may not replicate the scents produced by older forms of extraction.

ACCORDS AND AROMACHEMICALS

When you open a bottle of something labelled "Gardenia" it is virtually guaranteed not to have any real Gardenia in it, because this flower is so difficult to extract that it is not commercially viable. "Gardenia" is made from an "accord" or "bouquet" of aromachemicals. Higher quality bouquets contain natural essential oils, such as Jasmine and Tuberose, to give the compounded fragrance more complexity and depth.

AT LAST! SECRET FORMULAS! BELIEVED LOST TO THE WORLD!! CAN NOW BE YOURS!

One of the biggest secrets is that there is no "one" or "authentic" formula for popular condition oils, just like there is no single authentic recipe for apple pie. However, there are historical recipes as well as variations developed by occult-shop owners.

The following traditional formulas are from Zora Neale Hurston's 1920s article "Hoodoo in America":

Marie LaVeau Lucky Hand: Geranium, Cinnamon

Marie LaVeau Essence of Peace: Geranium, Cinnamon, Cedar

Father Simms, the Frizzly Rooster's Lucky Hand Oil: Anise, Geranium, Violet, Lavender, Verbena, Bay Rum

Ruth Mason's Business Oil "to bring a crowd": Van Van, Geranium, Lavender

And from the New Orleans Pharmacy Museum Formulary come these two:

Red Fast Luck: Cinnamon, Vanilla, Wintergreen

Fast Luck: Cinnamon, Bergamot, Lemon Grass

Popular 19th-century colognes like Florida Water and Hoyt's were adopted by spiritual workers. Here are two other old colognes that were used in hoodoo:

Jockey Club "to make love and find work": About a hundred years ago, this cologne was so popular that at least forty different companies made versions of it. There are many formulas, but they generally all had citrus, white flowers, and an animalic base. One example: Bergamot, Rose, Jasmine, Tuberose, Civet.

Bay Rum for uncrossing, luck, health: The Bay Rum tree (Pimenta racemosa) is a relative of Allspice, not to be confused with Bay Laurel, Bayberry, or California Bay. It is native to the West Indies, where it is known as Bwa Den (Bois d'Indes or Wood of India). Originally the leaves and berries were distilled directly into rum. Later, cheaper versions consisted of essential oil, alcohol, and imitation rum flavour made from caramelized sugar. The original, traditional recipe is Bay Rum, Allspice, and Orange oils in rum. Variations include added Bergamot, Clove, and Cinnamon.

HOODOO INCENSE HISTORY

"May my prayer be set before you like incense..."
— Psalms 141

Fragrant resins, woods and plants have been burned in the spiritual traditions of tribal cultures on every continent, and as part of the religious rituals of ancient Egypt, Babylon, and India. Frankincense, the most celebrated incense in the western world, has archeological evidence dating its use back at least 8,000 years, and it merits more than twenty mentions in the Bible.

The Bible's incense references mainly detail the practices of early Judaism, in particular the burning of the sacred incense, Ketoret, in the Temple in Jerusalem as described in the Book of Exodus. This was specified as a mixture of Frankincense, Storax, Galbanum, and Onycha. At first the Christian church forbade the use of incense because of its Jewish and Pagan associations, but this was later reversed around the 4th century during the reign of Constantine. By the Middle Ages, incense was used extensively during liturgical services and also on special occasions to sanctify persons, places, and things. It became an important part of the veneration of the saints, along with the lighting of candles. Mostly Frankincense was burned, though later it was combined with Myrrh and other resins.

By the 17th century, due to the secular influence of the perfume industry, church incense blends started to include flowers, spices, and woods, until eventually certain religious orders, like the Trappist and Benedictine brothers, became celebrated for their special compounded incenses, much like they were known for their liqueurs. Several of these blends, with names like "Gloria," "Pontifical" and "Mellaray" are still available today in religious supply stores and are used by spiritual workers.

The use of incense in hoodoo is inspired by Biblical lore, European folk magic, 19th-century hermeticism, 20th-century occult supply catalogues, and the craze for "Oriental" incense in the 1920s. Though some of the ingredients originated in Africa (like Myrrh), it is challenging to tease out what incense traditions might or might not be properly considered African traditions, though the same could be said for the use of incense in contemporary Voudon, Santeria, or Obeah. Even in contemporary Africa, most of the incense is purchased in the marketplace and often includes spices and resins that are not native to the continent.

By the 20th century, most hoodoo practitioners had access to church incense and common resins like Frankincense, Myrrh, Benzoin, Camphor, and Dragon's Blood. At some point, probably due to the popularity of powdered incense, such as the tins of "Temple Incense" from the oriental specialty firm Vantine's, occult catalogues began to offer compounded condition incenses. Stick and cone incense, usually from China, Japan, or India were also popular and inexpensive.

MATERIALS

The most common ingredients used in incense include resins, woods, spices, herbs, roots, flowers, minerals, sweeteners, animal products, and fragrant oils.

Tree and plant resins are the oldest and most universal incense materials. They are rich in sweet and balsamic essential oils which rapidly fill a room with fragrance, and almost every region has a wild source of resins (such as pines) available.

Compounded incenses are usually made from wood flour, perfumes, and a burning agent, such as potassium nitrate (saltpeter), rendering them "easy-lighting." According cultural norms, they may be formed into logs, cones, briquets, thin sticks, coils, or left loose in powder form.

TECHNIQUES

The word "incense" comes from the Latin "incendere" which means to set on fire. Fire requires heat, oxygen, and a combustible material. With incense, the goal is to smoulder slowly. Fires that are too rapid will scorch the ingredients and produce a lot of smoke with little smell. The advantage of ready-made combustible incense that already has saltpeter in it is that it has been designed to burn slowly and all you need to do is to apply a flame.

The non-combustible incenses, including blends of tree resins and compounds lacking saltpeter require an external heat source. In the past, rootworkers burned incense on the top of their wood burning stoves. Nowadays, charcoal is the norm, but it can be tricky to light and because the large pieces get very hot, some people prefer to use aluminum foil on top to control the burn. In traditional Japanese ceremonies, a plate of mica is used over the coal.

Another method is to restrict the oxygen supply by placing a slotted lid over the burner (though this can stop the whole thing if you are not attentive). When you are making your own compounded incense or customizing a commercially prepared powder, you can slow down the burn by adding extra woody materials, and speed it up by adding oils, which act as an accelerant.

RITUALS

Incense is burned on the candle altar as part of the process of setting lights. One simple hoodoo ritual noted by an informant of Harry Hyatt's was to recite a prayer out loud three times while the incense smouldered, or to sound out a command ("Come to me!"). A petition can also be placed under the burner, or incense can be placed on the petition paper and burned directly on charcoal.

INCENSE FORMULAS

The following recipes are from Zora Neale Hurston's "Hoodoo in America" and represent hoodoo practices from the 1920s.

Marie Laveau's Uncrossing Incense: Frankincense and Dragon's Blood

Ruth Mason's Business Incense "to bring a crowd": Frankincense, Dragon's Blood, Bay Leaves, sugar; put ashes in the four corners.

Ruth Mason's Uncrossing Incense: Cloves, "Spices" (probably Pumpkin Pie Spice, which contains good luck ingredients), Frankincense; smoke yourself for seven mornings after a Cinnamon bath.

These incense recipes are from the DeLaurence catalogue of the 1920s:

Temple Incense: Rose scent, likely blended with Sandalwood, and perhaps inspired by a classic Rosicrucian incense. DeLaurence suggested that it be used for all spiritual work, and could be combined with Cloves and other materials for various purposes.

Black Incense: Wistaria

Dr. James Dotson's workshop on "Hoodoo Perfumes and Incenses" was one of the most well-thought-out classes of 2009. A true classicist, James supplied a wealth of documented historical information, and then we got to make sample products.

THE ART OF HOODOO CANDLE MAGIC
catherine yronwode

A BRIEF HISTORY OF CANDLE MAGIC IN AMERICA

Oil lamps stretch back to ancient times and have long been used in both religious ceremonies and magical rites, but only after the Civil War did candles became readily available as a commercial product, sold in general stores, rather than being made at home or on the farm.

By the early 20th century, paraffin candles, with a relatively high melting point compared to tallow candles and much less expensive than beeswax candles, were transported by rail nationwide — and with the invention of aniline dyes, they were soon made available in many colours.

1924-1940: THE SONG-WRITER AND THE FOLKLORISTS

The 1924 song "Hoodoo Blues" written by New Orleans native Spencer Williams (1889-1965) and recorded by Bessie Brown contains one of the earliest mentions of candle conjure. Shortly thereafter, the systematic use of candles in African American folk magic was noticed by folklorists such as Newbell Niles Puckett, Zora Neale Hurston, and Harry Middleton Hyatt.

Puckett, writing in 1926, stated with conviction that candle magic had originated in New Orleans, where Roman Catholic candle burning combined with African-American folk magic to produce an emergent style of work.

Hurston, in the 1930s, described public candle rites such as the "pea vine drill" which took place in Spiritualist churches in New Orleans.

Hyatt interviewed practitioners all over the South from 1936 through 1940, a full ten years after Puckett, He noted that candle magic had spread North to Memphis, and that Southern conjure doctors in Georgia were buying candles from mail order houses in Memphis and Chicago. However his documentary work remained unpublished until the 1970s.

Meanwhile, in 1936, candle magic suddenly went national.

1936: LEWIS DE CLAREMONT, GODFREY SPENCER, AND MR. YOUNG

The first printed instructions on how to dress a candle and burn it on an altar in the hoodoo manner appeared in the 1936 book "Legends of Incense, Herb, and Oil Magic" by Lewis De Claremont / Louis DeClermont, who also wrote under the name Godfrey Spencer. A Jewish man, perhaps named Mr. Young, he owned the Oracle Products Company in New York City, the first supply service to nationally distribute oils and candles to the African American market via mail order. His catalogue included menorahs, shofars, mezuzahs, yads, and other Jewish religious goods.

Read about Mr.Young's candle rituals:
- **"Legends of Incense, Herb, and Oil Magic" by Lewis De Claremont**
- **LuckyMojo.com/young.html**

1941: MIKHAIL STRABO AND SYDNEY J. ROSENFELD STEINER

In a series of three books published from 1941-1943, the writer Mikhail Strabo described the use of candles in the Black Spiritualist churches of New York City. These ground-breaking works — "A Candle to Light Your Way," "How to Conduct a Candle Light Service," and "The Guiding Light to Power and Success" — were sold via Black-owned newspapers. They opened up a nation-wide conversation on the increasing importance of conjure work with candles.

My own research has uncovered the fact that Mikhail Strabo was a pen name of Sydney J. Rosenfeld Steiner (1894-1971), the Jewish American proprietor of Guidance House, a New York publishing company. Steiner was a participant-documentarian who respectfully sourced his information. Earlier observers of candle rituals in Spiritual churches, like Zora Neale Hurston, had placed a typical folklorist's emphasis on singular incidents. Steiner, on the other hand, collaborated with an African American minister, Rev. Adele Clemens, to compile a complete manual of candle altar services, which had an enduring impact.

Read about Mikhail Strabo's take on Spiritualism:
- **"The Guiding Light to Power and Success" by Mikhail Strabo**
- **LuckyMojo.com/strabo.html**

1937-1943: REV. ADELE CLEMENS AND THE BLACK SPIRITUAL CHURCHES

"How to Conduct a Candle Light Service" features an introduction by Rev. Adele Clemens, pastor of Divine Harmony Spiritual Church, which was probably located in Harlem. I have been unable to find further print or online mention of this church, but that is not unexpected, as material on the African American Spiritual Church Movement is spotty at best. Indeed the very existence of the Spiritual Church Movement and its inter-denominational umbrella organizations, such as the Coloured Spiritualist Association of Churches (CSAC), remains largely unknown outside of the African American community, and has not been celebrated by the wider religious world.

This ignorance was self-imposed by European American observers. The CSAC was formed in 1922 when, in line with the institutionalized racism of the era, the National Spiritualist Association of Churches (NSAC) expelled all affiliate churches with Negro congregations. Later, when Harry Middleton Hyatt, a White Episcopalian minister, interviewed 1,600 Black rootwork practitioners during the 1930s, he met several Spiritualist mediums with candle ministries, including a pastor who described the quadrennial CSAC convocations. However, despite this clear evidence, Hyatt opined that Spiritualist observances, including public candle services, were being held in "private churches."

Tantalizing glimpses of Black Spiritualism during the era of Sydney Steiner and Rev. Adele Clemens can be found in Gordan Parks' 1942 photographs of Saint Martin's Spiritual Church in Washington, D.C., as well as in the 1937 "March of Time" feature "Harlem's Black Magic." The latter is a racist and inaccurate news film which nevertheless includes clear images of signage for a number of Spiritualist churches in Harlem.

Read more about the Spiritual Church Movement:
• **"Mules and Men" by Zora Neale Hurston**
• **"Hoodoo Conjure Witchcraft Rootwork" by Harry Middleton Hyatt**
• **"The Spirit of Blackhawk" by Jason Berry**
• **"Spirit World" by Michael Smith**
• **"The Spiritual Churches Of New Orleans" by Claude F. Jacobs and Andrew J. Kaslow**
• **"Black Magic" by Yvonne Chireau**
• **ReadersAndRootworkers.org/wiki/Category: Working_Within_the_Spiritualist_Tradition**

1942: HENRI GAMACHE AND JOSEPH SPITALNICK A.K.A. JOSEPH W. KAY

"The Master Book of Candle Burning" by Henri Gamache, published in 1942, was widely advertised in Black-owned newspapers like the *Chicago Defender*. It is still carried today by all the major mail-order spiritual suppliers. This work delivers exactly what it promises: detailed instructions for spiritual doctors, rootworkers, and private practitioners on "How to Burn Candles for Every Purpose," including how to select candles, anoint them, arrange them on an altar, and burn them with appropriate Biblical Psalms. Gamache offered a unique Creole melange of Southern hoodoo, Jamaican obeah, Christianity, Jewish kabbalism, and Spiritualism. His other books are equally interesting. In particular, his "Long Lost 8th, 9th, and 10th Books of Moses" is a fascinating take on Marcus Garvey's theory that the Jewish leader Moses was a Black African, "the Great Voodoo Man of the Bible."

However, Henri Gamache was a pen name, either for the Jewish American hoodoo shop owner Joe Kay (born Joseph Spitalnick; 1889-1967), or, according to my personal conversations with Kay's son Ed Kay, "a young college-educated Jewish woman who worked for my father and wrote books for him." Like Sydney Steiner, "Henri Gamache" carefully and respectfully documented the work of African American Spiritual Church ministers and private practitioners, providing us with an excellent teaching manual in hoodoo candle magic.

Read more by and about Henri Gamache:
• **"The Master Book of Candle Burning" by Henri Gamache**
• **LuckyMojo.com/young.html**

1979-1980: ANNA RIVA AND CHARMAINE DEY

In 1979 and 1980, hoodoo candle manuals were published by Charmaine Dey (June D. Zabawsky, 1922-1983) and Anna Riva (Dorothy Spencer, 1923-2005). Both authors blended Southern conjure and Spiritual Church customs with Gardnerian Wicca, Theosophy, and New Age beliefs.

Read how Neo-Paganism influenced hoodoo:
• **"The Magic Candle" by Charmaine Dey**
• **"Candle Burning Magic" by Anna Riva**

This is a short excerpt from "The Art of Hoodoo Candle Magic," a 96-page book given to students in my 2013 MISC workshop of the same name. The book also includes candle spells and church services. It is on sale at LuckyMojo.com.

CANDLE-BURNING BASICS
catherine yronwode

COLOUR SYMBOLISM OF CANDLES

Candle symbolism varies, but here are some of the more common attributions given to offertory candles.

White: Spiritual blessings, purity, healing, peace, rest, drawing in new love.

Pink: Attraction, romance, friendship, clean living, reconciliation.

Red: Love, affection, sexual passion, bodily vigour, luck, energy.

Orange: Changing plans, opening the way, new roads, prophetic dreams.

Yellow (and untinted Beeswax): Devotion, prayer, rewards, money (gold), cheerfulness, attraction.

Green: Money (paper currency), gambling luck, business success, steady job, good crops.

Blue: Peace, harmony, kindliness, marital fidelity, joy, healing.

Purple: Mastery, power, ambition, success, control, command.

Brown (and untinted Beeswax): Court cases, mediations, neutrality, animals, the natural world.

Black: Repulsion, dark thoughts, sorrow, evil, harm, hurt, curses.

Metallic Gold: Money (gold), success, gambling luck, prosperity, the Sun.

Metallic Silver: Money (silver), psychism, emotions, development, the Moon.

Red and Black ("Double Action"): Love-unjinxing, returning evil to the sender.

White and Black ("Double Action"): Spiritual healing, returning evil to the sender.

Green and Black ("Double Action"): Money-unjinxing, get money owed.

Black-over-Red ("Reversible"): Return every kind of evil to the sender.

COMMON FIGURAL CANDLES

Figural candles are burned for special purposes. When available in a range of colours, their symbolism follows that of offertory candles.

Adam ("Nude Male"): To influence the life of a man; colour symbolism as for offertory candles.

Baphomet ("Sabbatic Goat"): Red for lust spells; black for worship of bestial or Satanic forces.

Black Cat with Tail Up: Black, for gambler's luck.

Bride and Groom, Groom and Groom, Bride and Bride ("Couple Candle"): Colour symbolism as for offertory candles.

Cross with Book, Keys, Flames ("Crucifix Candle"): Colour symbolism as for offertory candles.

Cross with Four-Leaf Clover ("Lucky Crucifix"): Colour symbolism same as for offertory candles.

Devil with Pitchfork: Red for lust and sex, black for harm; green for money owed or for gambler's luck.

Divorce: Black only; to cause a couple to break up or to cause one's own marriage to end.

Gargoyle: Protection; four of them faced outward signify protection of a magical or sacred space.

Eve ("Nude Female"): To influence the life of a woman; colour symbolism as for offertory candles.

Lovers (nude embracing couple): Red for sexual passion; white to attract a new love affair.

Penis ("Male Member"): To control the sexual behaviour of a man; colour symbolism same as for offertory candles.

Seven Knob Wishing Candle: Red for love, green for wealth, white for wishes, black for harm.

Skull: To influence another's thoughts; colour symbolism as for offertory candles.

Vulva ("Female Member"): To control the sexual behaviour of a woman; colour symbolism as for offertory candles.

TYPES OF SEVEN-WAY CANDLES

CANDLE DIVIDED BY SEVEN NEEDLES

I believe that this is the oldest form of the seven-way candle. You make it yourself.

Take a regular candle and seven needles (or pins). Poke the needles into the candle, dividing it into seven equal parts (the seventh needle can go at the top or at the bottom, but no one i know ever uses SIX needles to divide the candle into seven parts).

Write your wish (or seven wishes) on a piece of paper. Turn the paper 90 degrees sideways and write your full name over the wish or wishes seven times, crossing and covering the previous writing. Place the paper under the candle. Dress the candle with an appropriate oil. Burn it for seven nights, pinching it out (NOT blowing it out) each time a needle falls.

Save the needles when they fall. When the last needle falls, stick the needles into the paper in the form of two X patterns and one double X pattern (that has two lines crossed by one line). Bury the paper and any leftover wax under your doorstep.

SEVEN KNOB CANDLE

I have seen ads for these under the name "The Famous 7-Knob Wishing Candle" dating back at least to the 1930s; they might be older, but i do not think so. They are mentioned favourably in Henri Gamache's "Master Book of Candle Burning" (written in 1942) and they are still very popular in the African-American community, which seems to indicate that they are efficacious.

Seven-knob candles generally come in four colours, with the usual symbolism implied by those colours (white for blessing or wishing, red for love or sex, green for money or gambling luck, black for power, destruction, or revenge).

Carve a brief wish on each knob — either the same wish seven times or seven different wishes, one per knob. Dress the candle with an appropriate oil. Put the person you have in mind's name and personal concerns under the candle.

Burn the candle for seven nights, one knob per night, pinching it out (NOT blowing it out) between burnings.

SEVEN-DAY VIGIL CANDLE

The Seven-Day Vigil candle resembles a Catholic Novena candle in that it encased in glass, but instead of a saint-picture, it bears good-luck and magical images, usually silk-screened in white on the glass. This style first became popular in the 1970s and there are hundreds of different types available. Place your written wish beneath the candle, dress the candle with oil, and burn in sections for seven days.

SEVEN-WISHES GLASS-ENCASED CANDLE

This style resembles a Seven-Day Vigil candle but it is made with seven layers of wax in different colours, poured into the glass container. Dress with oil and burn one layer each day with appropriate prayers or wishes.

SEVEN CHARM SORTILEGE CANDLE

This is a hand-made candle that originated in Latin America. It contains seven tiny metal charms (milagros or ex-votos) inside, which are revealed one per day as you burn the candle over the course of seven days. The charms are religious as well as lucky, and may include a cross, the powerful hand of God, a man's head, a woman's head, and so forth. After the charms are collected, they are strung on a string and the string is knotted with seven knots to seal the seven wishes.

"Candle Burning Basics" was Lucky Mojo Hand-Out Sheet No. 1, crafted in 2002 from material that i had previously put online in 1995 as part of my book "Hoodoo in Theory and Practice," at LuckyMojo.com/hoodoo.html. The particular web page that this hand-out was drawn from is "Candle Magic," at LuckyMojo.com/candlemagic.html — but it went on to have a life of its own outside of that context, because this simple introduction to candle magic has been given away with tens of thousands of Lucky Mojo Curio Company candle orders and it is one of the stock "store flyers" that our walk-in customers can pick up for free as they shop with us. Additionally, from 2005 onward, it has been distributed in the instructional flyer packages given to students at every Missionary Independent Spiritual Church workshop that has touched upon the subject of flame, including all of my own candle workshops and all of the candle and lamp classes that have been presented by my colleagues. In 2013 i modified, edited, extended, and incorporated this text into a portion of my book "The Art of Hoodoo Candle Magic," which is available for separate purchase at LuckyMojo.com/mojocatbooks.html.

DIVINATION SIGNS FROM BURNING CANDLES
catherine yronwode

WHAT TO DO WHILE WAITING FOR YOUR CANDLE SPELL TO WORK

When we set lights, we often watch and wait for divinatory signs that tell us how the work is going to come out — that is, whether the spell will be a success or not.

Some of the common signs we observe are so-called "coincidences" (especially names and subject matter that relate to those in the spell). We can also consult a system of divination, such as using a pendulum or a Jack Ball, reading or cutting playing cards or tarot cards, or employing Bibliomancy (divination by means of a book such as the Bible). Another easy way to get a divination on candle-burning spells is through ceromancy — divination by wax. In this case, the wax we "read" is the wax of the candles themselves, both as they burn and after they are finished and the wax has cooled.

Not every magical practitioner takes heed of the manner in which ritual or spell-casting candles burn, but for the most part, in my experience, it is people who work in African-American and African-Caribbean traditions often pay attention to the way a candle burns and can draw conclusions about it. In particular, spiritual workers who set lights for clients make a habit of noticing the manner in which the candles burn.

Of course, it is important to note that some candles are simply poorly made and will burn badly no matter what you do with them (for instance, if the wick is too thick they may burn sootily). Also, the temperature in the area, the presence of wind or a draft, and other external factors may play a part in how candles burn. You should not worry over-much about how candles burn until you have burned a lot of candles and gained some perspective on the matter.

DIVINATION SIGNS FROM CANDLES

THE CANDLE GIVES A CLEAN, EVEN BURN

This means things will go well with the spell or blessing and that one will most likely get what one wishes for. If a glass encased candle burns and leaves no marks on the glass, that is best. If a free-standing candle leaves little or no residue, that is best.

THE CANDLE FLAME FLARES, DIPS, GUTTERS, AND FLARES AGAIN, REPEATEDLY

This is often seen as a sign that the person on whom you are working is subconsciously aware of your actions and may be responding partially, then fighting off your influence, then responding again.

Be sure, however, that this behaviour of the candle flame is not caused by the mundane fact that you have set the candle in a draft. If necessary, move the candle somewhere else and see if the repeated flaring up and dying away stops; if it does not stop, then it is to be considered a sign, and not simply a physical coincidence.

THE CANDLE FLAME HISSES, SIZZLES, POPS, OR MAKES OTHER NOISES

This is usually interpreted — especially by those in the Spiritual Church Movement — as a sign that spirits (of the dead, of angels, or of other entities) are trying to "come through," that is, to communicate. Pay attention! You may learn something important.

THE FLAME GOES OUT BEFORE THE CANDLE IS DONE COMPLETELY BURNING

This is generally a bad sign because it indicates that someone very strong is working against you or against the person on whose behalf you are setting the lights. It may also indicate unresolved issues from the past (known or unknown) are stopping the work. You will have to start the entire job over from the beginning and you may need to use stronger means than you first employed.

THE CANDLE BURNS UP OVERLY FAST

Generally a fast burn is good, but an overly-fast burn (compared to other times you have used the same kind of candle) means that although the work will go well, it may not last long. You might have to repeat the job at a later date.

If you have set lights for several people and one person's candle burns faster than the others, then that person is most affected by the work, but the influence may not last long enough to produce a permanent change.

THE CANDLE TIPS OVER AND FLAMES UP INTO A FIRE HAZARD

Not only will the spell fail but there may be increased danger ahead for you or the client. In order to accomplish anything, you will have to start the entire job over from the beginning — but first do a thorough Uncrossing spell for everyone involved and ritually clean the premises before setting any more lights.

A FREE-STANDING CANDLE RUNS AND MELTS A LOT WHILE BURNING

This gives you an opportunity to observe the flow of wax for signs. For instance, if you are burning a bride-and-groom candle for love, and the woman's wax runs all over the man's, then the woman desires the man more than he desires her. If you are burning a green money candle and the wax melts and runs down onto the monetary offering, then the spell is "eager to work" and the candle is "blessing the money."

Some people try to influence the way melting wax runs. They do this as an intentional part of the spell-work, to increase the likelihood that things will go their way. Others prefer to let nature take its course and to watch running wax for signs, without interfering in its movements.

A FREE-STANDING CANDLE BURNS DOWN TO A PUDDLE OF WAX

When this happens, most workers will examine the shape of the wax for a sign. You may see something of importance there, for the shape may suggest an outcome regarding the matter at hand. For instance, a heart-shaped wax puddle is a good significator if you are burning red candles for love spells — and a coffin-shaped wax puddle is a good significator if you are burning a black devil candle against an enemy. Wax puddles come in all kinds of shapes; many candle-workers treat them like tea-leaves when they "read" them, working according to the standard cultural symbolism attributed to tea-leaf or coffee-ground patterns.

A GLASS ENCASED CANDLE BURNS HALF CLEAN AND HALF DIRTY

This indicates that there is hidden trouble with the person for whom the lights have been set or that someone is working against your wishes. Things will not go well at first, but by repeated spells you may get them to go better.

A FREE-STANDING CANDLE LETS OUT A LOT OF SMOKE BUT BURNS CLEAN AT THE END

Again, hidden trouble or someone working against your wishes. Things will not go well at first, but with repeated work you will overcome.

A DIRTY, BLACK, SOOTY BURN MESSES UP A GLASS ENCASED CANDLE

This means things are going to go hard — the spell may not work, the blessing may fail, the person is in deeper stress or trouble than you thought. If the work is being done against an enemy and the enemy's candle burns sooty and dirty, then it is likely that the enemy is fighting your influences.

A GLASS ENCASED VIGIL CANDLE CRACKS OR BREAKS, SPILLING WAX

This is never a "good" sign. That does not mean, however, that it is always a "bad" sign. You need to consider what kind of candle it is in order to interpret the meaning.

A broken Love Me candle and dripping wax could mean tears and separation. A broken Money Stay With Me candle with dripping wax could mean inability to control outflow of money. A broken Separation candle might signify a compete and abrupt break-up (with tears). A broken Cast Off Evil candle might signify that the evil spell was suddenly broken (possibly with tears, bloodshed, or God-all-knows-what). In other words, the symbolism of a broken candle varies based on the type of candle.

In any case, when a candle breaks, the action i personally would take would be to set another of the same sort of light on the same situation; that is, i would re-do the work because i would not consider a broken candle and spilled wax to be a positive outcome unless the candle was lit for a negative petition, and even then it would have negative side-effects (tears, blood, loss).

"Divination Signs from Burning Candles" was Lucky Mojo Hand-Out Sheet No. 2, published in 2002. Like "Candle Burning Basics," it has been a stock workshop flyer ever since it was lifted more or less intact from my 1995 online book "Hoodoo in Theory and Practice" at LuckyMojo.com/hoodoo.html. The particular URL this text was drawn from is the popular "Candle Divination," page located at LuckyMojo.com/candlemagicdivination.html — and a more complete version of this text can be found in my 2013 book "The Art of Hoodoo Candle Magic."

SOME THOUGHTS ABOUT CANDLES
catherine yronwode

CHOOSING YOUR LIGHTS

OIL LAMPS

Before there was candle magic, there were oil lamps — fueled by butter, Olive oil or other vegetable oils, Whale oil, or kerosene (also called coal oil).

The advantages of oil lamps over candles:
• They burn for very, very long periods of time
• The reservoir can be refilled while the lamp burns
• They tend to be fairly safe if left unattended

The disadvantages of oil lamps:
• They may give off unpleasant odors
• They are difficult to read for divinatory purposes

FREE-STANDING ALTAR, OFFERTORY, JUMBO, AND TAPER LIGHTS

Early candles were made of beeswax or tallow (animal fat), but they are now made of paraffin (petroleum wax), hardened vegetable oil, or a blend of any of these. Modern chemistry techniques and the rise of the aniline dye industry in the early 20th century gave us the choice of candle colours. Because many spiritual suppliers to the African-American market in the 1940s were Jews, they naturally offered white Sabbath candles, branched menorah candle holders, and multi-coloured Hanukkah candles to their customers, imparting a festive kabbalistic glow to hoodoo altar rites which has persisted to this day.

Modern candle shops usually carry 4" altar lights (chime candles), 6" offertory candles (household candles), and 9" jumbo candles in at least ten symbolic colours, plus gold and silver 12" tapers.

The advantages of free-standing candles:
• They are inexpensive
• They have fairly predictable burn times
• They come in a variety of colours
• They are quickly prepared and dressed
• They can easily be rolled in an herb-wax mix

The disadvantages of free-standing candles:
• They are not safe to burn unattended
• Purchasing candle stands is an extra expense

DOUBLE ACTION AND REVERSIBLE CANDLES

A double action candle is generally butted — that is, the end is cut off and a new tip is carved at the other end. It is then burned on a mirror to reverse conditions. The green and black double action candle for reversing bad luck in money can be burned on thursday, a day good for money. The red and black double action candle for reversing bad luck in love can be burned on Friday, a day symbolic of love. The white and black double action candle for reversing bad luck in health and well-being can be burned on Sunday, a day symbolic of health or blessings.

The advantages of double action candles:
• They are inexpensive

The disadvantages double action candles:
• They are not safe to burn unattended
• Butting them and carving new tips is a job of work

FIGURAL CANDLES

In addition to stocking offertory candles, spiritual suppliers, as early as the 1930s, provided figural or "image" candles for special uses. More expensive than plain offertory candles, figurals are preferred by many practitioners when working unusual or extremely strong spells, because their visual symbolism is easy to see, and by carving names or other features in them, they can be personalized to represent individuals, in what amounts to a cross between working with candles and working with doll-babies or poppets. The stock of figural candles varies greatly from one supplier to another, as the moulds for most of these candles are registered with the U.S. patent office, and copying them is forbidden.

The advantages of figural candles:
• The images are an aid to concentration and focus
• They are ideal for moving candle spells
• They can be used as doll-babies and still burned
• They produce piles of wax for use in divination
• They come in a variety of colours

The disadvantages of figural candles:
• They are relatively expensive
• They are more breakable than plain candles
• They have variable and unpredictable burn times

GLASS VIGIL LIGHTS

Catholic style glass-encased votive, vigil, and novena candles made little impact on conjure until the late 1970s, when a wave of Latin-American immigrants brought Catholic customs to America and American makers designed the first secular or magical glass-encased candles, silk-screened all over the glass with lucky, protective, and aggressive images. The silk-screening machines were expensive, and the entire field of imprinted vigil candles was controlled by less than a half-dozen factories nation-wide, but in the 1990s, with the increased availability of colour printing, suppliers all over America began to design their own conjure candles with paper labels, which broke the near-monopoly on vigil candles for the hoodoo market.

The advantages of glass-encased candles
• They are relatively safe to leave unattended
• They leave signs of smoke and wax for divination
• They come in a variety of colours

The disadvantages of glass-encased candles
• They are heavy, and hence costly to ship
• They sometimes break or explode while burning

TRIMMING WICKS

Candle wicks are trimmed BEFORE lighting, if necessary. Some candles have very long wicks — maybe you have not had the experience of seeing these, but i have seen figural candles with up to 2" of free wick. I am not talking here about factory offertory candles, but figurals and such that are made by hand.

Attempting to light a 2" long wick is just a waste of time — it cannot draw the wax up it. You have to trim it first.

LOADING, INSCRIBING, AND PETITIONING

To load a candle, insert into it some personal concerns of the target of your spell. Once filled, the hole may be sealed with wax.

To inscribe the candle, write names or words on the candle, using a needle, pin, or nail. The words need not be legible to be effective.

A petition or prayer may be inscribed on the candle or written on a paper that is set beneath the candle or candle-stand, or taped to the candle.

ANOINTING, DRESSING, PRAYING, SEALING, AND KNOCKING

Once your candle has been inscribed, it should be anointed or dressed with an appropriate oil or combination of oils. Dress upward to draw and downward to repel. Dress double action candles both ways from the middle. Dress figural candles as if they were the figure they represent.

An awl can be used to poke holes in the wax of a vigil light, as can a screw driver, a nail, or a stick. It has been my practice to use a special tool dedicated to this task, and to keep it stored in a small tool kit in a drawer or box beneath my altar. This tool is also useful for straightening up wicks, carving "runlets" in free-standing candles to keep them from drowning, and fishing out pieces of wooden matches that have fallen into the deep wells of tall candles. I have used the same antique screw driver to work with my altar lights for 43 years now.

The candle should then be prayed over and sealed or knocked to fix it. There are several ways to seal a candle, by tapping it on the altar, by knocking on the top, and by holding it up and reciting a prayer over it.

DO YOU NEED TO CLEANSE YOUR CANDLES?

Candles do NOT need to be cleansed before burning. I'd say that 99% of folks DON'T cleanse their candles, and they get good results. The idea of cleansing candles is associated with the religions of Santeria, Voodoo, and Palo. Most Catholics of the USA and European type and most Protestant hoodoo practitioners do not cleanse candles before use. I don't think Hindus do either. Nor Jews, nor Muslims— at least none of them have ever instructed me to cleanse a candle before use. At my shop and in my church we just prepare a petition, affix it to the candle or lay it under the candle, dress the candle, pray over the candle, seal or knock the candle, and light the candle.

Whatever you do, don't get water on your candle — there are whole rafts of people who washed their candles with water and then felt they'd gotten a "bad sign" because the residual water put their flame out. Silliest thing i ever heard — 'cause OF COURSE water drowns a fire. If you feel the need to cleanse a candle before use, use Hoyt's Cologne. It'll evaporate quickly and won't put your flame out.

"SAVING" BAD CANDLES

When a free-standing candle is in danger of drowning, i abandon my natural inclination to use the candle in an accessory rite of wax divination, and with an awl, screw-driver, or pen-knife i carve a runlet to save having to do the spell over again.

Most folks almost instinctively do this for free-standing candles, but there is hesitancy among new practitioners to save badly burning vigil lights. One reason may be that they lack proper tools for addressing a candle that is well down inside an 8" tall glass tube. This is remedied by getting and using dedicated candle tools. Another reason newcomers are reluctant to salvage badly burning vigil lights is that they are learning about smoke-pattern divination in the glass, and somehow they get the idea that signs in the glass are only valid if they develop naturally, without meddling. They think that touching the candle may mess up the divination. However, vigil candles are spells-in-progress as well as divinatory aids, and if the wick forms a knot, it always ends up smoking the glass — so why settle for a bad divination and set a second light when you can correct the candle as it burns?

I always remove polyp-like knots on the ends of wicks and remediate bad wick placement to forestall cracked glass. I use splint-wicks to relight candles that go out, making a hole with my awl as close to the drowned wick as possible, inserting the splint, lighting it with additional prayers, and watching it closely. If the original wick catches after a while, i use my hemostat to extract the splint-wick, in order to avoid a messy double-wick burn. I trim, groom, and work my vigil candles to get the results i want. Many people don't — God bless them — but then they have to light more candles, until they get one to burn right. For me, it's like raising animals — if one falls sick, i don't just buy a second one to replace it. I nurse it back to health.

If you want to passively WATCH a candle burn, then let the knots stay, watch the twin flames, watch the wax run, watch the glass break and spill wax all over. In my church we call these candles "test candles" — that is, candles burned for the sole purpose of divination by wax or smoke reading.

If you want to WORK the situation through candle magic, you do not have to sit back and watch knots, runny wax, or out-of-control flames. Get the message the candle gives — and then rectify the unfortunate candle signs. This is YOUR WORK, and you can make the outcome of the spell as good as possible.

DISPOSING OF THE PETITION PAPER

Disposing of a petition paper in fire after burning a candle is a fairly individual practice. Not everyone does it the same way. The most popular method is to burn the paper in the candle flame right before it goes out. I do not always do this, and i'd like to explain why:

If you are burning a free-standing, offertory, jumbo, or figural candle, setting the petition paper alight at the end is a great conclusion to the ritual. All it requires is having a brass dish on the altar in which to drop the burning paper, lest you scorch your fingers. The ashes from the petition paper can then be mixed with sachet powder and used to further the intention of the spell, according to the many ways in which powders are customarily employed.

However, if you are burning a glass-encased vigil light and wish to perform a divination on the glass after the candle is finished, either via ceromancy (wax reading) or capnomancy (smoke reading), then burning your petition paper inside the candle glass will definitely smoke the glass up and change the signs you would have seen had you left the glass alone. Because a clear, clean candle glass portends success, it would seem counter-productive to smoke up a clear glass at the end of the rite, by tossing the petition paper into it and setting it alight.

If, for this or any other reason, you do not want to dispose of the petition paper in fire, you should not feel bound to do so. There are many cases in which you might find it a good idea to save the petition paper for further use rather than to dispose of it. Such future use may include setting it under another candle, but that need not necessarily be the case. For example, depending on the kind of spell work you are performing, you may wish to wear the petition paper in your shoe, carry it in your wallet, hide it over a door-frame, set it loose in running water, or save it for a continuation of the candle rite at a future date. The latter is especially the case if the petition has taken the form of a packet rather than a mere paper and contains personal concerns or herbs that your be difficult to replace if it were burned.

I wrote "Some Thoughts About Candles" for distribution at my 2011 candle workshop because i wanted to toss in some new ideas to accompany the earlier hand-outs. These new ideas led me to consider more new ideas, and thus was born an entire book, "The Art of Hoodoo Candle Magic," in 2013, in which this text is included.

OIL LAMPS IN HISTORY AND IN HOODOO
Professor Charles Porterfield

A BRIEF HISTORY OF OIL LAMPS

An Oil Lamp is a vessel that burns fuel to produce light continuously for a period of time. The flame is usually confined to a combustible material called the wick, to prevent the entire fuel surface from igniting. The word lamp is derived from the Greek word lampas, meaning torch.

The use of oil lamps extends from prehistory to the present day. The first lamps were made from naturally occurring objects such as coconuts, sea shells, egg shells, and hollow stones. The first shell lamps were in existence more than 6,000 years ago, during the Neolithic or Later Stone Age, c. 8500 - 4500 BCE.

It is thought that the first man-made lamps were carved from stone. Carved stone lamps have been found that date back as far as the Mesolithic or Middle Stone Age, c. 10,300 - 8000 BCE.

Early fuels for lamps consisted of olive oil, fish oil, whale oil, sesame oil, nut oil, and similar substances. These were the most commonly used fuels until the late 18th century when drilling for petroleum oil began, which led to kerosene — also known as coal oil, paraffin oil, and lamp oil — to become the most popular lamp fuel. The light given by an olive oil lamp is significantly brighter than a candle, but significantly less than that of kerosene lamp.

Lamps that burned olive oil as their fuel were in wide use throughout the Mediterranean well into the 19th century. Although mass-produced out of metal, they were otherwise little changed in design from the stone or clay lamps of some 2,000 years earlier.

The evolution of lamp forms moved from bowl-shaped to saucer-shaped, generally with a loose or unfixed wick, then from a saucer with a nozzle or wick-guide to a closed bowl with a spout or otherwise fixed wick, and finally to a mechanical system for regulating wick height, called the burner.

In 1780 the Argand lamp was invented by Ami Argand, a Swiss chemist, and quickly replaced the ancient form. It was, in turn, replaced by the kerosene lamp in about 1850. In small towns and rural areas these lamps continued to be in use well into the 20th century.

Most contemporary oil lamps are provided with a small wheel that moves the wick up and down so the user can adjust the light. Common modern lamps include the farmer's lantern, made of metal and glass, and the hurricane or parlour lamp, made of glass with a metal burner. In addition, some lamps are equipped with a mantle of non-flammable incandescent woven material which sheds more light.

RELIGIOUS USE OF OIL LAMPS

IN JUDAISM

Lamps appear in Jewish spirituality as lighting the way for the righteous, the wise, and for love and other positive values. In Judaism fire is often described as being destructive, but light is seen as being spiritually constructive and meaningful. Oil lamps are used in several traditional Jewish spiritual rituals and the oil lamp and its light has become an important ritualistic item.

"And you shall command the people of Israel that they bring to you pure beaten olive-oil for the light, that a lamp may be set to burn continually." (Exodus 27:20)

"A lamp is called a lamp, and the soul of man is called a lamp." (Babylonian Talmud, Shabbat 30B)

IN CHRISTIANITY

In the Orthodox Church and many Eastern Catholic Churches oil lamps are still used both on the altar and to illuminate icons on the iconostasis and around the temple. Orthodox Christians will also use oil lamps in their homes to illuminate their icon corner.

Traditionally, the sanctuary lamp in an Orthodox church is an oil lamp. It is lit by the bishop when the church is consecrated, and ideally it should burn perpetually thereafter. The oil burned in all of these lamps is by tradition olive oil.

"Your eye is the lamp of your body; when your eye is sound, your whole body is sound, your whole body is full of light; but when it is not sound, your body is full of darkness." (Luke 11:34)

"He was a burning and shining lamp, and you were willing to rejoice for a while in his light." (John 5:35)

IN ISLAM

According to the Koran:

"God is the Light of the heavens and the earth. The parable of His light is, as it were, that of a niche containing a lamp; the lamp is [enclosed] in glass, the glass [shining] like a radiant star: [a lamp] lit from a blessed tree - an olive-tree that is neither of the east nor of the west the oil whereof [is so bright that it] would well-nigh give light [of itself] even though fire had not touched it: light upon light! God guides unto His light him that wills [to be guided]; and [to this end[God propounds parables unto men, since God [alone] has full knowledge of all things." 24:35

IN HINDUISM

Oil lamps are used in Hindu temples as well as in home shrines. In Southern India, the most common lamp has only one wick, whereas in Northern India, a five-wick lamp is used, usually fueled with ghee (clarified butter).

Traditionally the lamps used in temples are circular with places for five wicks. There will usually be at least one lamp in each shrine, and the main shrine may contain several. Normally only one wick is lit, with all five lit only on festive occasions.

In home shrines, the sacred lamp is different, containing only one wick. The back of the lamp is typically composed of a piece of metal attached to the lamp which has an embossed image of a Hindu deity upon it, to whom that lamp is dedicated. In many homes this lamp burns all day, but in other homes it is lit at sunset. The home shrine lamp is supposed to be lit before any other lights are turned on in the home.

IN CHINESE FOLK RELIGION

Oil lamps are lit at traditional Chinese shrines before an image of a deity or a plaque with Chinese characters giving the name of the deity. Such lamps are usually made from clear glass and resemble western drinking glasses; they are filled with oil, sometimes with water underneath.

A cork or plastic floater containing a wick is placed on top of the oil with the bottom of the wick submerged in the on. Such lamps are kept burning in shrines, whether private or public, and incense sticks or joss sticks are lit from the lamp.

MAGICAL LAMPS

Oil lamps are used for magic, prayer, petition, and spell casting especially within the traditions of the African Diaspora, Ceremonial Magick, and Jewish Mysticism — and e can distinguish magical lamps from religious lamps because although magical lamps may be used in conjunction with veneration, devotions, and prayers to deities or to Spirit, they are also used in spells to effect changes in the lives of practitioners and their clients.

"A man's soul is the lamp of God, which searches the chambers of one's innards." (Proverbs 20:27)

HOODOO AND CONJURE LAMPS

Within the tradition of African American hoodoo, a lamp used for magical or spiritual purposes is normally a regular glass-reservoir kerosene lamp with a chimney, which has been fixed by placing minerals, herbs, roots, zoological curios, powders, and/or oils into the lamp's reservoir and then adding lamp fuel. Olive oil and other rustic lamps fueled with vegetable oil may be used as well, but since they are not bright lighting sources, they are not as common as kerosene lamps in the American South.

LATIN AMERICAN AND CARIBBEAN LAMPS

Practitioners of the magical traditions associated with African Diasporic religions such as Santeria, Lukumi, Palo Mayombe, and Quimbanda tend to craft lamps both as religious offerings and a requests for the aid of deities and spirits. These lamps are generally fueled with vegetable oils of various types and may be of the open or bowl style or have their wicks fixed in place.

INSIDE THE LAMP

Here are some lists of curios and botanical items that can added to lamp reservoirs in the creation of various hoodoo and conjure lamps:

PEACEFUL HOME LAMPS

- Angelica Root
- Basil
- Lavender
- Peaceful Home Oils
- Rosemary
- Sandalwood Chips
- Southern John Root

MONEY LAMPS

- Cinnamon Sticks
- Coins:
    - 3, 7, or 9 silver dimes
    - A coin for each person in the house
    - An array of coins totalling your own age
    - The change from your first cash sale
    - A penny, a nickel, a dime, a quarter, a fifty-cent piece, and a silver dollar.
- Devil's Shoestring (nine pieces tied together)
- Five Finger Grass
- Gator's Paw
- John the Conqueror Root
- Lodestone
- Money Drawing Oils
- Pyrite

LOVE LAMPS

- Adam and Eve Roots, a pair
- Balm of Gilead Buds, a pair
- Blood Root (He Coon and She Coon), a pair
- Cinnamon Sticks
- Cowrie Shells
- Ginger Root
- John the Conqueror Root
- Love Drawing Oils
- Matched Lodestones
- Munachi Stone or other carving of a couple
- Queen Elizabeth Root

PETITIONS

Petition papers can be placed loose into the lamp's reservoir or pinned to the wick of the lamp before lighting. They may also placed under the lamp, with or without other papers, such as copies of the Psalms, Solomonic or Mosaic seals of power, maps, photographs, drawings, or business cards. When crafting money lamps you can also create an unworded petition by carving your initials onto each of the coins that will be added into the lamp.

CLEANING THE CHIMNEY

Over time smoke and soot build up in the glass chimney of hurricane or farm style kerosene lamps, dimming the light, so every few days you should remove and clean the chimney. You may leave the lamp burning while you do this, but be aware that it will smoke. Hand wash the chimney in soapy water, just as you would a fine wine goblet or drinking glass.

TRIMMING THE WICK

To keep a kerosene lamp "in good trim" you will need to occasionally use the little wheel to roll the about 1/2 inch of wick up from the burner and trim the charred tip off the wick with a pair of scissors. There are three basic shapes for wicks, flat, pointed, and crowned, and each produces a different type of flame. One easy way to trim the wick is to round the corners to conform to the dome of the burner.

COLOURING LAMPS AND LAMP OIL

It is quite common in modern magical practices to associate certain colours with symbolic conditions, deities, or states of mind. In order to prepare a light that accords with a symbolic colour, simply purchase a lamp with a coloured glass reservoir; red for love, green for money, blue for a peaceful home, brown for court cases, clear for blessings, etc. If you can't find lamps made with appropriately coloured glass reservoirs, you can use pre-tinted lamp oil to produce the symbolic colours. Many hardware stores carry tinted lamp oil; if yours does not, you can order liquid soap dyes to colour your oil any hue you wish.

CONCLUSION

The creation and maintenance of magical oil lamps can be a little trickier than using modern day magical candles, but it is well worth the extra time and effort, because their influence and effectiveness is unquestionable. Before the bright, warm glow of a lamp we are in the world of our ancestors linking us back to the past and grounding us. Oil lamps continue to be an enduring token of humanity's desire to conquer darkness and the Philosophy of Fire.

"Oil Lamps" was written by the remarkable root doctor Professor Charles Porterfield of Denton, Texas, an old-school worker with impeccable taste and manners. This hand-out accompanied his 2009 MISC workshop presentation, at which he also raffled off a splendid example of the lamp-maker's art. In addition to his facility as a teacher, Professor Porterfield is a writer, and as such he was my constant telephonic colleague during 2009, the year that we created the Association of Independent Readers and Rootworkers (AIRR) web site. The two of us spent many happy evening hours together writing quietly across the lines. Professor Porterfield presently devotes his time to the study and practice of Hasidic Judaism and hoodoo; he can be reached at ProfessorPorterfield.com.

RUSTIC HOODOO OIL LAMPS
Dr. E.

HISTORIC LAMPS

Fire has always held spiritual meaning. The creation and maintenance of fire were of chief concern to ancient people for their very lives depended on it. The need for a constant source of fire and light led to the development of the lamp. With the invention of the lamp, people added more hours of productivity to their day and rapidly sped up our evolution as a species.

Within religious practices, fire was used as a sacrificial tool for burnt offerings, or as symbolic and literal representations of divine light. Fire's ability to pierce through the darkness of night and provide safety, illumination and warmth represented the protection of the divine. Places of worship around the globe utilized lamps as a sign of the eternal presence of the divine and its power. (As well as a practical tool for light during the night time hours.)

The earliest lamps were simple: a stone with a natural depression that acted as reservoirs to hold oil and a wick. Later, lamps were crafted out of clay and moulded to hold more oil, and better position the wick against the side for maximum light, or adding handles or chains for easier handling. These lamps were maintained with the addition of oil and the replacement of wicks as needed. Lamps were made from virtually every non-flammable material including sea shells, Coconut shells, clay, stone, and metal. The most commonly used form of a lamp was shallow and wide likes a bowl, with an opening on the top into which oil could be poured, and one or more shallow pointed spouts on which a fiber wick could rest.

These early lamps were fueled by naturally occurring oils like olive oil, fish oil, nut oils, castor oil, or ghee (clarified butter). Wicks were made from natural fibers: linen, flax, rushes, or cotton. The thickness of the wick affected how easily the fuel was drawn up into the flame, and the length of the wick dictated how large the flame was. A larger flame burned more fuel and often created a smoky burn, while a smaller flame burned fuel more efficiently, gave less light, and didn't emit as much smoke. Within places of worship, the maintenance of sacred lamps was a job reserved for spiritual leaders and keepers of the sacred place.

MODERN LAMPS

Up until the invention of the gas-powered lamp, oil lamps were the primary source of light in most homes. With the development of petroleum refining, and the invention of the kerosene lamp in 1850, lamps became even more simple to maintain. The traditional kerosene lamp with a glass chimney (or glass globe) and metal knob to adjust the wick became the favoured lamp in the United States. These lamps were still used for regular lighting well into the 20th century in areas of the country that had not yet received electrical wiring, and many families still keep a kerosene lamp on hand for emergencies.

Many rootworkers utilize kerosene lamps as a way of working spells over long periods of time. The reservoir of the lamp can be filled with various curios appropriate for a magical goal. The lamp is then filled with plain kerosene, prayed over, then lit. As the fuel is consumed, the top can be unscrewed and more fuel can be added without extinguishing the flame. This way of keeping a perpetual light working for a magical goal is very reminiscent of the eternal flames kept in religious places of worship.

While most modern rootworkers prefer to use candles, the use of lamps is far older and more closely tied to magical practices of Africa. Candles are simply unpractical in tropical climates. They melt, warping their shape, and burn too quickly. In these climates, the use of lamps was far more common in religious services and magical spells. The making of magical lamps filled with curios and powerful objects was found in most of the tribes of West Africa. With the slave trade, the magical use of loaded lamps came with the Congolese people to the Americas and became part of many African Diasporic Religions, as well as hoodoo.

The Congo people used oil lamps well after the introduction of candles. They created lamps in clay saucers or metal bowls filled with objects for their gods (like nails, stones or fish hooks), pieces of roots, and herbs with the magical powers needed for their goals. They were filled with palm oil (or olive oil in the Caribbean), wicked with dried palm fiber or cotton, and set before their sacred shrines as a petition to their gods for help, protection, health, or to curse an enemy.

HOW TO MAKE A RUSTIC OIL LAMP

Rustic hoodoo oil lamps can be made in almost any fireproof container. My container of choice is a one quart glass Ball or Kerr canning jar with a metal lid and rim, but I've also made lamps in ceramic bowls of the appropriate colour for my magical goal.

The Container: Remove the top of your canning jar and make sure the jar is clean. Separate the lid from the rim. Carefully cut the lid using a sturdy pair of kitchen shears or tin snips. (See diagram.) Be careful with this step as the lid is very sharp and can cut you. Bless the container by smoking it with an appropriate incense, and dress the inside with a corresponding condition oil.

The Curios: Any fully-dried plant curios, mineral curios, charms or other items can be added to the jar. Lightly dress each item with an appropriate condition oil and pray over it as you add it to the jar. See the list of recommended curios for suggested items to use.

The Oil: Selecting a vegetable oil associated with your magical goal is one of the benefits of using a rustic hoodoo oil lamp. Fill the jar with the appropriate oil while you pray a selected psalm for your needs. Leave 1/2 inch of space between the oil and the lid. You do not want the two touching. Add a few drops of your selected condition oil to the jar. You may dye your oil with oil-based pigments to match your magical goal.

The Wick: Because vegetable oils are heavier than kerosene it is important to use a loose natural fiber wick. The best material is 100% cotton woven bandage from a drug store. (Do not use cotton wool or cotton balls.) Tightly roll the bandage along its length.

ASSEMBLING AND USING THE LAMP

Rub the wick with a condition oil, then submerge it into the oil in the jar. Pull 1/4 inch of wick through the slit in the metal lid. Place the lid on the top of the jar and screw the threaded rim in place to tighten it down. Pray over your lamp and light it. Take a moment to observe your lamp and make sure it is burning properly. It may take a while for the oil to start wicking.

Think of your rustic hoodoo oil lamp as an eternal flame. Place it atop any item you wish to work in a spell.

Lucky lamps can be placed atop lottery tickets. Protection lamps can be placed on a photo of the family. Money lamps can be placed on $2.00 bills or in a dish of gold dollar coins. Cursing lamps can be placed on your enemy's personal concerns, or you can make a clay doll-baby and submerge it inside the lamp to keep an evil flame burning on your enemy. Lamps can also be set as constant beacons for power and protection on your hoodoo working altar.

Top off your oil lamp on a daily basis, or more frequently if needed. The wedge shape cut out of the lid allows you to easily pour more oil in or add curios and condition oil as needed. The wick must be pulled up through the lid as it is consumed. I use a small pair of tongs to do this. Never let the oil get lower than 2 inches below the flame or the oil won't pull up the wick and the flame will self-extinguish. When your wick runs out, roll a new one and replace it in your lamp.

CURIOS FOR OIL LAMPS

Love: Lodestone, Lovage, John the Conqueror, Queen Elizabeth root, Cubeb, Ginger, Raccoon bone.

Money: Lodestone, Pyrite, Cinnamon, Nutmeg, Allspice berries, Sassafras bark, Irish Moss, coins.

Protection: Ginger, Devil's Shoestrings, Angelica, Bay leaf, Dragon's Blood, evil eye beads, a cross.

Curse: Graveyard dirt, Chilis, Peppercorns, Vandal Root, Brown Mustard seed, coffin nails, black salt.

Luck: Lucky Hand root, Alligator tooth or paw, John the Conqueror, Nutmeg, Pyrite, dice or coins.

Healing: Angelica root, Buckeye nut, Eucalyptus leaves, Althaea (Marshmallow) root, Ginseng root.

VEGETABLE OILS FOR OIL LAMPS

Love: Olive Oil, Sunflower or Safflower Oil
Money: Corn or Peanut Oil
Luck or Success: Sunflower Oil
Protection or Healing: Olive Oil or Canola Oil
Cursing: Castor Oil

Dr. E. is a member of the Association of Independent Readers and Rootworkers and Hoodoo Psychics, founder of the Santería Church of the Orishas, and creator of Dr. E. Products. He is available for consultations through his web site ConjureDoctor.com. "Rustic Hoodoo Oil Lamps" was presented at his 2013 workshop of the same name.

MOJO HANDS FOR MONEY, LOVE, AND LEGAL WORK
catherine yronwode

Going to the Louisiana bottom
*   to get me a hoodoo hand*
Going to the Louisiana bottom
*   to get me a hoodoo hand*
Gotta stop these women from taking my man.

— Ma Rainey
Louisiana Hoodoo Blues, 1925

BACKGROUND

A mojo is the staple amulet of African-American hoodoo practice, a flannel bag or, less often, a muslin tobacco sack or leather bag containing one or more magical items. The word is said by some to be a corruption of the English word "magic" and others think it may be related to the West African word "mojuba," meaning a prayer of praise and homage, because It is a "prayer in a bag" — a spell you can carry.

Alternative names for the mojo bag include hand, mojo hand, conjure hand, lucky hand, conjure bag, trick bag, root bag, toby, jomo, and gris-gris bag. In the Memphis region, a special kind of mojo, worn only by women, is called a nation sack. A mojo used for divination, somewhat like a pendulum, is called a Jack, Jack bag, or Jack ball.

The word "gris-gris" looks French (and in French it would mean "grey-grey"), but it is simply a Frenchified spelling of the Central African word gree-gree (also sometimes spelled gri-gri). Gree-gree means "fetish" or "charm," thus a gris-gris or gree-gree bag is a charm bag. In the Caribbean, an almost-identical African-derived bag is called a wanga or oanga bag, from the African word wanga, which also means "charm" or "spell" — but that word is uncommon in the USA.

The word "conjure" — as in "conjure work" (casting spells) and "conjure woman" (a female herbalist-magician) — is an old alternative to "hoodoo," thus a conjure hand is a hoodoo bag, one made by a conjure doctor or two-headed doctor.

Likewise, the word trick derives from an African-American term for spell-casting — "laying tricks" — so a trick bag is a a a bag that contains a spell.

The word "hand" in this context means a combination of ingredients. The term may derive from the use of finger and hand bones of the dead in mojo bags made for various purposes, from the use of a root called Lucky Hand root in mojo bags for gamblers, or by an analogy between the mixed ingredients in the bag and the several cards that make up a "hand" in card games.

In the 1920s and '30s, as the manufacture and distribution of hoodoo spiritual supplies became a full-scale industry, the word "mojo" was adopted as a brand name for a variety of goods. For instance, Mojo Brand Oil, Genuine Mo-Jo Brand lodestones, Lucky Mojo Jickey Toilet Water, and Lucky Mo-Jo Good Luck Perfume were all made by the Chicago-based mail order firm Famous Products — which manufactured Lucky Brown hair dressing and Madame Jones skin brightener under the company-name Valmor Beauty Products, and distributed hoodoo supplies under the name King Novelty Company.

Although most "Southern Style" conjure bags are made of red flannel, some root doctors favour the colour-symbolism employed in candle-burning magic and thus use green flannel for a money mojo, white flannel for a baby-blessing mojo, red flannel for a love mojo, pale blue flannel for a peaceful home mojo, and so forth. Leather bags are seen less frequently than flannel; they are associated with Native Americans and with West Indian obeah, another form of folk magic closely related to African-American hoodoo.

Mojos made for an individual are usually carried on the person, always out of sight. They are rarely worn on a string around the neck, fairly commonly pinned inside a woman's brassiere, and much more commonly pinned to the clothes below the waist or carried in a pants pocket. Those who make conjure bags to carry as love spells sometimes specify that the mojo be worn next to the skin. Mojos intended to purify or protect a location are generally placed near the door, hidden in such a way that they cannot be seen by strangers.

Keeping the mojo from being seen is important because if another person touches it, the luck may be lost. This is called "killing the hand." The proscription against touching is far stronger in the case of the woman's nation sack than in any other kind of mojo.

29

IT'S IN THE BAG

What is contained in a mojo hand? Well, that varies a lot, based on what the wearer hopes to accomplish by carrying the amulet and what the maker finds effective or customary to use in preparing it. A mojo carried for love-drawing will contain different ingredients than one for gambling luck or magical protection. Generally there are at least three items in a simple hand, and many root doctors try to ensure that the total number of ingredients comes to an odd number — 3, 5, 7, 9, or 13 — although sometimes mixed herbs are counted as one item.

Once prepared or "fixed," the mojo is "dressed" or "fed" with a liquid of some kind. It may also be "smoked" in incense fumes or the smoke from a candle, or breathed upon to bring it to life. The most common liquids used to feed a hand are alcohol, such as whiskey; a perfume, such as Hoyt's Cologne or Florida Water; bodily fluids, such as spit or urine (or sexual fluids for a love-drawing hand); or with a specially-prepared condition oil. The bag is not generally soaked through, but simply dabbed with the liquid, although some old-time poker players i knew during in my youth, during the 1960s, used to say that to get a gambling hand to really work for you, you had to have your lover pee all over it out in the alley between rounds of play.

The objects most commonly found in mojo bags are roots and herbs, plus a variety of animal parts such as dyed feathers — green for money, red for love, orange for anger, blue for spiritual peace — rattlesnake rattles, dried frogs, swallow hearts, and bat wings. (Urban practitioners may substitute a toy plastic bat for the latter). Coins, metal lucky charms, crystals, good luck tokens, carved stones, and written papers may also be added for extra power. Some root workers top off their mojo bags with parchments upon which are printed medieval European seals and sigils of talismanic import, particularly the seals from the Greater Key of Solomon and The 6th and 7th Books of Moses, both of which are sold as sets of seals printed on parchment paper, and are used without reference to the rituals given in the texts of the books.

Here are a few representative mojo hand ingredients and the conditions for which they would be prescribed. To make a simple but effective mojo hand, you may select any three ingredients from any of these lists. It is also customary to add a name-paper or wish-paper signifying the person for whom the work is being done, as well as some personal concerns, if available.

SUGGESTED INGREDIENTS

FOR MONEY LUCK
in a Green Bag

- Pyrite
- Alfalfa leaf
- Nutmeg, whole
- Cinnamon chips
- Sassafras chips
- Blue Flag root chips

FOR LOVE LUCK
in a Red Bag

- Lodestone grit
- John the Conqueror root chips
- Queen Elizabeth root chips
- Cinnamon chips
- Damiana herb
- Love Herbs Mixture
    (nine herbs dressed with nine love oils)

FOR COURT AND LEGAL WORK
in a Yellow Bag

- Little John to Chew root
- Calendula flowers
- Deer's Tongue herb
- Cascara Sagrada bark chips
- Poppy seeds
- John the Conqueror root chips
- Lemon Grass

This material was adapted from my online book "Hoodoo in Theory and Practice," specifically the page called "Mojo Hand and Root Bag," located at LuckyMojo.com/mojo.html. It was written to accompany Dr. Kioni's 2008 workshop, which was held at the Home of Truth Spiritual Center. Participants climbed the steep wooden stairs to the second floor and entered a room where Dr. Kioni and his wife Marilyn assisted them. They were given a colour-choice of flannel bags and as the ingredients listed above were passed around, each person took what was wanted and made his or her own hand. When the bags had all been completed, Dr. Kioni shared his own way to fix a mojo in the smoke of incense or tobacco. Hanging the bag by its tail — the drawstring that held it closed — he called and chanted to it and commanded it to work. In the years since that long-ago workshop, i have talked to many people who can still recall that chant: "I am a money magnet! Money loves me! Money comes to me!" It was an inspiring demonstration of the conjure arts.

MAKIN' MOJO BAGS
Dr. E.

WHAT IS A MOJO BAG?

A mojo bag (also called a "hand," "jomo," "trick bag," or "gris- gris bag") is a magical charm bag constructed of various mineral, herbal or animal curios, and personal items belonging to its owner. By carrying a mojo bag, a person is centering the area of magical effect squarely on his physical body. But a mojo bag is far more than a charm bag, it is a private magical ally that is conjured to work on the behalf of its owner. No one should see, nor touch a person's mojo.

My philosophy is that mojo bags are conjured to life, not just constructed. They have a body, a mind and a soul. A powerful conjure doctor will use his alliance with the spirit of each curio that goes into the bag to conjure spirit medicine — "mojo" — that is more powerful than the mere sum of its parts.

WHAT GOES INTO A MOJO BAG?

To truly understand the structure and composition of a mojo bag, one must think of it as an entity with a body, mind and soul.

THE BODY

The body of the mojo bag is the contents of the bag and the bag itself. This can include any combination of dried roots, minerals, dried herbs and flowers, animal bones, coins, and other items of power. Each of these items has a unique spirit medicine that it brings to the body of the mojo bag. I'll discuss how to conjure that medicine later.

Typically mojos are contained in flannel bags (red being the most common and default colour), silk bags, or occasionally in leather. A material of a colour appropriate for the magical goal is usually selected. The bag may or may not be decorated with a sewn-on charm, according to the interests of the maker.

THE MIND

The mind of the mojo bag is the magical purpose written out in the form of a petition paper, name paper, scriptural prayer, affirmation, Solomonic or Mosaic seal. or other instruction set for the mojo.

The petition paper should be written out clearly in positive terms as if you have already attained your goal. For example: "I have a great paying job" for a job-attaining mojo bag.

Avoid statements that begin with "I will" for they place your desired goal perpetually in the future and out of reach. State what you want as if you already have attained it.

THE SOUL

The soul of the mojo bag is two-fold.

First, it includes a personal bodily concern that connects the bag to its owner, like a strand of hair, a fingernail. a photograph, or a dried drop of blood on a piece of tissue.

Second and most importantly there is the magical conjuration that breathes the bag to life and makes it an entity all its own. This critical part of the conjuration calls up the spirit medicine of the various parts of the bag and unifies them in purpose and magnifies them in strength.

The conjurer's life breath is breathed into the bag, summoning it to life and putting it to task. This breath is the animating force, and keeping the mojo private and hidden is key to preserving its power.

THE BODY: ROOTS, STONES, AND BONES

A unique trait of hoodoo is the pairing of minerals and herb curios in the conjuration of magic. For these reasons I typically like to include at least one mineral element in my mojos. Additionally, I prefer to use roots for their more powerfully grounded spirit medicine. All ingredients in a mojo bag should be dried to prevent moulding or rotting.

THE BAG

This is the skin of the mojo bag, and red flannel is the most common and typical material used, although historically yellow silk, leather, metal, or folded and sewn paper have also been used. You can select a bag with a colour that aligns with your magical goal.

MINERALS

I like to think of the mineral items in a mojo bag as the bones of the body. They are the solid frame upon which everything else is built. I put them into the bag first as they are the heaviest items. Common minerals used include chunks of pyrite, lodestones (naturally magnetic iron ore pieces), chunks of alum, or granular minerals like salt. Crystals and other gemstones are not traditionally used in hoodoo, but coins have always had an important part to play in the construction of mojo hands.

ROOTS

The next items I include in a bag are roots. When given a choice of an herb in root or leaf form, I will always select the root form first. Roots store the life force of plants, and consequently often have the most powerful spirit medicine available. I think of roots like the heart of the mojo bag. I prefer to use whole roots, but chopped root bits will do in a pinch.

SEEDS AND NUTS

Seeds are a wonderful addition to mojo bags and pack a nice punch of energy in them. Within a seed or nut, a plant stores potential energy for the life that will emerge from it once it germinates. Similarly, seeds and nuts have energetic and lively spirit medicine for us to use. Most of the spices used in cooking and hoodoo are some form of seed or nut. They are the muscles and tendons of the mojo bag, working hard for our benefit.

ANIMAL BONES, TEETH, AND CURIOS

While not everyone likes to use animal curios in their mojo bags, they are traditional in hoodoo. Animal curios can include bones, teeth, claws, paws or fur. Human bones — especially finger bones — are not uncommon in mojo hands, either. These curios draw upon the spirit medicine of that type of animal to give your mojo bag a powerful and unique punch. They are the teeth and claws of the mojo bag.

DRIED HERBS AND FLOWERS

Abundantly available and lightest in weight are dried leaves, herbs, and flowers. These are the nerves and connective tissues of the mojo bag. They are usually strongly scented, giving your mojo a unique scent. They are bulky and allow you to round out both the shape of your mojo bag, and balance the spirit medicine contained within.

THE MIND: PETITION PAPERS AND NAME PAPERS

Every mojo bag needs an instruction set, a mind, a program to follow. This keeps your mojo focused on its intended task and helps you to narrow your magical approach with accuracy. The best way to do this is with a petition or name paper. One should be created, smoked, dressed with an appropriate condition oil, folded up and added to the mojo bag before it is breathed to life.

Petition and name papers are typically written on some kind of "virgin" paper. It is traditional to use a piece of brown paper bag that has no printing on it, and has been hand-torn on all four edges. Crisp fresh currency can be used as a writing surface if the petition is for money. Optionally, different kinds of paper can be used for your goal, including paper of a shade similar the owner's skin colour, photographs of the intended owner, prayer papers, or even samples of an intended target's handwriting.

You can write your petition using a pen with an ink colour that is appropriate for your magical goal (a red pen for love, a green pen for money, etc.) or you can use a plain pencil with no eraser, "so you can't go back on your words."

PETITION PAPERS

Petition papers are easy to make. They are a small piece of paper (no bigger than 4 x 4 inches in size) on which you have written your intended desire or wish. You may write this in your own words, or in the form of a prayer, or you may quote an appropriate portion of scripture as your petition. Your petition need not rhyme or be expressed in fancy language. It is simply your wish or desire, committed to paper.

It is important to write your desire as if you have already attained it. Use positive language and describe what you want. Avoid describing what you don't want.

If you are creating a mojo bag for prosperity, a good example might read, "Prosperity builds in my life and my wealth is abundant." A bad example would read, "I will not have any debt and I will make lots of money." The bad example not only states things in the future (*I will*) but also describes things in the negative form by focusing on what the person doesn't want, and then mixes positive and negative together in one contradictory sentence.

NAME PAPERS

Name papers are a unique way to connect the intended magical goal to its owner. Like petition papers, they are no larger than a 4 x 4 inch piece of paper on which the intended magical goal of the bag is crisscrossed with the owner's name.

For a money draw mojo bag, as an example, you could write "Money Comes to Me" three times stacked on the paper, then turn the paper 1/4 turn clockwise and write the owner's name three times stacked and across the previously written goal. This is done so that goal will cross that person's path. For a love attraction mojo, the names of both parties may be written across or on top of each other, to bring them into proximity. Name papers are particularly effective when drawn on the back of the owner's photograph.

After you have completed writing out the petition or name paper, it is important to smoke the paper by passing it through incense smoke, then dressing it by either dusting it with a sachet powder or condition oil that is in harmony with your mojo bag's intended magical purpose.

Once the paper has been dressed, fold it in half toward you three times, turning it 1/4 turn clockwise each time you fold. This paper will be included in the mojo bag after the curios have been put into the bag.

THE SOUL:
PERSONAL ITEMS AND CONJURING THE MOJO'S MEDICINE

There are two parts to the soul of a mojo: The personal concern and the conjuration of spirit medicine. The personal concern powerfully connects a mojo bag to its intended owner. The conjuration of the spirit medicine is done for every item while it is being placed inside the bag.

PERSONAL CONCERNS

Personal concerns should tie or link to a person's unique body or characteristics. The more personal and intimate an item is, the more powerfully it will affect its owner.

The most personal items would be blood or sexual fluids; they carry the person's life force within them.

Less personal yet still effective items would be hair, fingernail clippings, saliva, sweat, etc.

Finally, the least personal items that would still work for a mojo would be swatches of clothing, writing samples, photographs, or a person's name on a name paper.

Personal concerns can be folded inside of the petition or name paper for safe keeping.

CONJURING THE MEDICINE

One by one, connect to each curio prior to placing them in the bag. Call out to the spirit of each item and ask for its consent to be added to the bag, clearly defining how it will help you. For example, "High John the Conqueror Root, I call to your spirit and ask for your assistance in this mojo bag. Lend me your spirit medicine that I may conquer my obstacles with this mojo bag."

Once every item has been added to the bag, finish with the petition paper and personal concern.

THE BREATH OF LIFE

Next, the mojo must be "breathed to life." Hold the bag up to your mouth and speak your prayer of intention into it. Give the bag a name, then take a deep breath and exhale into the bag, cinching the bag shut to catch your breath inside. This breathes the bag to life making it an entity all its own.

FEEDING AND EMPOWERING THE MOJO

Tie off the mojo bag with three square knots, then wrap the thread around the neck of the bag and tie it off to prevent any spillage. Dab an appropriate condition oil on the four corners and center of the bag to feed it and keep it strong (this will be done every week).

Finish by holding the mojo over smouldering incense while praying intensely for the mojo to come to life and work for its owner. Hold it over the incense until it swings in a steady circle. Snatch it up while at maximum swing to catch the magic. It is now alive and working. Keep it hidden.

Dr. E. taught "Makin' Mojo Bags" at the MISC workshops in 2012. A member of the AIRR Tech Team, a graduate of the my Hoodoo Rootwork Correspondence Course (#1266G), and the founder of Dr. E. Products, he can be reached for readings and rootwork consultations through his own ConjureDoctor.com web site.

CATHOLIC SAINT PACKETS FOR LOVE, MONEY, BLESSINGS
Lou Florez

WHAT IS A SAINT?

What distinguishes Catholic saint packets from other cloth-contained spells, such as mojo hands, is that they are dedicated to — and decorated with — the images of saints. On seeing these mojo-like bags and packets, hoodoo practitioners who are unfamiliar with the Catholic religion often ask, "What is a saint?"

A saint is a person who has been called to this state of presence and who has performed miraculous works which have been recognized by this or her religious community of worship. Within the Catholic tradition, saints are seen as intercessors in Heaven who carry the prayers of humanity. In addition, certain saints are granted "patronage" over certain occupations, locations, and human conditions. The practice of honouring and petitioning saints, spirit helpers, and miracle workers within rootwork and conjure has a long history and a vivid presence in the South among those who profess the Catholic faith.

A CONJURE MINISTER'S PERSPECTIVE

Growing up practicing folk Catholicism meant that my introduction to Christianity was less about going to church and learning the Bible than it was about developing a relationship with the Virgin and the saints, who were seen as invisible members of the family, readily available to offer guidance, advice, love, and comfort, as well as to act as healers, protectors, and defenders against the diseases, injustices, and ills of the world. The saints were real people who lived, breathed, and knew what it was like to be alive. Because of this, they want to help and uplift the lives of their communities. Even after death they continue to work for those same principles, and it is because of their humanness that they know the specific nature and urgency of our needs.

As a reader and rootworker, I am continually astonished and brought to awe by the miracles I see manifest in my life and my client's lives through traditional rituals, formulas, and novenas meant to invoke and evoke the spiritual power and grace of the saints. A receptive heart and honest communication are all that is needed to start opening the doors to blessings in your life.

ROOTWORK AND THE SAINTS: HOW DO I CHOOSE?

If you have ever googled "saints" and found yourself overwhelmed, I completely sympathize. In the Catholic cannon alone there are estimates of about 8,050 holy women and men who have been recognized, and that's not including "venerables," "servants of God," and Jewish archangels such as Michael and Raphael, who have also have been granted sainthood within the Catholic church. Add to that list the countless folk saints and spirit helpers who each are recognized within their spiritual communities and the number is astounding!

There are many methods by which practitioners select a saint to work with, and I will outline a few:

Saintly Patronage: Traditional Catholics often selects saints as allies through their roles as patrons of specific causes, locations, or areas of expertise. For instance, because of her association with invisible transmissions, Saint Claire is the patroness of psychics, mediums, clairvoyants, television, and radio. I would petition Saint Claire to receive the gifts that she was given and in order to have my psychic senses open and receptive to the presence of Spirit.

General Purpose Saints: Some saints, like Saint Joseph, can be called upon in multiple ways. Joseph is petitioned to sell property, to find a husband, for a good death, for job-getting, for the payment of child support, for a happy family, and to bear children. All of these attributes stem from varied incidents in his life.

Family Affiliation or Hereditary Transmission: Certain families and confraternities affiliate with particular saints. Reception of such a saint may occur during the Confirmation ritual of the Catholic Church.

Spiritualist or Hoodoo Head Readings: In some heterodox Catholic-influenced Spiritual churches, seekers may be given readings which outline the metaphysical gifts, talents, and personal saints that they will be called to work with throughout their lives.

Direct Visions: A more mystical way of identifying the right saint to work with is through direct visions given from the Saint during waking or sleeping life.

LATIN AMERICAN PACKAGE AMULETS

Latin American package amulets are square or rectangular packets filled with magical and/or religious articles and wrapped in cellophane, vinyl, foil, or cloth. They may be carried on the person, secreted in a drawer, or kept on an altar. Like North American mojo hands or medicine bags, they may contain written prayers, scriptural text, minerals, herbs, roots, or curios. Some common fillings for package amulets are grains (for prosperity), Lodestone grit to draw money, herbs or seeds for use in varied magical operations, and scented herbal incense mixtures appropriate to the conditions for which the packages are made.

Package amulets are usually decorated with metal charms, beads, crocheted edging, sequins, or glitter. Not all package amulets are saint packets; the latter can be identified by small external printed images of saints, called "estampas" (stamps). Specialized saint packets are made for specific purposes, such as the following, for domination in love:

SAINT MARTHA THE DOMINATOR'S DOMINATING HAND

You will need the following ingredients:

- Red bag
- Picture or statuary representation of Saint Martha
- Petition paper
- A piece of red string
- Saint Martha Oil
- Small figural representation of the target's genitals
- A small strip of fabric from the target's underwear
- A strip of fabric cut from inside your own left shoe
- Licorice root
- Catnip herb
- Dried Orange peel
- * Calamus root
- Sampson Snake Root
- Five Finger Grass
- Estampa for the outside of the packet

Place your representation of the saint so she looks over your working space. Anoint her lightly with her oil three times in the shape of a cross, one beneath the other, while saying, "Holy Virgin Saint Martha who entered the mountain and tied up the beast with your ribbons, hear my petition and watch over this working as The Lord watched over you."

Write a dominant, authoritative petition describing the situation, and how it needs to be addressed.

Keep your petition short, and remember that sometimes the strongest prayer can be said simply. Anoint the paper in a five spot pattern, fold it three times towards yourself, and place it to the side.

Tie the cloth from your target's underwear onto or around the genital representation while saying, "As a servant knows their master, so shall you know me."

Anoint the tied genital representation with Saint Martha oil, saying, "As Saint Martha knew the Dragon, I know the snake. [Name]'s words and actions brought them here, and so shall they stay till I release them."

The tied genital representation, the petition, and the piece of fabric from your left shoe will next be bound with the piece of red string. Start by anointing the string with Saint Martha Oil by drawing it toward yourself while saying, "As the holy ribbons bound the beast, so shall this string bind my beast"

Next take the petition paper, the tied genital representation, and the piece of cloth fabric cut from the inside of your left shoe, making sure the shoe fabric is enough to cover the representation, and bind everything together with the string three times. Tie the string, then say, "Let [Name] not sit in a chair, nor lie in a bed until they are at my feet. Holy Martha, hear me, help me for the love of God."

Anoint the bundle with Saint Martha oil until it is completely covered. Place it in your left hand, and sprinkle it lightly with each of the herbs, saying, "Holy Virgin Martha, I dedicate this packet to you so that you may relieve me of all my miseries and help me to overcome all difficulties. As you dominated the beast at your feet, give me health and work so that I may provide for my needs." Place the packet in the red bag.

Address the image of Saint Martha that has been watching you work: "My Mother, grant me that [Name], may not live in peace until they come to stand at my feet. In this way, my Mother, for the love of God, grant my petition and eliminate my suffering. Amen." Place the image above the charm, looking down on it. Sew or tie the bag closed, and decorate it. Wear it close to your person and feed it every Tuesday and Saturday with Saint Martha Oil.

"Catholic Saint Packets for Love, Money, Blessings" was the hand-out at Lou Florez's 2013 MISC workshop of the same name. Lou is a Church Deacon and Candle Minister at Missionary Independent Spiritual Church and a member of AIRR and Hoodoo Psychics. He can also be contacted for readings at his LouFlorez.com web site.

MAKING DOLL-BABIES FOR RITUAL USE
Dr. E.

WHAT IS A DOLL-BABY?

A doll-baby is a human effigy, usually constructed out of cloth, wax, clay, or some other pliable or mouldable material, tied to a specific person through the use of personal concerns (hair, fingernail clippings, blood, semen, etc.), and enlivened through prayer and ritual. It is used to affect your intended target powerfully on a very physical level. Doll-babies can be used for harmful or helpful magic, but in every case they are ritually connected to the target person's physical, mental, and spiritual condition.

DOLL-BABY, VOODOO DOLL, OR POPPET?

Historically, the practice of using a doll to affect a target with magic originates in Indo-European folk magic, not in the West African and Haitian religion of Voudoun. Regardless, the name "voodoo doll," described and portrayed in countless movies, has firmly established itself in our language.

"Poppet" is an older spelling of "puppet," meaning a small child or doll. Primarily a British-English term, it is not commonly encountered in the USA.

Within African American hoodoo, the terms "doll-baby" and "dollie" are most commonly used. These words do not convey the prejudice that surrounds the name "voodoo doll," nor do they require the affected use of a British term unfamiliar to most Americans.

MATERIALS FOR CONSTRUCTION

There are many ways to make a doll-baby, all of which have their advantages and applications.

CLOTH

Cloth doll-babies are easy to construct and afford you the opportunity to use cloth of a corresponding colour to the spell's intent. For greater potency, you can also utilize used clothing scraps from your target's wardrobe to make the doll. A commercial cloth doll can be improved if a button from the target's clothing is sewn onto it. Cloth dolls are easy to stuff with herbs and easy to bind with string or wire and stab with pins.

STICKS

Doll-babies made with sticks and plant material add a very rustic feel to your work. They can be made using twigs from herbs corresponding with your goal, such as Licorice sticks for domination or Cinnamon sticks for money-drawing. Doll-babies made from sticks can also be lashed together with used clothing scraps that belonged to your target, or even their used dental floss.

CLAY

My favourite way to make doll-babies is by sculpting them out of clay. It recalls God making mankind out of earth (Genesis 2:7) and allows for a more realistic representation of the person. You can use polymer clay and bake it in your oven for rigid doll-babies, or plasticine modeling clay for flexible doll-babies. Herbs can be finely ground and kneaded into the clay along with personal concerns. Clay doll-babies are sturdy and hold up to being submerged in liquids and being stabbed with pins or needles.

CORN HUSKS

Doll-babies made out of corn husks have a natural rustic appeal. They husks should be soaked overnight to make them flexible, and can then be woven into a human shape. Herbs can be stuffed inside the doll-baby along with personal concerns. Corn husk babies are very flammable and light - great for hitting someone with nasty curses.

WAX

Soft beeswax or wax cheese rinds can be kneaded with herbs and formed into a doll. Wax figure candles can be loaded by carving out a small hollow, stuffing in herbs and personal concerns, and melting the wax that was removed back into the cavity to seal it.

ROPE

Two lengths of common manila rope, knotted at both ends, make a serviceable doll. One length defines the length of the arms from hand to hand, the other runs from foot to head and down to foot again. A lashing of string holds the pieces in place. Clothing cut from the target's wardrobe completes the doll.

CONNECTING THE DOLL TO YOUR TARGET

In the process of constructing your doll-baby, it is imperative that you connect it to your target using some type of personal concern. Personal concerns vary from extremely difficult to obtain bodily items (like blood, semen, and vaginal fluids) to easily obtainable items that are related to the person (used clothing, hair, a writing sample, their signature, a photo, used napkins or cigarette butts, etc.). The item's power is directly proportional to how personally connected it is to your target and how difficult it is to obtain.

To affect your target on a more powerful, physical level you will want to use personal concerns from their physical body. For example, a bit of your target's dried blood on a used cotton ball or bandage links directly to your target's physical health, their circulation, and the blood that courses through their veins.

In addition to a personal concern, I like to give the doll-baby a stated purpose — instructions if you will — in the form of a name paper. I prefer to make the name paper, dress its four corners and center with an appropriate condition oil, then lay the doll on top of the paper, instead of putting it inside. This lets me use the doll (or the paper) for other spells in the future.

BAPTIZING THE DOLL-BABY

Once your doll has been assembled and connected physically through the inclusion of your target's personal concerns, you need to put a little magic to work to enliven the doll. The idea here is to use the personal concern as a physical conduit to capture that person's spirit in the doll. Here is one way to capture a spirit in a doll-baby:

You'll need:

- A Bible
- The prepared doll-baby
- Whiskey
- A hoodoo condition oil appropriate to your magical intent

Open the Bible to the book of Genesis, Chapter 2. Place the doll-baby on top of the Bible, face up. Mentally and emotionally connect to the personal concern within the doll-baby, and feel an energetic trace back to your intended target.

Holding the doll over a bowl or sink, dribble a bit of whiskey over the doll's head, "In the Name of the Father, the Son and the Holy Spirit. Amen!" Now, recite Genesis 2:7. Pray the Lord's Prayer, and state:

"You are no longer clay, you are now flesh and blood, the very body and vessel for the spirit of [Name]."

BREATHING LIFE INTO THE DOLL-BABY

Now, inhale deeply and as you do so, draw the spirit of the intended target from a distance (by way of the personal concern inside), into your belly and hold it there. As you exhale, breathe over the face of the doll and expel the spirit of that person into the doll while you intone the person's name. Repeat this breathing and intoning process three times until you feel the person's spirit captured in the doll. Then recite:

"[Name], I hold you in my hands, your body is mine to control, your will is mine to affect, and your fate is mine to determine. In the name of the Most Holy!"

Then intone the name of God:

"YOD HEH VAV HEH!"

The doll-baby is now enlivened. Dress its forehead, chest, genitals, hands, and feet with the appropriate condition oil. It is now ready for use in spell work.

CONSIDERATIONS WITH DOLL-BABIES

Once a doll-baby is enlivened, it has become a person's physical body. Treat it with great care. It's important to make sure the target of the doll never touches it. This will disempower the doll and you'll have to start from scratch. The other thing to consider is that your target might be able to perceive your activities in a vision or dream, so it is important to conceal harmful, attack magic by blindfolding your doll-baby. That way, if your target goes to get a consultation, they will be unable to see what you're doing.

If you want to effectively conceal your activities from another rootworker, you can easily lay down a small stack of a Bay leaf, a mirror and a Devil's Shoestring at the four corners of your working surface, and work during the dark or new Moon.

SPELL IDEAS FOR DOLL-BABIES

RECONCILIATION

Make two pink doll-babies, one for each person in the relationship, fill them with ground balm of gilead, damiana and licorice. Include a lodestone within the heart of each doll so that they will stick together.

Enliven the dolls and tie them together with their heart lodestones connected. Place them in a box full of dried Rose petals under your bed to draw your lover back home to you.

MIRROR BOX REVERSING

Make a small coffin out of a cardboard or wooden box. Cover the interior of the box with mirror shards making sure to avoid capturing your reflection in the mirror. Create a black coloured doll-baby for your enemy stuffed with Blackberry leaf. Blindfold the doll, hog-tie its arms and legs, and place it in the coffin. Cover the doll with Crab shell powder, Agrimony herb and sulphur powder.

Seal the box carefully, position it on top of a face-up mirror and place a jumbo reversing candle at each of the four corners of the coffin. Place a length of Devil's Shoestring root between each candle to box in your enemy and prevent them from escaping their repercussions.

Burn down the four candles, gather up the remnants and the coffin, bury it in the grave of a police officer or soldier who has agreed to work with you. Pay the spirit with a bottle of whiskey and a silver dime for their assistance. Return home by a different route.

PROXY UNCROSSING

Make a white doll-baby (either polymer clay or wax) for the person you intend to cleanse. Every day, you will make up a batch of Uncrossing Bath, and use it to bathe the doll. Air dry the doll, then dress it with Protection Oil.

Wrap the doll-baby in white cloth or rolled cotton and light a white candle dressed in Protection Oil and set it to burn at the head of the plate. Repeat this for the course of thirteen days and the person will be thoroughly cleansed of any evil. This working can also be done with herbal or mineral healing baths and Blessing Oil to help a person recover from a disease or affliction.

HOODOO WAR WATER TORTURE

Make a black doll-baby for your enemy, stuffed with Spanish Moss, Vandal Root, or Mullein. Place the doll-baby in a glass jar along with nine needles, a generous dusting of sulphur, Black Peppercorns, and Red Pepper. Take a bottle of War Water and carefully puncture a hole in the lid. Suspend the bottle over the open jar so that the War Water will drip over the doll-baby's head like a "Chinese water torture."

Curse your enemy while the water drips on his head. Once the entire bottle of War Water has been emptied into the jar with the doll-baby, cap the jar. Every day, swirl the jar so that the pins stab the doll baby with pains, and the dark whirling waters cause confusion in your enemy's life. When the time is right, dress a black candle with Crossing Oil and burn it down on top of the jar. This spell can be worked in perpetuity or you can do it for one month and bury the jar near your target's doorstep to hit him every time he walks over or around it.

DISASSEMBLING A DOLL-BABY

You may come to a point where you no longer want to continue using your doll baby. You cannot simply throw it out. It is important to ritually disempower the doll baby and disassemble it. Do this by washing the entire doll baby with whiskey and praying The Lord's Prayer over the doll. Say:

"You are no longer flesh and blood! I return you to the simple materials of which you were originally assembled and disconnect any spiritual, physical, or magical connection you had to [Name]! In the most Holy Name!"

Then intone the four names of God:

"Yod-Heh-Vav-Heh, Eheieh, Adonai, Ah-geh-la-ah."

The doll is no longer connected to the person. You can then either disassemble the doll (removing the personal concern) and burn each of the parts separately (scattering the ashes at the crossroads), or you can bury the doll at a crossroads where its energy may be scattered to the four corners of the earth. The doll baby is now disassembled.

"Making Doll-Babies for Ritual Use" was a hand-out at Dr. E.'s 2011 workshop. Dr. E. is a member of AIRR, and Hoodoo Psychics, the founder of Dr. E. Products, and is available for rootwork consultations through his web site ConjureDoctor.

HOW TO MAKE AND USE BOTTLE AND JAR SPELLS
catherine yronwode

HISTORY AND DEFINITION

A bottle spell is defined as a magical spell that is contained within a bottle, and which, when finished, is expected to work for the ends one desires. There are many types of bottle spells used in folk magic traditions from around the world.

Among the earliest bottle spells known are those called witch bottles. They are buried under the threshold or hidden up in a chimney to keep witches or evil-intentioned people away from your home. Examples of witch bottles have been found in England that date back to the 1600s at least.

A typical witch bottle contains sharp, jagged items like bent pins, shards of glass, nails, or even broken razor blades, a hair, and the urine of the person who wishes to be protected.

Some of the ancient witch bottles found sealed by archaeologists in England have been opened and all of them that still contained liquids tested positive for the presence of urine.

HOODOO BOTTLE SPELLS

Bottle spells are made in glass bottles with narrow mouths. appropriate herbs and minerals are placed in bottle along with a petition paper and it is customary to burn a candle in the mouth of the bottle before sealing it.

ATTRACTION, BLESSING, PROSPERITY, FAST LUCK, AND PSYCHIC VISION BOTTLE SPELLS

These are designed to draw what you want, bring about positive changes, get luck in a hurry, or help you to make money.

When a bottle is made for success, healing, wealth, or luck, a petition paper may be made made by writing your desire or command first and crossing it with your own name written out nine times. The paper is placed in the bottle with herbs and roots.

A small candle of the appropriate colour, dressed with an appropriate oil, may be burned in the mouth of the bottle before sealing it.

COME TO ME, LOVE ME, RECONCILIATION, PEACEFUL HOME, LAVENDER LOVE, AND STAY WITH ME BOTTLE SPELLS

These bottles are created while working on relationships in which there are two or more people involved and the object is to unite them.

In these cases, you may wish to write out a petition paper with your name repeated nine times on top of the name of the other party, to rule them.

A candle dressed with an appropriate formula oil or an all-purpose oil such as Special Oil No. 20 may be burned in or on the bottle, if desired, before sealing it.

COMPELLING, STOP GOSSIP, OR BOSS FIX BOTTLE SPELLS

These are intended to make someone keep a promise, shut them up, or demand that they change their ways.

The petition may be made by writing their name on paper, crossed by your command, folding the paper with herbs such as Licorice and Calamus that are used to rule and control people.

A candle dressed with appropriate oil is burned in the neck of the bottle if desired, before sealing it.

BREAK UP BOTTLE SPELLS

These bottles are intended to break up a couple. They are widespread in African American hoodoo, and, interestingly, their contents are related to "divorce from demons" spells inscribed in bowls found in ancient Jewish ruins.

The petition may be made on a piece of paper which is cut apart to symbolize the coming break-up of the couple. Other ingredients are included to promote disagreements and arguments.

After a Break Up bottle is prepared it may be buried at the couple's home where they will step over it, or it can be shaken up daily as you name them and call down curses on their relationship.

Read more about hoodoo bottle spells here:
LuckyMojo.com/bottlespells.html

RELIGIOUS BOTTLE SPELLS

Religious bottle spells are a special form of prayer-in-a-bottle. Our bottles include images and painted decorations. Styles available include:

- Anima Sola (lonely soul) Bottle Spell
- Archangel Michael Bottle Spell
- Niño De Atocha (infant of atocha) Bottle Spell
- St. Christopher Bottle Spell
- St. Expedite Bottle Spell
- Guardian Angel Bottle Spell
- St. Jude Bottle Spell
- Just Judge Bottle Spell
- Mano Poderosa Bottle Spell
- Martha the Dominator Bottle Spell
- St. Martin Caballero Bottle Spell
- Infant of Prague Bottle Spell
- Santisima Muerte (Holy Death) Bottle Spell
- Seven African Powers Bottle Spell
- The Holy Trinity Bottle Spell
- Maria Dolorosa Bottle Spell
- O.L. Guadalupe Bottle Spell

The bottles are made to hold your wish or petition, written on paper, along with herbs and minerals deemed relevant to the case, such as Rose buds if calling upon the Virgin, two Balm of Gilead buds if petitioning Saint Anthony to mend a broken relationship, or Frankincense and Myrrh in making a petition to the Infant Jesus.

Once these items are in the bottle, a candle of the appropriate colour is inserted in the neck of the bottle and dressed with oil — either a named Saint oil or Holy Oil — and then lit. One candle alone may be sufficient, but some people burn several, one per day, until they achieve satisfaction.

Read more about religious bottle spells here:
LuckyMojo.com/bottlespells.html

HOODOO HONEY JAR SPELLS

Honey jar spells are generally used for helpful magic only. They are worked in a wide-mouth jar rather than a bottle and if a candle is burned, it will be set upon the metal lid of the jar. They are typically made by writing names on paper, folding it around some personal items, herbs, or curios, and placing it in the honey to create sweet conditions. Small candles dressed with oils may be burned on the metal lid of the jar.

Boss Fix, Court Case, Crown of Success, King Solomon Wisdom, Love Me, Money Drawing, Peaceful Home, Reconciliation, Steady Work, Stay With Me, Stop Gossip, Influence, and Forestall Foreclosure honey jar spells are used when you want people to be sweet to you. If you don't know the name of the person you want to sweeten, substitute the person's job description: "School Staff," "Bank Loan Department," and "Parole Board" are all appropriate terms of address. Company logos are also useful.

See more information here:
LuckyMojo.com/honeyjar.html

WORKING WITH AND DISPOSING OF BOTTLE AND JAR SPELLS

If your spell is ongoing, you may make a "shaking" bottle of it before you seal it. After the candle burns, add vinegar (for a harmful spell), Florida Water (for blessing), or Hoyt's Cologne (for good luck) and seal the bottle. Hold it between your thumb and middle finger and shake it rhythmically, as you would a rattle, while you call aloud your blessing, wish, prayer, or curse. Do this every day or once a week. Your words should be improvised and cadenced, like preaching, toasting, or rapping. Honey jars are generally not shaken, but are kept going by burning candles on them Monday, Wednesday, and Friday.

When you are done with a bottle spell, prayer bottle, or honey jar and feel that the work is completed, it may be buried, thrown into a crossroads or running water, or kept on an altar, depending on what your intention was.

If the spell or prayer was to rid yourself of some person or condition, dispose of the bottle in earth, water, or fire, as appropriate to the case.

If your intention was to keep someone close but not let them know what you are doing, bury the bottle in your back yard.

If the petition or prayer was for love, money, or luck, and you maintain an altar, keep the bottle on the altar where it will continue to work for you.

See more information here:
LuckyMojo.com/layingtricks.html

"Bottle and Jar Spells" was Lucky Mojo Shop Hand-Out No. 14 in 2002 and is adapted from my 1995 book "Hoodoo in Theory and Practice."

CONTAINER SPELLS IN THE HOODOO TRADITION
Lara Rivera

TYPES OF CONTAINER SPELLS

Container spells are spells in which curios and prayers are physically contained within something, such as a bottle, bag, bowl, jar, etc. Let's take a look at the various types of container spells used in the hoodoo tradition:

HONEY JARS

One of the most well known container spells in modern hoodoo is the honey jar spell. A jar of honey containing petition papers, plus optional herbs, roots, and prayers, is used to "sweeten" a person or situation in favour of the practitioner or client. Other forms of sweet liquid can be used in place of honey; Karo Syrup, Crystal Syrup, home made brown sugar syrup, Log Cabin Syrup, Vermont Maple syrup, molasses, etc. The sweetener may later be used in cooking.

SUGAR BOXES, BOWLS, AND JARS

A sugar box, bowl, or jar spell also sweetens those whose names are added. Different types of sugar may indicate the skin colour of those involved: brown sugar for dark skin; white sugar for light skin. Sugar spells may include popsicle sticks on which people's names are written; rotating them in the sugar does the work. The sugar may be removed later and used in cooking.

BOTTLES AND JARS

All manner of bottles and jars are used to contain spells. The bottles can be clear, painted, glass, pottery, ceramic, or clay. Gourds are used in a similar manner. Herbs, roots, curios, petition papers, powders, and oils are added to the bottle which is then shaken to get the work going, or buried to deploy or to dispose of the work. A European version of this is the English witch bottles used to keep witches away from the home.

RED APPLES OR RED ONIONS IN A TIN

Hollowed-out red apples or red onions are used as containers in spells to sweeten a person or a situation like a court case, loan application, or conflict at work. The apple or onion needs to be of a size that fits in a tin, such as a coffee can. It is then cored and filled with name papers, herbs, and a sweetener such as honey.

FLOWER POTS

Putting an Apple or Onion sweetening spell into a flower pot is an effective method for deployment, done to keep the work going while out of sight, which makes the flower pot a container. Flower pots can also be used for the disposal of ritual remains when no natural or outdoors earth is available.

MOJO BAGS

A mojo is a small red flannel bag, or a tied-up bit of red flannel that contains herbs, roots and minerals, which is then dressed with a condition oil or perfume. Other regional names for similar bag spells are hands, gris gris, tobies, jomos, and nation sacks.

EGGS

When items are introduced into an egg for the purpose of spell work, the egg is a container. Ingredients within the egg can be selected for anything from love to hot-footing. In some spells breaking the egg is part of the rite.

COFFIN, MIRROR BOX, OR CIGAR BOX SPELLS

Small wood or cardboard boxes have many uses: miniature coffins to "send someone to the graveyard," mirror boxes to reverse evil, old prescription bottles and cigarette containers to remove addictions, etc.

POPPETS AND BABY DOLLS

Cloth, porcelain, or clay dolls or statues can be used to create a container spell, if filled with curios.

OIL LAMPS

A condition lamp is a form of fire magic in a container. Traditional glass kerosene, paraffin oil,or vegetable oil lamps may be used. The well of the lamp is filled with herbs, roots, curios, condition oils, and other ingredients before the lamp is lit.

LOADED CANDLES

Another form of containment involves hollowing out and loading a candle, typically a figural candle, with herbs and petition papers prior to the candle being lit.

SELECTING YOUR CONTAINER AND INGREDIENTS

CONTAINER

Determine which kind of container you are going to use. This is often as simple as choosing what you have on hand. Set the container on your workspace, altar, or handkerchief as you select your ingredients.

HERBS, ROOTS, AND CURIOS

See *Hoodoo Herb and Root Magic* by catherine yronwode for lists of herbs used for various conditions.

COLOURED CANDLE

A 4" candle appropriate to the work is all that is necessary. If the container has fire-safe surfaces, the candle may be burned on top or inside the container; otherwise it is set on the altar or the container is placed under an overturned bowl and the candle is lit atop that.

DRESSING OILS AND CONDITION OILS

Van Van Oil is used to dress roots and curios. Other choices include John the Conqueror Oil for John the Conqueror root, Lodestone Oil for Lodestones, and Court Case Oil for Little John to Chew root. Or select an appropriate oil, such as Healing, Reconciliation, Fast Luck, Money Drawing, Love Me, Pay Me, etc.

INCENSE

Cloth containers, including poppets and mojo bags, may be smoked to fix them. With other containers, you can simply light an appropriate incense on the altar as you work to aid in concentration and success.

WAX

You can use soft wax to quickly create a baby doll or poppet to be used in box spells, coffin spells, and some jar spells, such as Hot Foot jars.

PAPER

A large paper holds herbs; a small piece is for your petition; or simply write the petition on the herb-paper.

LIQUID OR SOLID "CARRIER"

Many containers include solid or liquid carriers such as sugar, dirt, perfume, honey, vinegar, or hot sauce.

THE RITUAL OF PREPARATION: A WAX DOLL INSIDE A CONTAINER

Select an appropriate condition incense and light it.

Select each of your larger roots or curios and "wake them up" by anointing them with Van Van Oil (or other appropriate oil), speaking to them in a voice of command or encouragement. Ask them to assist you in the spell work, and breathe on them to give them "the breath of life." Pass them through the incense smoke and set them aside as you finish. Repeat for all the larger individual roots or curios.

Set the herbs out on the white piece of paper. You may mix them together or leave them in separate piles if they are very different from one another. Hold your hands over the herbs and speak to them, asking for their help in your working. Name each herb and call upon its magical usage: "Five Finger Grass, I call upon you to aid me in all things lucky that may be accomplished with five fingers." You may then put a few drops of your condition oil on the herbs, or pass the paper with the herbs on it through the incense.

Form your wax poppet into human shape, then name and baptize it. You may also add some of the herbs to the wax, working them in with your fingers.

Write out your petition paper carefully, using a pen, a bridge pencil, or ink and quill. You may then dress the petition paper with the condition oil, some of the herbs, or with sachet powder. Fold the paper towards you to draw in, or away from you to send away, according to your work.

Put the herbs, roots, curios, wax poppet, and petition paper into the container you chose. Tie, close, or seal the container according to its tradition. For example, mojo bags are tied closed, cloth poppets are sewn closed, and bottles and jars are corked or have the lids tightly secured, with or without the addition of carrier solids or liquids.

Finally, depending on the type of spell you are doing, you will smoke the item, or burn a candle on it or beside it while saying your prayers or curses before deploying it.

Lara Rivera's "Container Spells" class in 2009 was one of those deceptively simple concepts that encompass a vast array of possibilities, all bound firmly within the tradition of Southern Christian hoodoo. Each participant made a container spell, for good or evil, and all were well pleased.

HOW TO USE YOUR LUCKY MOJO HONEY JAR SPELL
catherine yronwode

WHY WE USE SWEETENING SPELLS

Sweetening spells can be worked on anyone's name you want to sweeten. Depending on what relationship the person has to you, what special items you put into the name-packet, the colour of candle you choose, and the oil you dress it with, this trick will cause the person you name to like you more, to love you more, to favour your petition, to want to help you, to be sympathetic to your cause, or to forgive any wrongs you have committed.

Sweetening spells can be used to influence and sweeten a judge in a court case, a loan officer at the bank, a boss from whom you want a raise, or a teacher in your school from whom you want a good grade. They can sweeten a lover whom you want back in your life, an in-law who has been back-biting you, or a friend who has cut you off because of a foolish quarrel. Use them to get hired, to bring in a proposal of marriage, or cause a pet to bond with you and other pets in the home.

A BRIEF HISTORY OF SWEET SPELLS

There are many variations of this spell. In the oldest version that i know, there is actually no "honey-jar," just a plain white cream-saucer in which you burn a candle on the person's name, surrounded by a poured-out ring of syrup. This old-fashioned method has the disadvantage of drawing flies, so, as packaged syrups and sweeteners became available from grocery stores during the late 19th and early 20th centuries, the honey-jar and sugar-jar versions of the spell gradually replaced the old cream-saucer version, and the candle was placed on top of the jar, not in a circle of sweetener. You can work it either way, but a jar is a lot neater, that's all.

Another old-fashioned variation makes use of plain white sugar. You lay the names of the people such as family members, neighbours, or church members whom you want to sweeten into a jar, with layers of sugar in between. Then you pray over the jar daily and use the sugar in preparing food for them, especially pies, cakes, or cookies. As the sugar runs low in the jar, you continually top it up and pray over it, and you may keep on making good things to eat from that sugar for as long as you wish.

In the old days, when skin colour was a lot more important to people than it is now, it was sometimes recommended that the colour of the sweetener match the skin of the person you wanted to sweeten. Thus, for a white judge, you might use Crystal Syrup or white sugar, and for a Latino loan officer you might use light brown sugar syrup or light brown sugar, and for a dark-skinned lover you might use Brer Rabbit Blackstrap Molasses or dark brown sugar. I was once told to use powdered sugar for sweetening babies, "because it looks like baby powder."

Frankly, these days specifying a person's skin colour is not as meaningful as it once was (for which we can all be thankful), and today many folks prefer to use honey for the spell, no matter what the target's skin colour is, because it is a natural sweetener and not man-made. I believe that if you just follow your own intuition and decide which sweetener you like the best, you can be confident that you have made the right choice.

Again, in the old days, when writing out our petitions, we were told to use white paper for a white person, tan paper for a high-brown, and rough old grocery-bag paper for a person of dark colour, but these days the type of paper you use can simply be a matter of personal style.

I use the smooth, tan-coloured light-weight shopping bag paper because that is my choice, based on the way i was taught, which was that such paper is "pure paper" and better than parchment from the art-supply store. I prepare my paper by tearing it neatly on all four sides so there is no machine-cut edge.

Of course some folks prefer parchment paper more, and they trim it square with scissors — and the spell still works for them.

MAKE SURE YOUR INTENTION IS SUITABLE FOR THIS SPELL

Sweetening spells work on living beings. They will not draw lottery winnings; they will not rid your home of a ghost, and they will not allow you to dominate, torment, or curse another person. They are for one thing and one thing only — making one or more people sweet to you.

WORKING WITH YOUR LUCKY MOJO HONEY JAR SPELL KIT

We have included the following items in your kit:

• A jar of honey in a glass container with a metal lid
• A piece of parchment paper
• Appropriate herbs and curios
• An appropriate candle-dressing oil
• A candle of appropriate symbolic colour
• A star-holder for the candle

You will also need:

• A pencil or pen
• A needle
• An optional pair of scissors
• Bodily concerns

Sweetening spells can be made with sugar, honey, Karo Syrup, Crystal Syrup, home-made syrup, Log Cabin Syrup, Vermont maple syrup, Brer Rabbit Blackstrap Molasses — as long as the sweetener is not so diluted with water that it will ferment. We have chosen honey and put it into a short jar with a metal (not plastic!) lid so you can burn candles on it.

We have included a sheet of parchment paper in this jar for you, but you can use paper bag paper if you wish. Once you have cut or torn your paper into a square, write the person's name three times on it, one name under the other like so:

John Russell Brown
John Russell Brown
John Russell Brown

Rotate the paper 90 degrees and write your own name across the person's name, also three times:

Abigail Samantha Little
Abigail Samantha Little
Abigail Samantha Little

The result will be that the two names are crossed over each other, like a cross or a tic-tac-toe grid, and the other person's name will be under yours. This is called crossing and covering their name.

If the sweetening is being done for love, you can use a red ink pen. Otherwise, the colour of the ink does not matter. You can use a pencil, if you prefer.

Now all around the crossed names, write your specific wish in a circle. If you need a guideline, lightly sketch the circle-shape with a pencil and then follow around it when writing with your ink pen.

Write your wish in one continuous run of script letters, with no spaces — AND WITHOUT LIFTING YOUR PEN FROM THE PAPER. Do not cross your t's or dot your i's. Just write the words in one run and be sure to join up the end of the last word with the beginning of the first word so the circle is complete. Then go back and cross your t's and dot your i's. To make it easy to connect the word together at the end, i have found it best to make my petition in the form of short commands, such as "help me favour me help me favour me" or "love me love me love me" or "forgive me come back forgive me come back." If you make a mistake — or if you lift your pen in the middle of writing your petition-circle — throw away the paper and start it all over again. You want it to be perfect.

Herbal ingredients are now added to the name-paper. These will vary based on the kind of kit you purchased — Court Case Root for a court case, Rose petals for love, Clove buds for friendship, Bayberry or Sassafras root for house blessing money, Five Finger Grass for a loan from the bank, Damiana for sexuality, small Lodestones to draw love, Deer's Tongue leaves for a proposal of marriage, Solomon Seal root for impressing teachers, and so forth.

If you are sweetening someone for love, then in addition to the name-paper and whatever herbs, roots, or minerals you add, you must also try to get one of the person's hairs and one of your hairs. Lay them crosswise to each other. In either case, place them on the name-paper. Don't ask me what to do if you can't get their hairs 'cause i can't help with that. Either work the spell without the hairs and expect a much lower rate of success or get the hairs! Don't load the paper up with lots of other stuff thinking that if you can't get the hairs that six different love-herbs and two lodestones will be as strong as two hairs. They won't be.

Fold the paper toward you to bring what you want your way and speak aloud your wish as you do so. Turn the paper and fold it again, and again, always folding toward you, to bring what you want your way. Speak aloud your wish each time you fold the paper toward you. Fold it until it will not fold any more.

Open the jar of honey or syrup. Push the folded paper packet down into the jar. It may float. Take out a spoon's or finger-tip's worth and eat it, saying, "As this honey is sweet to me, so will i become sweet to John Russell Brown [or the name of the person you are working this on]" and close up the lid. You can do this three times — taking out three small dips of sweetener and speaking your wish aloud each time.

Your kit contains a candle of a colour appropriate to your work. Bend the prongs on your star-holder to grip the candle tight. Inscribe your wish or the name of the person you are working on into the candle with a needle. It is traditional to do this in the form of a spiral, like the stripes on a barber pole. Next, dress the candle with the oil — such as Love Me, Court Case, or Reconciliation — which is included in your kit. Stand the candle in the prepared star-holder and set it on top of the lid. Pray over it before you light it.

Let the candle burn all the way out. Do this every Monday, Wednesday, and Friday, for as long as it takes. Add each new candle on top of the remains of the last one. I have seen people's syrup-jar spells like this done for court cases that were continued for so long and required so many candles that you could not see the jar under all the dripped-on wax!

Honey will naturally crystallize or "candy" in cooler weather, especially if it is organic honey with a high pollen content. If your honey jar spell kit was shipped to you during cold weather, it may arrive crystallized. Crystallized honey is not ruined or bad. You may leave it as it is, or you may warm it in a hot water bath — or just zap it in a microwave for 15 to 30 seconds. If you microwave your honey, remember that metal must never go into a microwave, so take the lid off the jar and place the jar on a microwave-safe plate. Process it for 15 seconds, stir, and process it for 15 seconds more. Be careful — the jar will be warm or hot. Handle with care. You may let the jar cool off to a little above room temperature before closing the lid.

Even if your honey arrived in liquid form, if you keep your honey jar spell kit in an unheated room, the honey may crystallize unexpectedly. Again, this does not mean that the honey has gone bad or that the spell has been ruined. Honey crystallization is a natural process. To keep your honey liquid, store your honey jar in a warm place, such as on a high shelf in your kitchen or pantry. Do not store it on the floor where it can be exposed to cold drafts. If it crystallizes, you may warm it as described above, but it is not necessary to do so.

THREE THINGS NOT TO DO WITH YOUR HONEY JAR

1) Do not add mean-spirited, cursing, ill-intentioned, or evil herbs such as Vandal Root, Devil's Dung, or Bitter Aloes to your honey jar. Honey is for sweetening, not for harming. If you want to "heat up" a sweet spell, use Ginger or Cinnamon, not Cayenne Pepper.

2) Do not add toxic herbs to your sweetening spell and expect to be able to use the sweetener in cooking. Keep all added herbs inside the name packet or packets. Cooking with your honey (or sugar) is traditional and effective.

3) Don't worry about opening the jar or letting people see it. A honey jar is not a mojo hand that must remain tied or is "killed" if it touched by another person.

DISPOSING OF YOUR HONEY JAR

You don't need to dispose of a honey jar. You can keep it around as long as you please, burning candles on it whenever you feel the need. (We sell dozen-packs of the same kind of candle you got with the kit, if you want to extend the work for a longer time.)

If the spell is working and you are satisfied, one of the best ways to "dispose" of the honey is to use it in cooking or to sweeten tea. This is especially appropriate if you are in a position to cook for the person on whom the jar was made.

If you are done with the spell and are far away from the one on whom you did the work, it is traditional to take the jar to an Ant hill, open it, and leave it as an offering for the Ants. In hoodoo there is a belief that Ants communicate with one another all around the world, so if you ask the Ants for help, your sweet spell will be conveyed to your friend, family member, or lover, wherever in the world he or she may be.

If you feel the spell did not work, or if you no longer care if that person is sweet to you, take the jar to a river, open the lid, and, holding the jar under water, scoop out the honey and release it into the flowing water, When the glass jar and lid are rinsed clean, take them home and put them in your recycling.

"Honey Jar Spells" was Lucky Mojo Shop Hand-Out No. 5 in 2002, adapted from my 1995 online book "Hoodoo in Theory and Practice." It was distributed at several workshops, and in 2010 it was replaced with this longer version, specifically designed to instruct our customers.

SPIRIT VESSELS AND SPIRIT TRAPS
ConjureMan Ali

SPIRIT VESSELS

Many traditions of magic teach that the universe is populated with unseen hosts of spirits who vary greatly in character, temperament, and purpose.

Benevolent spirits can become powerful allies and helpers to the individual who can properly petition and invoke their power.

Malevolent spirits, on the other hand, bring trouble and harm to people who do not employ protective means to ward off their influence.

Therefore, how to interact with these spirits varies according to the nature of the entities themselves. Among these teachings is the idea of using physical objects to either house or trap spirits.

SPIRIT HOUSES

Those spirits who are considered helpful and beneficent are potentially very powerful allies. One of the ways that their power is invoked is by giving them a place where they can live. Another way is by offering them food and water.

Spirit houses are found around the world in various cultures and are seen as a means by which to manifest the power of the spirits, to propitiate them, and to seek their aid and assistance.

Homes for spirits can range from statues meant to give the disembodied a body, to miniature homes complete with luxury furnishings, to necromantic pots designed to give the dead the power over life.

SPIRIT TRAPS

In contrast to welcoming spirits into your home by giving them a place to reside, or offering them a pleasant house in which to dwell, spirit traps are used to protect a person or place from the disruptive influence of evil and malicious spirits by capturing them. These spirits are viewed as dangerous and capable of causing miscarriages, death, nightmares, and other tragedies and so cultures the world around have employed various objects to trap and thus stop the intrusion of these spirits into home and life.

Some spirit traps are meant to provide permanent protection and others are temporary and have to be remade after they have fulfilled their purpose. Remaking them often involves seeking out a specialist who is able to craft another spirit trap.

SPIRIT VESSELS AROUND THE WORLD

In this brief survey, we will look at several popular types of spirit vessels from many cultures, both ancient and contemporary.

SPIRIT VESSELS IN ASIA: THAILAND

In Thailand it is believed that the spirits that dwell in nature can be displaced and may become unhappy or angry if human habitations are built on their land.

Therefore small spirit houses or spirit temples, each about the size an American doll-house, are built for the spirits and kept outdoors. Offerings of fruit and flowers may be placed around the spirit houses for the spirits.

SPIRIT VESSELS IN AFRICA: THE CONGO

In the magical practices of the Congo we find a wide variety of spirit vessels, such as the nkisi ndoki, nganga, bwete, and other minkisi. These may take the form of statuary, pots, or tied packets, and are generally crafted by priests or magicians with the intent of housing spiritual allies, thereby giving the individual who possesses them a direct physical link to those spirits and their powers.

In contrast, evil spirits are often trapped using knots and nails which are then put into containers like gourds and sent down a body of water to remove their influence. Acts of spirit removal are often performed by a specialist or priest who knows how to employ knot magic to bind the spirit that may be bothering an individual, trap it within a specially made gourd, and then send it down-river to the place which all spirits came from. Alternatively, once trapped, the spirit may set on fire to remove it.

SPIRIT VESSELS IN THE NEAR EAST: MESOPOTAMIA AND THE LEVANT

In Mesopotamia and the region of the Levant, the spirits of the desert and the night have long been considered some of the most dangerous beings. Ancient entities like Lilith and Pazuzu were feared spirits reputed to cause miscarriage and disease. They are associated with the untamed deserts that border on the edge of the civilization of cities.

In order to keep these dangerous spirits from entering into the domicile, the people of the ancient Near East hired specialists to craft demon bowls that drew in the wandering and disruptive spirits and cut them off from the house. These protective demon bowls were used by the early Jewish people in dealing with Lilith and were one of the ways to stop her from causing sudden infant deaths or miscarriages.

To make demon bowls, professional magicians and scribes use a spiraling magical script that includes secret words of power and languages known only to the writer. The spirals lure the demons into the bowls, which are then either buried on the property or placed in the four corners of a home.

SPIRIT VESSELS AROUND THE MEDITERRANEAN SEA: NORTH AFRICA AND THE MIDDLE EAST

Borrowing the techniques that had developed in the Levant and Mesopotamia, the magicians of North Africa and the Middle East employ djinn bowls to deal with the invisible race of beings known as djinn.

Some djinn are believed to be helpful, while others are dangerous. Those associated with the dangers of the desert are often considered to be malicious. To ward off and keep these djinn from bringing disasters like illness, the evil eye, or sand storms, the people of North Africa and the Middle East employ djinn bowls which are made with a spiraling Quranic script and blessed with prayers. These are filled with water which will capture the djinn, who are then taken back out to the desert, where the water is poured out.

The idea is that the djinn will be lured by the spiraling script and trapped by the water. This allows the magician to dispose of the spirits away from the home and therefore keep their dangerous influence away.

SPIRIT VESSELS IN EUROPE: GERMANY AND ENGLAND

The witch bottles of England and Germany are bottles filled with magically charged items which capture haunts, ghosts, and revenants by luring them into the device. Sometimes it is believed that these malevolent forces have been sent by enemy witches and from this they draw their name. If the right items are placed in a witch bottle, the spirit is drawn into the bottle. Once it enters it is trapped. Witch bottles are placed in windowsills, buried at the threshold, or hidden up the chimney to prevent spirits from entering the house.

Impromptu and temporary spirit traps are made by placing a flour sifter or sieve beneath the bed or scattering mustard or poppy seeds on the floor, forcing the spirits to count the holes or the seeds all night long, while the inhabitants sleep soundly.

SPIRIT VESSELS IN THE UNITED STATES: CONJURE, ROOTWORK, AND HOODOO

Hoodoo spirit vessels and spirit traps vary from region to region. Their forms derive from the cultures that have contributed to African American folk-magic.

- **The Black Hawk buckets** seen in African American Spiritualist churches are a form of spirit vessel, reminding us of the clay pots and iron cauldrons of the Congo that similarly house spirits, and of their Afro-Caribbean counterparts.
- **Louisiana spirit houses made out of bottles** are used for work with ancestors or friendly spirits of the dead, another African custom.
- **Spirit traps made within bottles,** using knots, things that spiral, and items believed to draw and trap dangerous spirits, embody the practices of Africa, Europe, and the Middle East.
- **Bottle trees** in the South-East and Texas are a form of spirit trap, and they often employ blue bottles, a colour harkening back to Middle Eastern protections against the evil eye.
- **Psalms 121 by the bedside, accompanied by a glass of water** (the latter to be thrown out in the morning), is a form of spirit trap that shows evidence of Jewish traditions in conjure.
- **A spirit-trapping flour sifter under the bed and seeds scattered on the floor** are hoodoo practices influenced by European folk-magic.

Spirit vessels and traps feature prominently in the conjure practices of Virginia, Georgia, South and North Carolina, Texas, and Mississippi.

ITEMS FOR A HOODOO SPIRIT BOTTLE

Spirit bottles within the tradition of conjure contain herbs, mineral, and man-made items that grant natural potency to the bottle to either ward off or trap evil spirits, depending on the maker's intentions and the cultural background being drawn upon. Reflective of the practices of hoodoo itself, conjure spirit vessels draw their influences from the full variety of folk magic traditions that have influenced African American culture.

Common items include:

- Red Pepper for protection.
- Knotweed to bind up and trap.
- Salt to protect and drive away.
- Black Pepper to ward off evil.
- Poppy Seeds to lure the spirit and trip it up.
- Mustard Seeds to lure the spirit into counting the seeds.
- Spanish Moss to tie up the spirit.
- Knotted strings to bind and tie the spirit.
- Urine for protection or to lure the spirit into the bottle.
- Nails to nail the spirit in place.
- Devil's Shoe String to tie up devils.
- Broken glass and broken mirrors to reflect back evil.

TO MAKE A SPIRIT BOTTLE

The idea behind spirit bottles is to draw the spirit into the bottle by forcing it to count items like poppy or mustard seeds, or by luring it down into the bottle with a spiral trail of herbs, knotted string, or nails. Then the bottle is filled with protective herbs and charms to keep the spirit from causing trouble.

Making a spirit bottle involves selecting the right herbs and curios for the purpose of trapping spirits, empowering these items with prayer as they are placed within the vessel, and then sealing the bottle to hold in that power.

While the process may seem straightforward, it does require a certain level of spiritual aptitude and knowledge to properly get the vessels to work. This comes down to ensuring that the right combination of elements is employed in the crafting of the bottle and that the components are each brought to life with prayer and the strong intention and focus of the one who is making the bottle.

When properly constructed and employed with prayers, spirit bottles become filled with power and can be used as potent defensive tools against the world of malevolent spirits. They may be hung from windowsills, buried in front of doors, placed up a chimney, or hung on trees, where they act as spirit traps and apotropaic charms.

HOW TO MAKE A BLUE BOTTLE TREE

Bottle trees are found in several areas of the rural South-East and Texas. There are regional variations in their mode of construction, but they all make use of blue glass bottles to trap evil spirits.

A "bottle-brush" or "coat-rack" form of bottle tree employs a dead tree with upward-angled branches. The trunk is cemented into the soil and bottles are jammed onto the ends of the branches. If a dead tree cannot be found, a "coat-rack" style holder is made from lumber and dowels, with the branches angled upward to receive the bottle-mouths. The bottles are open at the mouths, unsealed, and may become a home for spiders. Uniform bottle size is desired, and wine bottles are the preferred type. Not all of the bottles will be blue, as they are difficult to find in that size. This kind of bottle tree is common in Texas.

A "hanging bottle" tree is made by wrapping baling wire around the necks of sealed empty bottles and looping the wires over the branches of a living tree so that the bottles hang suspended like fruit. To keep the hanging-wires from cutting into the bark of the tree, short arcs of used rubber tires are positioned over the limbs for padding. Each bottles' wire is threaded up through a hole in a rubber piece, from the underside to the top, across the pad, then down through a second hole. In this way the branches never come in contact with the metal wire. Practical considerations, in addition to spiritual tradition, require the bottles to be sealed lest rain water fill them and provide a breeding ground for mosquitoes. Blue bottles of all sizes and shapes are displayed, including small perfume flasks, Milk of Magnesia bottles, and wine bottles. This type of bottle tree is common in the South-East.

"Spirit Vessels and Spirit Traps" was written for ConjureMan Ali's 2012 workshop of the same name. The ConjureMan is a member of AIRR and Hoodoo Psychics, and tata of the House of Quimbanda church. He can be reached for readings and rootwork consultations at his web site, TheConjureMan.com.

SKULL SORCERY: USING SKULLS AND SKULL CANDLES
ConjureMan Ali

INTRODUCTION TO SKULL MAGIC

In African-American hoodoo the use of the skull dates back to early roots in African and European magical practices. With the popularization of different colours of figural and candles, it has evolved into the use of skull candles loaded, prepared, and used for a variety of conditions.

This brief survey will examine skull sorcery around the world and discuss how hoodoo workers continue this practice today.

SKULLS IN TIBET AND ASIA

In Tibetan Buddhist practice the image of the skull is prevalent in religious iconography, and skull bones are used in the manufacture of prayer beads. The kapala (a Sanskrit loan word meaning skullcap), is an actual human skullcap, often inlaid with silver or other metals, carved, or otherwise decorated. The kapala is often used to hold special offerings and libations to wrathful deities. Its use derives from older indigenous practices of blood sacrifice in which the blood was kept in the kapala. Its most simple function is that of begging bowl.

In addition to their religious function, kapalas and skulls are used for meditative and magical purposes, to elevate the thoughts, and to perform rituals. The purpose and potency of a skull is determined according to whose the skull it was — the skull of a murderer, for example, would have a unique potency.

While Asian culture is not strictly part of traditional hoodoo, years of contact with Asian immigrants in cities like Oakland and New York City brought some Asian influence into local hoodoo culture, especially through spiritual supply shops.

SKULLS IN EUROPE

The use of skulls as magical objects is also found among various peoples in the European continent. While mostly forgotten by the modern western occult tradition, the use of skulls was rather prominent among the various indigenous magical traditions, especially those that involved ancestor veneration and/or necromantic practices. Skulls were used to commune with familiar and ancestral spirits.

Another European belief centered on oracular heads, sacred idols or objects used for the purpose of prophecy. As late as the Christian era, it was stated that the beheading of John the Baptist was done as part of an act of fashioning an oracular head and gaining the power of prophecy. During the Medieval era and later, European ossuaries often featured elaborate displays of skulls, memento mori intended as spiritual aids to meditation.

SKULLS IN THE NEAR EAST

While the use of skulls and body parts in spiritual practice was forbidden by Jewish halacha, magical skulls made an appearance among the early Israelite people as well. Skulls have been found dating from the Talmudic period in Babylon which are inscribed in Aramaic, not unlike demon bowls.

According to Jewish magical traditions, inscribed skulls can be used for the necromantic purpose of summoning the shades of the dead to act as familiar and oracular spirits. Ancient Jewish skulls which were used for necromancy generally were inscribed on the outside surface of the skull whereas those which had the writing on the inside, like a bowl, were used as spirit traps.

SKULLS IN AFRICA

The use of skull imagery and skulls is prevalent in many African nations and religions. Focusing on West and Central Africa, from which hoodoo draws its roots, the skull was used to represents spirits of the dead, ancestors, and those deified. This idea continues on in several of the African Traditional Religions, such as Quimbanda, Palo, and Voudoun.

In addition to serving a symbolic religious function, the skull was also used to house a spirit familiar. In the creation of spirit vessels to house spirits, as practiced today in the ATRs, one can find a skull. Because of this, the skull is a highly prized and valuable magical object — used to house a spirit familiar, to influence the spirits of the living, and as the means to communicate with the realm of the dead. Today that value remains and there are reports of people unburying the dead for their bones and especially their skulls.

THE USE OF SKULLS IN HOODOO

While spiritual practitioners in African nations preserved the bones and skulls of their ancestors and placed them in vessels so that they might continue to work for the living, this idea was strictly taboo in mainstream America, and so the practice went underground. Drawing from European and African necromantic practices, African American hoodoo doctors continued to use skulls when they could obtain them, or fashioned them from clay or wood, which would then be loaded with magical herbs and dusts to enliven them with power.

With the popularization of figural candles from the 1930s onward, skull candles entered hoodoo, merging the power of candle magic with the traditional use of skulls to engage the spirits of the dead, for prophecy, and to influence the spirit and mind of another.

HOW TO WORK WITH SKULLS AND SKULL CANDLES

Bone, clay, and resin skulls and wax skull candles can be used for a variety of situations, from communing with and housing a familiar ancestral spirit to influencing the mind of another, but the common theme here is spirit. The skull represents spirit and mind.

To create a vessel in which to house, and through which to commune with, a spirit, you will need:

- Graveyard dirt from the spirit
- Bay leaf
- Tobacco
- Mullein
- Althaea

Skull candles are loaded from the bottom with spiritually potent materia magica, but in addition to putting them on an altar as a focal object, the wick is lit and therefore worked as a form of candle magic.

To influence the mind of another you will need to include a personal concern from that person, along with herbs that match the intent for which you are influencing them. For example, to influence a person to love you, you might combine Calamus to compel, Rose Petals for romance, and Damiana to spark passion. Or to influence someone toward a life of self-destruction, you may use Red Pepper to harm, Poppy Seeds to confuse, and Black Pepper to curse.

The skull candle should then be dedicated to a purpose. If it used to represent the mind of a person, a baptism or christening ceremony may be done to name the skull candle for that person. As a magical act this will draw the spirit of that person and link them to the skull candle which holds their personal concern.

To work the skull candle, begin by holding it in your hands and talking to it as if to the person it represents. Then your commands are to be inscribed directly on it as if carved upon their soul. It should be lit with prayers, and incense should be offered up before it. Use an appropriate self-lighting condition incense to which you've added Tobacco to help create the spirit connection. Pray with intent while blowing incense smoke onto the lit candle to influence the mind, compel the spirit, and pluck the strings of the heart. As with a doll baby, what happens to the skull candle happens to the person, so if you stick it with pins, you could cause pain, but if you whisper lovingly in its ear you could warm the heart to romance.

If a skull candle is to be used to commune with spirits, then you can scry using the flame of the candle, or speak through the smoke, letting the spirit feed from flame and smoke to commune back. This is excellent for acts of prophecy or can be used to convey commands to a spirit who then goes forth and carries out the work. It is also perfectly fine to keep the unlit candle on an ancestral altar if it is to serve as a vessel for your ancestor.

The key is to remember that the skull candle becomes the focal point of your prayers and intent, for it contains within it either a familiar spirit of the dead, or the spirit and mind of a person whom you wish to influence. What is said to the skull candle or done to it will be heard and felt by the spirit which resides within.

Skull candles are arguably one of the most potent tools of the conjure worker for they are containers that can hold a spirit and they can be direct links to a person's mind, all with the firepower of a candle.

In the hands of a skilled conjure worker the skull candle can raise the dead, or control the living.

"Skull Sorcery" was written by ConjureMan Ali for his 2013 MISC workshop of the same name. The co-host of the weekly Lucky Mojo Hoodoo Rootwork Hour on Blog Talk radio, and a member of Hoodoo Psychics and the Association of Independent Readers and Rootworkers, ConjureMan Ali can also be contacted for readings and rootwork at his web site, TheConjureMan.com.

HERB USE METHODS FOR KITCHEN WITCHERY
Sister Robin Petersen

Conjure cooking will add a delicious dimension to your magical repertoire. There is almost nothing that you cook that wouldn't be better with magical herbs, especially if you pray (or curse) over the food as you work, to bring about the results you desire.

BEGIN WITH CLEAN TOOLS

First off, always work with utensils and gadgets that are dedicated to food preparation. Everything should always be clean — pots, pans, utensils, food, and herbs. Impurities can create a bad taste and may also make you sick. Always prepare glass storage containers by washing with the hottest soapy water possible and rinsing with the hottest water possible followed by a boiling water bath similar to the sterilization process used in home canning.

INFUSIONS

Infusion is the process of putting the flavour of one thing into the other. The liquid or solid that receives the essence is called the host. The host can be water, vinegar, oil, alcohol, syrup, honey, sugar, or any of a number of other edible components of cookery.

HOT WATER INFUSIONS

To many of us, the most common infusions are Tea and Coffee. In the case of Tea, the water, which the host, is brought to a boil, poured over tea leaves, and allowed to steep. You may have noticed that Tea tastes bitter if it steeps too long and tastes like brown hot water if it is not steeped long enough. According to Tea aficionados, 4 minutes is the correct time to steep the infusion for a perfect cup of tea; no more, no less.

Unlike Tea, the best Coffee is made from water that has been brought up to the temperature just under boiling and then removed from the heat. This is poured over the ground Coffee, which imparts its flavour to the host water very quickly and needs no steeping.

When herbs are infused in hot water, they are called tisanes. In making a tisane, it is important to actually bring the water to a full boil. Herbs can be steeped longer than tea, according to your taste, but a minimum of 4 minutes is suggested.

VINEGAR INFUSIONS

Vinegar is another host that works well with infusion. It is important to use non-metallic pans and containers when preparing vinegar infusions, and the prepared product is best stored in a glass container that has a non-metallic lid. Vinegar naturally cures food, so you may use either fresh or dried herbs for your vinegar infusions. If you are making an infusion in which vinegar is the host, it is not necessary to heat it up first but you can heat it to coffee temperature in a microwave to accelerate the infusion. Herbs may be left in the vinegar bottle for a 'terrarium'-like presentation, similar to the Lucky Mojo Curio Company anointing oils, or the herbs may be strained off when the desired taste is acquired.

ALCOHOLIC INFUSIONS OR TINCTURES

Technically, an infusion in alcohol is called a tincture. The host may be plain grain alcohol but at the present time distilled alcoholic beverages, such as whiskey, gin, brandy, rum, or vodka, are popular liquids in which to infuse fruits, vegetables, and herbs. Use a jar that does not have a paper or metallic lid for your blending jar. Sterilize the jar as described above.

Some fruit or vegetable ingredients need to be cored, peeled, seeded, and cut into chunks before infusion in alcohol. Fresh herbs and spices can be prepared by only using the leaves and discarding the twiggy parts. If you use dried herbs, you will probably need a coffee filter to strain the herbs through when decanting into a bottle. "Discard the bitter and use the flavourful" is a good rule.

Put ingredients in the jar and cover with the liquor of your choice. Start by using a modest amount of flavour material, then check after a day. If it tastes weak after 24 hours, add more. Be prudent until you get your relationship with your ingredients going. You are in a learning curve, so waste not, want not. Seal the jar and store in a cool, dry place, tasting daily. When the desired taste is acquired, you're done.

However pretty the herbs look in your jar, resist the temptation to leave your liquid unstrained. The taste you found perfect will only stay that way if you stop further infusion. Strain the liquid using a sieve lined with a coffee filter. Decant into a decorative bottle.

OIL INFUSIONS

Oil may also be infused, but a few precautions are necessary. If you want to use fresh herbs in your oil infusion, for on-the-spot flavouring and scenting of a cooking oil, plan to cook with the oil immediately. You may heat the oil just up to boiling for an accelerated infusion, and the herbs may be strained off or left in the oil while cooking. However, because oil that contains even a trace of water from fresh herb pieces can become a breeding ground for the anaerobic bacteria that causes botulism, you should discard any unused oil after preparing the meal.

When making oil infusions that are not to be consumed immediately, only dried herbs should be used. The herbs should be completely air-, oven-, or food dehydrator-dried before use. As with a fresh herb oil infusion, you may heat the oil just up to boiling for rapid uptake of fragrance and flavour, and the herbs themselves may be strained off or left in the oil. It is still suggested that even with these precautions, herbed oils should be refrigerated before use.

HERB GARNISHES

Fresh herbs make beautiful garnishes for beverages. Try Apple Mint or a few leaves of Borage with its starry blossoms. The leaves of Master of the Woods, Lemon Balm, Lemon Thyme, Sage, and scented Geranium are also attractive to use.

CHIFFONADE OF HERBS

A chiffonade is comprised of fresh herbs or leafy vegetables cut fine and employed as a garnish. A chiffonade of herbs for soup is simple to make and adds wonderful flavouring. To each pint of soup stock, use 1-2 tablespoons of fresh herbs and 2 tablespoons of greens like Parsley, Sorrel, or Lettuce. Add the herbs to a small quantity of the stock in a blender and blend well. Combine this into the remaining stock. If you have no blender, mince the herbs very, very fine.

BLACKENING SPICES

Make a magical blackening spice mix for fish or chicken with 1 tablespoon Paprika, 2 teaspoons salt, 1 teaspoon Onion powder, 1 teaspoon Garlic powder, 1 teaspoon Cayenne Pepper, 1/2 teaspoon White Pepper, 1/2 teaspoon Black Pepper, 1/2 teaspoon Thyme, 1/2 teaspoon Oregano, 1/2 teaspoon Sage, 1/2 teaspoon Lavender, and 1/2 teaspoon Basil. Rub meat with the mix before sautéing.

SPRINKLING HERBS

You may sprinkle Fennel, Caraway, or Anise seeds on your cookie sheets before baking cookies on them and they will give an interesting 'adult' taste to the cookies and infuse them with magic as well.

SWEET INFUSIONS OR ELECTUARIES

An electuary is a pasty compound made with syrup, honey, or a mixture of powdered sugar and water into which finely powdered herbs have been introduced. The term comes from medicine, and the original purpose for creating such a mixture was to disguise the bitter taste of medicinal herbs, but recipes for electuaries can also found in old cook books, and they are suitable to use in magical cookery as well. If the herbs are strained or sifted out of the sweetener, the flavour will remain, resulting in a sweet infusion.

To infuse sugar, layer superfine sugar with solids such as whole Vanilla beans, herb stalks, large leafed herbs, or fragrant edible flower petals, in a airtight container. A good ratio to use, for example, is one cup superfine sugar to a handful of Rose petals. Keep in a cool dark place for 24 hours. When the taste is strong enough, remove your flavouring agent. You may repeat with a new batch of fresh herbs the next day, if a stronger fragrance is desired. Only Vanilla beans are commonly left in sugar for a longer time; in days past, it was common to store a Vanilla bean in the sugar jar for later use, thus scenting the sugar and preserving the bean until it was needed.

To infuse syrups with herbal essences, the herbs are boiled in a water-sugar combination called simple syrup. Magical syrups can be used to sweeten iced tea or tisane, or added to sparkling water or club soda. Combine 1 cup fresh herbs or flowers, 2 cups white sugar, and 4 cups water. (If using Rose petals, substitute half the water with Rose Water.) Bring the sugar and liquids to low boil. Reduce heat and simmer for 45 minutes, stirring often. Add the herbs, remove from heat, and cool to warm temperature. Strain off the herbs and pour into bottles to store.

"Herb Use Methods for Kitchen Witchery" was Sister Robin Petersen's 2010 intro to MISC's annual Conjure Cook-Off and Recipe Round-Up. It was also distributed in 2011. Sister Robin is the shop manager of the Lucky Mojo Curio Co. and pastor of the Santisima Muerte Chapel of Perpetual Pilgrimage at SantisimaMuerteChapel.org.

GROCERY STORE MAGIC
catherine yronwode

When people think of edible magic, they tend to imagine recipes for cooking, especially foods made with herbs and spices well known in conjure. But not all food magic is cooked. Some fruits, vegetables, and meats are used "as-is" in conjure, right off the grocery store shelves. This is everyday magic that's accessible to you every time you go to the store.

THE ONION

Red Onions are powerful, but some folks say that you have to steal one from a grocery store to get the best use of it.

KEEP A MAN, LOSE A MAN

If your Man threatens to leave, write his name on paper. Bore a hole in a Red Onion with a nail, roll the name-paper tight, push it into the hole, and carry the Onion in your pocket to make him stay. If you want him gone, pull the Paper out of the Onion, soak it in vinegar, dress it with Red Pepper, reinsert it, and bury the Onion. When it rots, he will leave.

HOLD A WOMAN

Get nine of your Woman's fingernail clippings, nine of her toenail clippings, and nine Hairs from the mould of her head. Cut a hole in a Red Onion, place the items inside with sugar, and stop the Onion back up. Bury it in the dirt on the East side of your house at sunrise.

PEACE IN THE HOME

Bore a hole in a Red Onion, fill it with sugar, tie a shoe lace around it, and hide it above the door so folks walk under it.

BURN RED ONION PEELINGS FOR LUCK

Folks burn Red Onion peelings because they are lucky for the home; because they draw in business to a bar, restaurant, or boarding house; because they keep the law away; and because they help in love affairs. For the last-named purpose, you can call your lover's name and say, *"Hold him tight to me; make him come under my command,"* three times as the Onion peels burn.

THE EGG

Eggs, especially eggs from a Black Hen, are used in many magic spells. For this reason, the musician Blind Willie McTell relates in an old blues song that his mother told him, *"Don't drink no Black Cow's milk; don't eat no Black Hen's egg."*

TO BREAK UP A COUPLE

Hard-boil a Black Hen's egg in your own Urine and cut it in half. Feed half to a Black Dog and half to a Black Cat. As you feed the Dog, say, *"As dogs hate cats, so will [man] hate [woman]."* As you feed the Cat, say, *"As cats hate dogs, so will [woman] hate [man]."*

FOR UNCROSSING

Roll an uncooked Hen's egg over the body to collect negative energy and messes; discard it by throwing into a crossroads or at a tree.

TO KEEP OFF BILL COLLECTORS AND POLICE OFFICERS

Empty a Black Hen's egg, crack up the shell, and toast it in your oven until it turns brown. Powder it, then put the powder under your front doorsteps. The collectors or officers may come around, but they will not be able to do anything to harm you.

MALE FIDELITY

Wipe a Hen's egg with a brand-new handkerchief, then wipe the Man's penis with the handkerchief, and hide it in his pillow.

GOOFERING AN ENEMY

Blow out an egg, fill it with Red Pepper, Goofer Dust, and Sulphur. Write your foe's name on the egg, and hide it under his house porch to hurt him. Throw it clean over the roof to move him out.

ENABLE A CHILD TO TEETHE WITHOUT PAIN

Take a raw egg, write the baby's name on it in ink, place it in a muslin Tobacco sack, and hang it over the door. The egg will dry out, and the child will teethe without pain.

TO FIND OUT A MURDERER

Bury the murder victim with a Black Hen's egg in each hand, and when the eggs rot and burst, the killer will return to town and inadvertently reveal himself.

THE CUCUMBER, ZUCCHINI, OR DILL PICKLE

Because of its shape, a Cucumber, Zucchini, or Dill Pickle can be said to represent a Man's penis, and hence his sexuality. It is possible to use these vegetables in positive magical spells, to enhance a man's sex-pleasure or fecundity, or in ways that are coercive or harmful to his life.

A FREEZER SPELL
TO MESS UP A MAN'S SEXUALITY

A large Dill Pickle is better than a mild Cucumber or Zucchini for this trick, because it is sour and will sour his sex life. In any case, slit the Cucumber, Zucchini, or Pickle, then insert his semen or his urine on a name paper, and add Alum powder to stop him from coming or from peeing. Add Red Pepper to give him a burning inflammation of the penis and Black Mustard seeds to harm his sexuality and his urinary tract. These are traditional minerals, roots, and barks from our long past history and give real power to the work. Why Alum powder? Try it on your tongue and be convinced as to why it shuts things up. Also be fully aware that if you do this, the Man won't be having sex with you either, and he may get seriously ill from urinary blockage. You will have frozen his penis. This is a grievous spell, and the intention is harmful, so the work must be carefully performed and you'd better be prepared to tell God why you did it.

THE FIG OR PEAR

A ripe Fig or Pear resembles a Woman's uterus or womb and can be used to affect her sexual and reproductive organs for good or for ill.

TO INCREASE A WOMAN'S
CHANCE OF CONCEPTION

Working from the bottom end, inject a ripe fresh Fig full of honey, and insert a tightly rolled paper on which is written, *"Baby, child of [father], born from the womb of [mother]."* Place it in a small jar of honey, stem-end up, and bury it in the yard where the Woman will step over it.

A FREEZER SPELL
TO MESS UP A WOMAN'S SEXUALITY

To freeze a Woman's sex drive, give her an infection, and stop her ability to bear children, slit open the Fig or Pear, and insert into it her menstrual blood or her urine on a name paper, and add Alum powder to stop her periods, Red Pepper to give her a burning inflammation of the genitals, and Black Mustard seeds to harm her sexuality and her urinary tract. This sexually damaging freezer spell can be wrapped up in aluminum foil, but for serious impact, first wrap it in the target's dirty underpants, wetted with her urine, then encase it in aluminum foil, shiny side in. Be prepared to tell God why you did such a mean thing to her.

THE GARLIC

The use of Garlic to ward off evil derives from European witchcraft and is especially popular in the Mediterranean and Eastern European regions. Due to centuries of American inter-racial friendship and marriage, and the broad reach of popular culture, its use of Garlic has made considerable inroads into the African-American community, and many hoodoo doctors work with it.

A PROTECTIVE PLANT

Hang a braid of Garlic in the kitchen to discourage troublesome visitors; use it as needed for cooking, and replace it every year. In Jamaican obeah practice, a large nail is driven down into the center of a single head of Garlic (where the central stem is) and a string is tied around it, held in place by the nail head, and this is used to suspend the Garlic.

THE STRAWBERRIES

Strawberries look like natural hearts, and thus they symbolized love. Being red and covered with seeds, they also symbolize a female's "blood love," the sexual passion of a fecund Woman.

MALE AND FEMALE IN UNION

Strawberries are customarily used fresh and uncooked to garnish sweet desserts whose white colour represents male semen. Strawberries on Vanilla ice cream, Strawberry shortcake with whipped cream, and Strawberry sundaes exemplify this. Strawberries are also dipped in Chocolate, which itself contains love-inducing chemicals.

THE WALNUTS

Black Walnuts, English Walnuts, or Persian Walnuts are used to break the power of the past and the hold of emotions that should be left behind.

TO FALL OUT OF LOVE

If you are having a difficult time leaving a relationship, bathe in a strong brown tea made by boiling nine Black Walnuts still in their husks or, if those cannot be had, nine English Walnuts boiled in 3 quarts of water until it evaporates down to 1 quart and turns brown. As you bathe, renounce all ties to your former lover, then throw the water out at a crossroads or against a tree. To make the spell stronger, you may write the ex-lover's name on paper, bathe by the light of a candle, and burn the name-paper in the candle flame.

THE COFFEE

Coffee grounds can be read in the cup the same way as Tea leaves can, and are popular for this in Eastern Europe and the Levant. Coffee bean husks are highly reputed for use in uncrossing and jinx-removing baths.

HOW TO KEEP A HUSBAND AND A KID MAN TOO

Brew three nails in Coffee. Drink the first cup yourself, give the second to your husband, and the third to your outside lover. Place the three nails in the form of a downward-pointing triangle, naming the top one for yourself, the one on the right for your husband, and the one on your left for your lover. Keep them hidden that way, and the two will stay friends, even if your husband catches you in bed with your lover.

THE POTATO

Potatoes, a South American plant, have acquired quite a reputation in European folk-magic. They are one of several items used to take off warts; they are also used in love-domination.

TO REMOVE WARTS

Cut a Potato in half and rub half on the wart. Bury it under the drip-line of the eaves of the house where the rain runs off. As the Potato rots, the wart will fall off.

FOR A HUSBAND TO DOMINATE HIS WIFE

Bore a hole in a Potato. Write your wife's name on a slip of paper and write your name over hers, to dominate her. Roll the slip up, place it in the hole in the Potato and bury the Potato in the back yard. You will be able to do whatever you want and your wife will not be able to speak against you.

THE SUGAR BOX OR SUGAR PACKETS

Sugar is used for sweetening up lovers, friends, and others.

FOR THE RETURN OF A LOVE

Write your absent lover's name on paper nine times and cross it with your name written nine times. Place the name-paper in a white saucer and fill the saucer with white Sugar. Buy nine small white candles and burn one, set upright in the Sugar, each day for nine days. If your lover has not returned after nine days, burn everything in a fire and start again with new materials, repeating the process nine more days. If your lover still does not come back, again burn everything, and make a third attempt. If this spell does not work after three tries, your lover will not return.

TO SWEETEN CO-WORKERS ON THE JOB

Write the names of each of your co-workers on a separate slip of paper, or collect all of their business cards. Layer the name-papers or cards in a jar of Sugar. Pray over the jar for kindness, sweetness, and friendliness on the job or, if there are back-biters or gossips, pray for sweetness to replace negativity. Sneak some of the Sugar into the break-room Sugar jar so they use it. If your break-room has all of the sweeteners in packets, "borrow" some packets and layer them in your Sugar jar with the name-papers or cards. After seven days, brush off the prayed-over packets and return them to the break-room.

THE APPLE

The Apple features in a particular kind of sweetening rite used for love. This sweetening spell has many variations, and in those where an Apple appears, it is both a receptacle for the sweetener and a magical agent.

TO CAUSE A COUPLE TO GET ALONG BETTER

Obtain a red Apple of a size that will fit inside an empty Coffee tin. On a square of paper no taller than the height of the Apple, write the squabbling couple's names, crossing them like an X. Around this X write the word "love" over and over again (lovelovelove) as many times as it takes to go around their names in an unbroken circle, never lifting your pen from the paper, and ending the final "e" so that it just runs into the first "l." It's okay to practice a few times to get this right — you want a perfectly done name-paper. Core the Apple with a regular corer, making a hollow cylinder down the center. Roll the name-paper into a tube, then slide it into the Apple, letting it expand to fill the space. Place the Apple in the Coffee tin, pour Cinnamon powder and a sweetener (Sugar, Syrup, Honey, Molasses, or whatever you prefer) into the hole, and put the lid on the tin. Hide the tin in a trunk or drawer, or bury it in the fighting couple's front yard. This will assist them to love one another again.

TO CAUSE A COUPLE'S LOVE
FOR ONE ANOTHER TO GROW

This spell is not generally performed by the people involved but is done on their behalf by a third party, either a family member or a professional root worker. Get a Red Delicious Apple and a clay flower pot large enough that the Apple will fit inside with lots of room to spare. You will also need a small living Fern plant. The species of Fern does not matter, but Maidenhair Fern and Male Fern are the two species most often used in love spells. On a square of paper no taller than the height of the Apple, write out the couple's full names, crossing them like an X. Around this X write your wish for their happiness over and over again (e.g. loveoneanotherloveoneanother) as many times as it takes to go around their names in an unbroken circle, never lifting your pen from the paper and ending the final letter of the last word so that it just runs into the first letter of the first word. Practicing this with a pencil on a scrap of paper a few times is fine, in order to get a neat final version. Core the Apple to make a hollow cylinder down the center. Roll the name-paper into a tube, then slide it into the Apple, letting it expand to fill the void. Place the Apple in the flower pot, pour Cinnamon powder and sweetener into the hole (Sugar, Honey, Syrup, Molasses, as you prefer), and top it off with regular potting soil. Plant the Fern with its roots in the soil on top of the Apple and water it with Holy Water. As the Fern grows, so will the couple's love for one another grow. It should only be watered with Holy Water as long as you wish to work the spell.

THE LEMON

The Lemon has two-fold symbolism: Because it is succulent and shaped like an eye, it can reflect the Evil Eye back to its sender, which makes it a protective plant; and because it has a sharp, clean scent, it is used in cleansing and clearing spells to separate a person from unwanted ties to the past.

CUT-AND-CLEAR RITE TO GET RID OF A MAN

If a Woman wants to cut a Man out of her life, she buys a brand-new knife and a Lemon. When she sees the Man, she uses the knife to cut the Lemon up as she walks behind him, unnoticed, dropping small pieces of the Lemon in his foot-tracks until the Lemon is gone. Then she turns and walks home in complete silence and buries the knife at her doorstep, blade outward, as she says, *"In the name of the Father, the Son, and the Holy Ghost, i hope i never see* [the Man's name] *no more."* If the Man notices her doing this or if anyone speaks to her while she is about her business, the spell must be repeated with another brand-new knife and Lemon.

BREAK-UP SPELL

Light a black candle dressed with Confusion Oil and cut a fresh Lemon in half. Write the names of the parties side-by-side, not touching, and cut them apart. Place the name-papers inside the Lemon, not touching, with Black Dog hair, Black Cat hair, and Red Pepper between them. Tie the Lemon up with black thread, seal it by dripping black candle wax all over it, and bury it in the couple's yard, so they will be sour-tempered and fight like Cats and Dogs. Variants of this spell specify submerging the Lemon in a jar of vinegar to sour the relationship or in a jar of Black Cow's milk to curdle and clabber their lives.

A PROTECTIVE CHARM

Sicilians stab a Lemon with nine nails, wind the nails with red thread and place this charm above a door to protect against the gaze of envious people. English people put the Lemon up the chimney.

"Grocery Store Magic" was written by me for Sister Robin Petersen's presentation of the 2012 Annual Conjure Cook-Off and Recipe Round-Up. Some of these spells and ideas can be found in slightly different form in my 2002 book "Hoodoo Herb and Root Magic" as well as in my 1995 book "Hoodoo in Theory and Practice," which is online at LuckyMojo.com/hoodoo.html.

NORDIC BREAD SPELLS
Dr. Johannes Gårdbäck

THE GRAIN CROPS

Rye, Wheat, Oats, and Barley are the cornerstone grain crops of Northern Europe. As food staples, they represent the basic economy, but in trolldom, the folk magic of Sweden, they are also sometimes used as offerings to spirits. For instance, they may be offered to the spirit of a troll bag (the regional equivalent to an African American mojo bag) or they may become a talisman inserted into the door post of a house in order to keep the spell strong.

A common ingredient in troll powders — especially those used to cure — is malted cereal grain. The malt is mixed with salt and a troll formula is spoken over the powder and it is then fed to a person in order to cure them from a spiritual malady.

PREPARING THE FLOUR: THE POWERFUL MILLS

Grist mills are regarded as places of strong spiritual power in Norse folk magic. An old mill is one of the places in which people go to do divination or perform magical rituals of various sorts, to hire spirits to become the house Tomte — guardians and helpers of a a house — or to dispose of troublesome Tomte spirits who are no longer desired in the household.

The mills go around to grind grain into flour and this circular motion has been regarded as spiritually powerful for thousands of years. In the old Pagan days, Thursday (Thor's-Day) was the sacred day of the the ancient five-day week and no acts or work of circular motion were allowed on that day, since this was considered disturbing to the spirits and deities. When the modern seven-day week was introduced, along with Christianity, Thursday remained sacred, but Sunday was added as a forbidden day. Thus flour milled on a Thursday or Sunday came to be regarded as magically and spiritually potent.

Quern-stones (small circular stone hand-mills) are also magical. Turned counter-clockwise (or magically backwards, for reversal), they are used to cause runaway servants or loved ones to return or to get a response in a lawsuit. Thieves are punished by putting a glowing coal in the side-hole of the quern to summon and then send demons after them.

TO GRIND AWAY A DISEASE

Querns can be used to grind away diseases and spiritual problems. The afflicted person first puts his or her hand on the quern, loosely, so that the hand does not follow the turning of the upper stone, but so that the skin of the hand is gently scratched by the turning stone underneath it. The quern is then turned counter-clockwise (backwards) while the practitioner says:

"I grind, I grind."

The afflicted person, who should be standing next to the practitioner, asks:

"What are you grinding?"

The practitioner then responds:

"I grind pain and suffering and everything away."

The procedure of asking and responding is repeated three or nine times.

THE ROUND HOLE-BREAD

In the bread spells of traditional trolldom, the bread referred to is the old Nordic style of bread, formed into a flattish circular loaf with a hole in the middle. The shape of the loaf resembles the powerful mill-wheels that ground the flour from the grain.

In Sweden, thick, soft, circular Wheat-Rye yeast bread with a center-hole is called Hålkaka (hole-cake or hole-bread). In Finland, Rye bread with a hole in the middle is called ruisreikäleipä ("Rye hole-bread"). Cracker-like Rye hardtack, which may also be baked in the form of a disk with a center hole, is called knäckebröd ("bread which can be broken") or hårdbröd ("hard or crisp bread"). After being baked, these round, holed breads were usually threaded on a horizontal pole suspended above the stove, where they were stored for later use, and this storage method also became part of the folk-magic tradition.

A recipe for traditional Swedish Hålkaka or hole-bread can be found in the "Hoodoo Food! The 2013 Conjure Cook-Off and Rootwork Recipe Round-Up," edited by SIster Robin Petersen of Missionary Independent Spiritual Church.

THE POWER PIECE: USING THE LAST PIECE OF BREAD TO INFLUENCE ANOTHER

In Scandinavian folk belief the last piece of a loaf of hole-bread is called maktbiten ("the power piece") and it contains all of the power of bread and a link to the physical and spiritual health and economy of its owner.

If stolen, the power piece can be used to take all the luck and power from the former owner as well as to gain any kind of influence desired over his health and economy. A common example of this would be to steal a piece of bread from a fellow-hunter during a hunt in order to take his hunting luck.

OLD SCANDINAVIAN SUPERSTITIONS REGARDING BREAD AND BAKING

When you bake, the side away from the body should not be thicker than that facing the body; if it is, then one becomes poor.

Take care not to eat the new Rye flour before baking with it, lest you become poor.

Smooth dough is important the first time a girl kneads the bread: "Ugly bread, ugly man. Smooth bread, handsome man."

If a maiden slaps the dough with her hand while she is baking, she will have an evil mother-in-law.

When you greet someone who has moved into new quarters for the first time, bring bread and salt for good luck, so they should not lack wealth.

If a round of bread dough is forgotten and not baked or if a bread is forgotten and burned to coal in the oven, death will come to someone during the year.

Bread should not be placed with the bottom side up on the table as this invites misfortune and means that bad people will gain power in the house.

Bread must not be placed in a basket with the hole oriented vertically, since this will invite the devil. They must be placed top-side-up in the basket.

The breads hanging on the pole must all have their top sides facing the door. This will invite luck, ensuring the attraction of good fortune in matters of love and money and anything drawn to the house.

A bread hanging on the bread pole with the bottom end facing the door means it is given to the Tomte — the spirit-guardian of the house — and should never be eaten.

A pinch of salt must always be offered to the oven after baking or evil will enter the house and the oven will be unusable for baking again.

If the bread breaks during baking, guests are to be expected.

If the dough makes a squeaking sound in the oven, guests will come from far away.

After baking bread, two logs of wood should be placed crosswise in front of the oven. This will ensure that the household will never be without bread (through the protection of the oven from the evil eye and other dangers).

Midsummer dew added to the bread dough will ensure a similar protection.

Bread dough is always cut with equal-armed crosses three or nine times while kneading, to protect the work from negative influences. Some old Scandinavian breads were carved with crosses, pentagrams, runes, or other symbols of protection, or decorated with symbols promoting good luck, increase in wealth, the growth of crops, and happiness.

Here, in English translation, is a Norwegian prayer from 1810 to be said while kneading the bread:

Cross and mark,
[make the sign of the cross over the bread]
God bless my day's work.

Cross and knock,
(make the sign of the cross and knock on wood)
So from me none can take.

HANDS-ON CURING WITH BREAD

This method was often used to cure both Cows and Humans from various spiritual problems. When used for a Human, replace the word "Cow" with the gender of the person you are working on or their name.

From a round hole-bread cut three triangles, which are each then cut with a slit in the back, and into the slit of each, add a little Garlic. Then, while reading the following formula, stab the pieces of bread with a knife, once each for each sentence:

I went on a road and met a Cow,
Who went and cried.

I asked:
"Why are you crying, my Cow?"

"They have stolen
Power and bravery,
Flesh and blood,
Marrow and bones."

"I will give you back
Power and courage,
Flesh and blood,
Marrow and bones.

"Through three names:
God the Father, Son, and Holy Spirit."

USING HOLE-BREAD TO CURE SKIN DISEASES

Circular hole-bread can cure skin rashes, eczema, and the like. The crust is used to draw a pentagram or a counter-clockwise circle around the troubled area while reading a magical formula out loud, such as:

"You shall fold as dew for day,
First a month, then a year,
Then as long as the world is standing."

In Swedish, this rhymes:

"Du ska vika som dagg för dag,
Först en månad, sen ett år,
sen så länge välden står."

The magical formula and the counter-clockwise procedure are repeated three or nine times and the bread is then given to an animal, ants, or birds to eat.

MELTING LEAD THROUGH A LOAF OF HOLE-BREAD TO CURE SPIRITUAL DISORDERS

Curing spiritual afflictions by pouring molten lead or tin through the hole in the loaf of bread is so old and common a method in trolldom that many professional practitioners — called by names such as "Blygumma" (Lead Old Woman), or "Smältgumma" (Melting Old Woman) — used only this way of curing. Some practitioners added their profession to their baptismal names, so they were called "Bly-Anna" (Lead-Anna), "Smält-Britta" (Melting-Britta) and the like.

Here is how the metal-melting cure is done:

Melt some lead or tin in a small sauce pan. Pour some water into a bowl. Preferably this should be well water bought from a well on a Thursday in a waning moon and paid for with an offering.

Put a hole-bread over the bowl of water and hold it over the head of the spiritually afflicted person as he or she lies down on a bed. Pour the melted lead or tin through the hole in the bread and into the water. Repeat the process, holding the bowl over the chest of the person, and then a third time, over the feet of the person. The bowl and bread are then put under the bed and the afflicted person sleeps there overnight.

The procedure should take place in absolute silence and no one must enter or exit the doors while it is going on. All windows must also be shut.

In the morning the water and bread are taken to a crossroads or cemetery and disposed of by tossing them in and walking away without looking back.

In some cases the remains are disposed of in four different places, representing the four elements. Mountains or hilltops represent air (or weather, which is the more correct description, according to the old folks of trolldom), The stove represents fire. A running stream or river symbolizes water. The cemetery stands for earth.

In other cases, the remains are disposed of in only one of the four elemental places. To determine which element should be used, the spirits of the elements are called out when pouring the lead and the strongest hissing sound produced by the hot lead hitting the cold water will be heard when mentioning the right element. The remains are disposed of only in a place representing that particular element and by doing so the malady is returned to the right place.

Occasionally various nature spirits are mentioned instead of elementals and the remains are then disposed of at the location of these spirits such as in the forests (forest spirits), cemetery (the dead), a neighbour's farm (the spirits of their farm or their Tomte), and so on. This can be translated to spirits of various places in an urban area as well.

Some workers add eight other things to the lead or tin while it is melting, making nine things in total. This goes back to an early bronze age Scandinavian belief that all things exist in nine worlds and must thus be countered by nines.

BREAD AS AN OFFERING TO SPIRITS

Making an offering to spirits in order to cure or rectify a spiritually caused problem is very common in trolldom. The offering is often made at ancient sacrificial stones – called Älvkvarnar or Elven Mills.

Älvkvarnar are blocks of stone in which small hollows have been carved out. Many of these Elven Mills date all the way back to the early stone age, about 9,000 years ago, and have been in more or less constant use by Scandinavian folk-magicians.

Small stones that are found with a small hole in the middle are sometimes also called Elven Mill stones, due to their resemblance to large mill stones and they can be used in the same manner.

When offering bread, it is often mixed with salt, in order to protect from the spirit and also to put the spirit at ease. In some cases bread is seen as representative of the earth element and, along with salt, it is used to ground something.

In a procedure similar to the hands-on methods above, we mix bread and a little something from each of the four elements — ashes from the stove, earth from the cemetery, and water from a running stream poured into a bowl filled with a beverage or alcohol. (In this spell, the air or weather element is only considered as a means of transporting the work at this point). The bread and the beverage are to please the spirit; the elemental parts are added in order to address the proper sources of the problem or the elemental spirits who are thought to be responsible for the problem.

Once the mixture is made, it is poured into another bowl — sometimes a bowl made of stone —and passed three times counter-clockwise around the body of a person afflicted by a spiritual problem. The afflicted person is then dismissed.

The following morning before sunrise, the practitioner goes outside and tosses the contents of the bowl in three different directions. In each direction. the material is tossed both upwards into "the weather" and onto the earth. While tossing, the spirits are addressed with the following words:

"Here you have got what you should have! Now give [Name] what [he or she] should have!"

This method is used for all kinds of diseases and problems with spiritual origins.

In a similar spell, bread and salt are chewed by the practitioner and spit into a tobacco pouch or similar cloth bag, passed around the the body of the afflicted person and then given to the person with instructions to go to a three-way crossroads, a sauna bathhouse, or the cemetery, and to throw it over the left shoulder and leave without looking back. Sometimes words are spoken while circling the afflicted person with items such as these, but what is said is usually just a description of what one is doing, like:

"I offer in order to cure the disease of [Name] and that [he or she] should have [his or her] health back!"

A TROLL BAG WITH BREAD TO PROTECT A HOUSE OR BARN

Similar to making an offering of bread to the spirits and asking for protection is the use of a protective trollbag made with bread. Here is one example:

Put salt, bread, and mercury in a magic bag and hang it up in the barn to protect it. Those who enter with malice will become upset and powerless.

Please note that mercury (quicksilver) is a VERY toxic substance and could be safely substituted by using another metal of protection, like iron or silver:

TO MAGICALLY FETTER ANIMALS
(Norway, 1780)

Mix lard (Pig fat), grated Rye bread, Camphor, the inner bark of a Buckthorn tree, and Onion. Boil it as thick as gruel. Walk in a circle around the area in which you wish to magically fetter the animals and for every ten steps, rub the mixture under the sole of your shoe. The animals will not be able to leave your circle.

A SPELL TO PROTECT YOUR MONEY
(Sweden, 1790)

Take two sticks from a Rowan tree cut in May. Lay them crosswise over the money, along with a small piece of Rye bread and salt. Your money will never be able to be removed without your knowledge.

A SPELL TO DESTROY A RIFLE

Bread in a rifle barrel will make it harmless and unable to kill, and it will hit nothing. Putting a Snake in the barrel will restore such a destroyed rifle.

SPELL TO CONTROL A RIFLE TARGET

If you put bread underneath a shooting target, no shots will be able to hit it.

BREAD SPELLS TO CURE LONGING

These kinds of spells are used when a person longs for another location, for another person, another partner, and so on.

A pinch of Barley meal is taken between the left hand thumb, index, and middle finger and sprinkled secretly down the neck of the person who is longing, between the shirt and the coat (not on the skin) while saying:

"You shall not long more than this longing" (meaning the pinch of Barley).

If a person longs for a former home when he has moved to a new place, he should eat a piece of bread brought from the old place, one bite each time he experiences the longing. This will end that feeling.

If you experience longing while travelling, bring a piece of bread on the trip and at the first place you stop, drop some of it unnoticed and secretly on the floor and step on it with the left foot. This removes the power that has taken hold of you.

The same sort of spell can be cast by serving a sandwich in which you have placed some scrapings from the dinner table of the new location or some spider web taken from the inner corners of the new house to the person afflicted by longing.

Another very old spell utilizes an iron rod with a loop in one end. The rod is stuck in the ground in the Northern end of a farm field in which the plow furrows run from North to South. Three pieces of bread are inserted counterclockwise three times through the loop at the top of the pole with the words, "You shall not long more than these things given by me." The pieces are then fed to the person afflicted with longing.

In a similar manner an earthbound rock can be used to cure longing. These rocks are usually called unlausan, meaning "not loose" and they represent stability and influence over the land. The bread is carried counterclockwise three or nine laps around the rock with the same words as above and is served to the afflicted person.

SPELL TO FIND A DROWNED PERSON

When someone has drowned in a lake and the body cannot be found, practitioners of trolldom often throw a circular loaf of bread into the water. It then floats until it stops and sinks where the dead person is. This was a very common practice in the past.

DREAMING TRUE USING BREAD

Tie a clove of Garlic and a piece of bread under the left arm, in the armpit, when you go to sleep and you'll see anything you wish in your dream or dream true.

DIVINATION WITH BREAD

Love-divination bread spells are often performed in order to see one's future spouse or partner. They are most often practiced by young girls, but men perform them as well. The same divinatory methods can be employed for other questions as well.

A RING-CAKE

Three girls bake a ring into a hole-bread (or any other kind of bread, bun, or cake). Once finished the hole-bread is divided into four parts. Whoever gets the ring will be married. If none of the three gets the ring, none of them will be married that year.

PYROMANCY WHILE BAKING

Start baking on a Thursday night, turning your back to the oven, in this case an old style oven with an open fire, not a modern one. Pull up your skirt and look between your legs and into the flames of the fire, in which the future partner will appear.

KÄRLEKSKAKA (THE LOVE BUN)

To see which one loves another the most, make a small round bun out the hole from the existing hole-bread dough as you bake. It should be no larger than 2"-4" in diameter. The love-bun must be made and flattened using only the left hand. Make a shallow slit in the middle. Name the halves after the two loved ones. Which side rises highest in the oven?

MAKING "VIPPEBULLE" (STRAW BUN)

A Rye-straw (rågvippa) is named for each family member and inserted in a row into an unbaked bread-bun. The straw which falls first or is burned first will show who among the family will be the first to die.

TRADITIONAL TROLLDOM LOVE SPELLS USING BREAD

DRAW LOVE THROUGH BLOOD AND BREAD

Prick your left ring finger and drip three drops of blood onto a piece of bread. Drop it at once down your neckline, inside your shirt, with the words: *"As close as this is to me, as in love so shall [Name] be."* Then serve it secretly to the one desired.

AWAKEN LOVE THROUGH SWEAT AND BREAD

To awaken love, a piece of bread is held under the left armpit until the sweat comes on it. Sweating three rounds on the bread is considered powerful.

THE THREE BITES OF BREAD LOVE SPELL

Three small pieces of bread are bitten and held in the mouth from three different loaves with the words, *"As close as this bread is to me, so close will [Name] also be."*

MAKE YOUR PARTNER FAITHFUL USING BREAD AND YOUR OWN HAIR

If another woman desires your husband collect hair from three locations (head, armpit, pubic), cut it fine and put in bread that you feed to the man and he should not long for anyone other than you.

SUMMONING THE FUTURE SPOUSE WITH A DREAM PANCAKE

There are several varieties of this method of seeing one's future husband and they all involve eating something extremely salty and then going to bed and trying to sleep without drinking anything.

As with many old methods of trolldom divination of this sort, what is important is not so much a matter of seeing the man or woman in a dream-vision as it is about summoning the Vard or Vålne — meaning the spirit of the person — to you.

This following is one very common way to do it:

Three maidens (or an odd number of participants of any gender) come on Midsummer Eve to jointly cook and eat a Swedish pancake. Using only their left hands each adds an equal amount of the Wheat flour and milk. They each break an egg into the other ingredients and stir them all together.

Then each one, instead of a pinch of salt, adds a whole handful of salt, and the salt must be plentiful in such a pancake, if it is to have proper effect. One thick pancake is baked and cut into three equal parts, and each must eat up her share, regardless of how salty it may be. They then go to sleep in separate places, taking great care not to drink anything at all before falling asleep. In their sleep their thirst will be so strong that they will attract their future husband, who will come and offer them something to drink.

Here is the conventional pancake recipe from which this spell is adapted:

CLASSIC SWEDISH PANCAKES (PANNKAKSRECEPT)

For four people you will need:

- 2 ½ cups Wheat flour
- ½ teaspoon salt
- 6 cups milk
- 3 eggs
- 3 tablespoons butter

Mix the flour and salt in a bowl. Whisk in half of the milk until smooth. Whisk in the remaining milk and the eggs. Let ingredients work together and swell for about 30 minutes.

Melt half the butter in a frying pan and whisk it into the batter. Use the remaining butter to fry thin pancakes.

How many people this serves varies of course, as all eat different amounts! The recipe is enough to fry about 16 thin pancakes of normal size (about 1/2 cup batter per pancake), resulting in four pancakes per person.

Attention! Many people find it difficult to cook pancakes. It is easy to fail at pancake-making before you get the hang of it. If you are a beginner, try using less milk and/or more flour for the pancakes; they will hold together better. An important tip is to really let the batter swell for a while before you cook the pancakes, it makes them easier to handle. Be sure to heat the pan so it is really hot before you start; the batter must react immediately when poured into the pan.

"Nordic Bread Spells" was Dr. Johannes Gårdbäck's contribution to Sister Robin Petersen's 2013 annual Conjure Cook-Off and Recipe Round-Up. Dr. Johannes is a member of AIRR and can be reached at TheRootDoctor.se.

MOON PHASES: WORKING WITH THE MOON
catherine yronwode

THE MOON'S INFLUENCE ON MAGIC

As a spiritual practitioner, you may wish to divine optimal times to work according to the Moon's phases, to add the power of the Moon to your spells. In order to know how to work with the Moon's phases, you'll need to know the cycles of the Moon. The Moon goes through an entire cycle of waxing and waning about every 28 days. This is called a Lunar Month. There are about 13 Lunar Months in a calendar (or Solar) year.

THE WAXING MOON

Let's start with a **Waxing Crescent Moon,** the kind that looks like a Man in a Moon drawing or a cute Christmas tree ornament with a smiling face and a long white beard. When the Moon is a Waxing Crescent; the dark side is to your left, more or less, and the bright Crescent is to your right. (Sometimes the Moon is tipped a little, so it may not be exactly right or left, but you will know what i mean if you go outside and look at it.)

THE WAXING CRESCENT MOON

- Rises after sunrise and sets after sunset
- Is only seen in the night sky for a short time after the sun goes down.

Every night the Moon rises in the East a little later and the thickness of the Waxing Crescent gets fatter, until the shape of the Moon is half a circle. This is the **First Quarter,** also called by some people the **Waxing Half Moon.** It is dark on the left and bright on the right

THE WAXING FIRST QUARTER MOON

- Rises about at noon
- Sets about at midnight.

After that, the Moon starts to look like it is pregnant — round on the right side, but bulged out past half-way on the left. This is the **Waxing Gibbous Moon.**

THE WAXING GIBBOUS MOON

- Rises in the middle of the afternoon
- Sets before well before sunrise.

SPELLS OF THE WAXING MOON

Spells that are worked to increase or expand something — to draw love or money to you, to bring you success on the job or in school, to draw customers to your business, to increase health — are often worked when the moon is waxing or growing bigger in apparent size. Folks who want their hair to grow thick and fast cut their hair when the moon is waxing. People plant crops grown for leaves, flowers, or seeds during the waxing moon. You can work these spells from Waxing Crescent to Waxing Gibbous Moon.

THE FULL MOON

It takes about 14 days of growing bigger for the moon to grow or wax full — that night you will see the **Full Moon** rise as a perfect circular disk.

THE FULL MOON

- Rises almost exactly at sunset
- Sets almost exactly at the next sunrise.

SPELLS OF THE FULL MOON

Many folks use the Full Moon for Lunar worship and for spells of love, romance, sex, marriage, and fertility. Because the Moon circles the Earth, the actual Full Moon moment may not take place directly over your head on any given month. Some people count the Full Moon as consisting of three nights, the one "before," the one "during" and the one "after" Full. Because the minute the Moon is fully "Full," it begins to wane, it is a good idea to plan your spell to culminate before the actual astronomical moment of fullness. Generally you will work spells the night of the approaching Full Moon.

THE WANING MOON

After its 14 days of waxing, culminating with the Full Moon, the process reverses and the Moon decreases in apparent size. It slowly begins to go dark on the right side, while the left side stays the same disk-shape it had when it was Full. This is the **Waning Gibbous Moon** — it looks perfectly round on the left side, but bulged out past half-way on the right.

THE WANING GIBBOUS MOON

• Rises in the early evening
• Sets some time after sunrise.

Every night the Moon rises in the East a little later and the Waning Gibbous gets thinner, until the Moon is half a circle. This is the **Last Quarter,** also called the **Third Quarter** or **Waning Half Moon.** It is dark on the right and bright on the left.

THE WANING LAST QUARTER MOON

• Rises about at midnight
• Sets about at noon.

As the shape of the Moon continues to shrink, night by night, the Moon becomes a **Waning Crescent**; at this time the dark side is to your right and the bright Crescent is to your left.

THE WANING CRESCENT MOON

• Rises between midnight and dawn,
• Fades out when the Sun comes up.

SPELLS OF THE WANING MOON

Spells that are worked to decrease or diminish something — to break up a love affair, to drive away an unwanted neighbour, to take off crossed conditions, to cut away former relationships, to banish poverty, and to rid oneself of disease — are often worked when the moon is waning or growing smaller in apparent size. Folks who want to keep a hairdo and slow down their hair growth cut their hair when the moon is waning. People plant crops grown for roots during the waning moon. You can work these spells from Waxing Gibbous to Waxing Crescent Moon.

THE NEW MOON

Finally, growing smaller still, the Moon has waned completely and it vanishes from the night-time sky. This is called the **Dark of the Moon** or **New Moon** — and on that night you will see no Moon at all, no matter how long you stay up and watch, because…

THE NEW MOON (DARK MOON)

• Rises at sunrise
• Sets at sunset.

SPELLS OF THE NEW MOON

Many folks say the only spells to be worked by the Dark of the Moon are death spells.

WAXING MOON AGAIN

About 3 days after the true Dark of the Moon you will see a tiny sliver of a Moon like a fingernail paring appear in the sky at sunset near where the Sun has gone down. Some people call this the **First Crescent.** Others call it the **Siva Moon,** because the Hindu god Siva is shown with a thin crescent moon in his hair.

THE FIRST CRESCENT

• Rises a little bit after sunrise
• Sets a little bit after sunset.

After that, the Moon grows (or waxes) to a nice, "Man in the Moon" type Crescent Moon again. And that's where we started out, with the **Waxing Crescent Moon.**

HOW YOU CAN TELL
WHAT PHASE THE MOON IS IN

To tell whether the Moon is waxing or waning is fairly simple. Basically, all you have to do is go outside at sundown and take a look — if you don't see the Moon then, you will have to go outside later at night and check again, or check during the day:

If the Moon is already up in the sky in the evening, when the Sun goes down, then the Moon is **Waxing.** Every night it will rise a little later and look a little fuller. At Full Moon it will rise like a circle almost exactly when the Sun sets.

If the Moon is not already up in the sky when night falls, but instead rises long after sunset, or if you see it faintly during the day, then the Moon is **Waning.** Every day it will rise a little later and look a little thinner. At New Moon it will rise almost exactly when the Sun does, but you won't be able to see it at all.

"Moon Phases" was Lucky Mojo Shop Hand-Out No. 15, from 2002. It was distributed at my "Astrology for Rootworkers" MISC workshop in 2008. The text is taken directly from the web page "Moon Phases" at LuckyMojo.com/moonphases.html, which is part of my 1995 book "Hoodoo in Theory and Practice."

ASTROLOGY IN THE DRUGSTORE, THE ZODIAC IN THE PANTRY

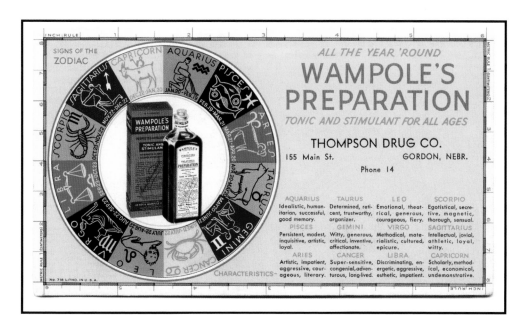

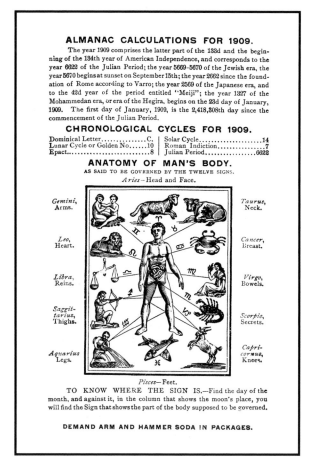

Top: Desk blotter advertisement for Wampole's Preparation, early 20th century, with signs of the Zodiac and brief descriptions.
Bottom: Cover and interior page from Arm and Hammer Almanac for 1909, with signs of the Zodiac and the Zodiacal Man.

SUN-SIGN ASTROLOGY FOR THE HOODOO PRACTITIONER

Page 23 from a circa 1945 mail order hoodoo supply catalogue of The Standard O and B Supply Co. of Chicago, Illinois.
Items offered for sale include Zodiac oil, jewelry, and lucky coins, astral candles; and a mojo bag containing a Sun-sign herb.

ASTROLOGY FOR CONJURE DOCTORS
catherine yronwode

BACKGROUND

The study of the movements of stars and planets is known world-wide, wherever people can gaze up to the night sky and keep records of such phenomena as Moon phases, eclipses, and the yearly interplay of Solar and Lunar periodicity as seen against the backdrop of the stars. Every culture has developed its own star-lore, its own names and shapes for constellations, and its own wisdom concerning how the movements of these cosmic bodies affect the lives of human beings.

Although few rootworkers think of themselves as astrologers, and some outsiders think that African Americans "don't use astrology," star-lore does play a definite part in conjure, and you can learn to use this traditional wisdom to enhance and empower hoodoo spells.

Many newcomers to hoodoo only understand African American folklore in the light of popular fictional films in which spooky, illiterate "Voodoo doctors" roam the night, mumbling strange incantations. The legends of rural rootworkers have been so romanticized as to eclipse the actuality that many conjures were educated, widely read, and multi-cultural in outlook.

The patronizing fiction that African Americans, being basically illiterate, could not understand the tenets of astrology, provides a framework in which the "primitive" is idolized at the expense of the "learned." Within this paradigm, it is earnestly attested that "hoodoo doctors don't do astrology," a false notion i intend here to thoroughly disprove.

THE NORTH STAR: LIBERTY TALISMANS

Historical evidence supports the notion that not only did African American slaves use the North Star constellation, "The Drinking Gourd," for navigation as they went North to freedom, they also used the North Star magically. That is, the image of the star that literally could guide one north to liberty became, when minted on a coin, the talisman that kept one's spiritual direction pointed ever in the direction of personal freedom and potential prosperity.

The coins favoured for conjure work in pre-Emancipation times were those bearing the image of Lady Liberty (preferably with the word "LIBERTY" included as well), plus the 13 stars that are used to symbolize the 13 original American colonies.

Very often, if the coin was arranged with the 13 stars above Liberty's head, the middle star, representing the North Star, would be drilled through, to make the coin into a hanging pendant. This sort of lucky talisman could be worn to guide, protect, and lead a person north to freedom — to the land of Liberty.

Four coins minted before Emancipation that could be used as conjure talismans for freedom: the 1816-1839 Coronet Matron Head Cent, 1839-1857 Coronet Braided Hair Cent, the 1849-1857 Coronet Half Cent and the Seated Liberty Half Dollar, first minted in 1831.

ASTROLOGY IN THE DRUGSTORE, THE ZODIAC IN THE PANTRY

As a teacher, author, and shop-keeper, i am continually frustrated by the contemporary belief that only today's counter-cultural New Age, Neo-Pagan, and Witchcraft communities have ever had the courage to face down the modern right-wing branch of Christianity which frowns upon the occult.

The truth is that until quite recently — and certainly within my memory — what now passes for "the occult" was accessible everywhere in America, and commercial enterprises of all types, from shoe stores to liquor distilleries, promoted their products with free advertising material featuring the signs of the Zodiac, along with the respective lucky days, numbers, gemstones, and the body parts they ruled.

I shall let two 20th century examples suffice, but trust me, there are at least a hundred in my collection:

Wampole's Preparation, a "tonic and stimulant for all ages" distributed a blotter (this was in the days of fountain pens) listing all of the Sun signs, their dates, and a short character analysis for the native of each sign.

Beginning in 1909, Church and Dwight, makers of Arm and Hammer Soda, an essential ingredient in biscuits, cakes, and cookies, produced a yearly almanac featuring the Zodiacal signs, a rulership chart of the human body by signs, and complete Sun and Moon sign tables for the year. The almanac was distributed in boxes of baking soda. Thus anyone who could read a cookbook could learn — and put to use — simple Sun sign and Moon sign astrology.

EDWARD A. LOWE, PROFESSIONAL HOODOO ASTROLOGER

Astrology was not only used in ad campaigns that reached into Black neighbourhoods and kitchens, astrologers also practiced hoodoo. The Standard O & B Company of Chicago distributed Zodiac-themed coins, oils, and candles to hoodoo rootworkers via mail order and Chicago was a major center for the promulgation of astrological conjure.

During the 1920s, Texas-born Edward A. Lowe (September 19, 1908 - December 17, 1987) migrated to Chicago's South Side "Bronzeville" district. There he cast natal and progressed horoscopes for clients, according to "the science of the Zodiac." The 1945 book "Black Metropolis: a Study of Negro Life in a Northern City" by St. Clair Drake and Horace Roscoe Cayton described Lowe's "jinx-removal candles" and "efficacious oils," as well as his "elaborate altar, where a rack of candles burns and a coloured glass bowl contains oil and water" for clients to touch in a ritual of purification.

Professor Lowe sold policy tickets for illegal betting, published his own "Spiritualistic Dream Book" for catching lucky numbers, compounded and marketed his own brand of Algiers Oil, and called himself an "Astro-Numerologist." Thus in Edward Lowe we see the perfect amalgam of the conjure doctor and the astrologer, putting the lie to the notion that Southern-born root doctors don't work by the signs of the Zodiac.

DR. E. P. READ, HOODOO HERB DOCTOR AND ASTROLOGER

People have asked me if Professor Lowe was a "fluke," the *sui generis* astrologer hoodoo doctor of his era. Quite obviously he was not. Let us examine next the person of Dr. E. P. Read, an herbalist, rootworker, and astrologer located on South Street in Philadelphia during the 1920s - 1940s.

Dr. Read ran the Indian Medicine Company. He made Hindoo Devil Chaser Incense. He sold John the Conqueror roots. He started an insurance company. He owned a mineral spring in Virginia where Black people could bathe in the healing waters that would have been forbidden to them at a White-owned spa of the era. And he was also an astrologer. I have in my possession the horoscopes of several members of his family, along with their interpretations.

MOON PHASES AND "THE CHANGE OF THE MOON"

In order to harness the power of the Moon influences, you need to know about the phases of the Moon. The Moon visibly waxes and wanes through a cycle that repeats about every 28 days. This cycle is a Lunar Month, and there are about 13 Lunar Months in a Solar calendar year.

The New Moon, or its first visible appearance as a crescent, after the Dark of the Moon, is called "the change of the Moon."

Spells for expansion, increase or acquisition — to draw love, to get money, for advancement and success on the job or in school, to bring customers to your business — are often worked right after the change of the Moon, when the Moon is waxing or increasing in apparent size. This time is sometimes called the "young" or "growing" Moon.

Spells for elimination, decrease or diminishment — to remove illness, break up love affairs, drive away unwanted neighbours, or undo crossed conditions — are worked when the Moon is waning or shrinking in apparent size. This time is sometimes called "the waste of the Moon" or the "wasting Moon."

THE MOON IN THE SIGNS OF THE ZODIAC

Every lunar month the Moon travels around the entire Zodiac, spending about two and a half days in each sign. In traversing the Zodiacal signs, the Moon picks up their vibrations. Each sign has its own symbolism and its own strengths and weaknesses, which in turn affect the transiting Moon — for instance, Aries is a good Moon sign for starting projects, but not for transplanting tender greens, Taurus is a good Moon sign for planting, but not for travel, Gemini is a good Moon sign for travel, but not for completing projects.

Traditional Zodiac Moon sign lore of this type — along with the dates of the Moon's entrance into each sign — is published in almanacs. It is an old hoodoo tradition to design spells according to the symbolism of the Zodiacal Moon signs. For example, a female root doctor in Fayetteville, North Carolina, interviewed in the 1930s by the folklorist Harry Hyatt, explained that to control a man's mind, you should work on him when the Moon is in Aries, the sign that rules the head, and thus the brain:

"Yo ketch dis [Moon] sign whilst it in dis man's brain, if yo' wants tuh change his mind fo' any purpose" ("Hoodoo - Conjuration - Witchcraft - Rootwork" Vol. 3, page 1915).

Another of Hyatt's informants, a man in Waycross, Georgia, whom he called "Dr. Yousee," revealed that a good rootworker should instruct his clients to work according to the times that he, the doctor, set forth for them, after consulting his almanac:

"We have tuh take de alm'nac an' go by de signs — see where de signs at, yo' see, 'cause signs is de biggest part of all […]." Giving an example of the Moon changing signs at 10:00 PM on a certain day, he said that, "Yo' take dat place den, see, where de sign is at [in the book], yo' see, an' after tracing [determining] de sign, yo' tell dat man [the client], yo' say, 'Yo' take dis at ten a'clock — yo' start in de night — at ten a'clock at night.'" (Ibid. Vol. 2, pages 1212-3.)

EFFECTS REPEAT AS THE MOON SIGN RETURNS

Work done with harmful intent is often thought to come back around and repeat on the victim every month as the Moon enters the sign it occupied when the spell was originally cast. This is said to be particularly true of jinxing tricks or messes designed to cause physical ailments, and, as a result, the victim takes a downturn each time the Moon re-enters that sign of the Zodiac.

Once you understand this concept of cyclical repetition, you can use it to your advantage, both in creating helpful spells and in counter-acting the work of bad tricks aimed at you.

For instance, to increase your ability to save money, perform a candle spell for this purpose when the Moon is in Taurus, a positive money sign with acquisitive tendencies. Thereafter, set a new light each time the Moon returns to that sign.

Likewise, If you come under enemy attack in a sudden and obvious way, make a note of the Moon's sign before you clean everything off — and stay alert for a renewed attack next month, when the Moon again enters that sign.

THE SUN, ITS RISINGS, AND ITS SETTINGS

The rising Sun is a symbol of good things to come. We often begin rituals with a spiritual bath at Sunrise, and as the rite concludes, we pour out the used bath water toward the rising Sun. Likewise, the setting Sun is a symbol for decrease, and water poured out toward the West at Sunset is appropriate for works of repudiation or removal.

The folklore collector Harry Hyatt wrote that, "The Sun […] has two timetables with variations — first, from midnight to noon; second, before noon and after noon. All evil is done with the setting Sun; all good, especially cures, with the rising Sun." He added that, as far as conjure is concerned, "The Sun starts rising at midnight."

PLANETARY HOURS, AN OLD SYSTEM MADE NEW

No evidence exists that slavery-era Southern hoodoo practitioners utilized the Chaldean system of dividing a day into planetary hours ruled by the Sun, Mercury, Venus, Moon, Saturn, Jupiter, and Mars — but by the early 1920s, modern Black root workers like Edward Lowe of Chicago were selling Professor A. F. Seward's planetary hour calculator for timing spells, so "the hours" have been a part of hoodoo for 100 years. Online software is now available to automatically perform the necessary calculations.

GIVE ASTROLOGY A TRY

Many rootworkers overlook the potential that astrology has to offer. They may feel that the subject is complex, that it requires an extensive knowledge of mathematics, and that it is "not traditional," but as the examples given here readily indicate, star-lore has long been a part of hoodoo, and almost any root doctor, armed with a current almanac, can link his or her work to the power of the stars.

I wrote this hand-out in 2008 and enlarged it in 2010, also adding a sheet of coloured illustrations at that time.

TEA LEAF READING, A BRIEF INTRODUCTION
catherine yronwode

HISTORY

Tea Leaf Reading is also known as Cup Reading, Tasseomancy (French "tasse" [cup] plus Greek "mancy" [divination]), Tasseography ("cup writing"), and "Tasseology" ("cup study"). As a form of divination, it is probably as old as the invention of cups. Some claim it originated in China, where tea was first commercially grown, but it seems to have been known in Scotland, Ireland, and England before trade with China developed, and probably developed there with herbal teas. In 1899, John Hanley, an American of Irish descent, described tea reading by "Figures and Signs as Interpreted by Our Grandmothers," implying that the art was already old in his era. Around the same time, Harry Roseland, a popular American genre artist, made several paintings featuring a Black female tea leaf reader divining for young While female clients.

In the early 20th century, tea leaf reading became a widespread form of divination. Women entrepreneurs opened tea rooms — small, cozy, domestic restaurants serving light lunches and non-alcoholic beverages. Getting one's cup read was a popular adjunct to dining out in such restaurants, especially between World War One and World War Two. Some tea rooms of that era featured fortune telling waitresses, who dressed as Gypsies and offered patrons "a free reading with every meal." In some tea rooms, the "Gypsy" waitresses also offered palm readings to guests.

HOW TEA LEAF READINGS ARE CONDUCTED

Tea leaf reading is almost always performed in person rather than by phone or email, as it is the cup of the client or "sitter" that is read. In addition to being conducted in the home by family members or between friends, it is also a form of divination for which one can seek out a professional "cup reader" who will brew the tea, perhaps drink a cup while chatting with you, and then tell your fortune in the leaves.

Tea leaf symbols are not read "intuitively." rather, each symbol has one or more traditional meanings. The amateur reader will have learned 50 or so, while a professional may have a repertoire of 100 to 200 symbols memorized.

SPECIAL TEA CUPS FOR TASSEOGRAPHIC READING

Tea leaf reading can be performed in a plain white cup, and many folks prefer that type of cup because the emblems are clearly discernable against a plain backdrop. However, since the late 19th century, designers and potteries have produced many forms of special "fortune telling cups." These generally fall into one of three types: Astrology, Symbol, and Cartomancy cups.

ASTROLOGY CUPS AND SAUCERS

Astrological cups and saucers are decorated with the twelve signs of the zodiac and symbols of the seven ancient planets. The tea leaves are read with their usual traditional meanings, but their imagery is combined with the meanings usually ascribed to the astrological symbols upon which the tea-leaves lay. For instance, a heart overlaying the symbol for the zodiacal sign of Aries may mean the love of a soldier, a mechanic, or an Aries man.

SYMBOL CUPS AND SAUCERS

Symbol cups and saucers contain popular signs from tea reading plus other omen-symbols, such as a snake, anchor, or horseshoe. The leaves are read with their usual meanings, but their imagery is combined with the meanings traditionally given to the images upon which the tea-leaf symbols lay. For instance, a heart overlaying the symbol of a ring may mean a marriage based on love.

CARTOMANCY CUPS AND SAUCERS

Cartomancy cups and saucers are decorated with images of scattered playing cards, usually either from a 32-card euchre deck (as used in Lenormand style card reading) or a 52 card poker deck (as used in Italian and English style card reading). The leaves are read with their usual meanings, but their imagery is combined with the meanings traditionally given to the playing cards upon which the tea-leaf symbols lay. For instance, a heart overlaying the card of the Queen of Spades may mean the love or a dark woman, a divorced woman, or a widowed woman.

SPACE, TIME, DANGER, AND THE STRANGER IN THE CUP

Cup reading proceeds in an orderly manner, following a prescribed pattern of examination.

HOME AND AWAY

The handle of the cup is the "home" and any signs found along its vertical axis relate to events close to the home. Across from the handle is "away" and its vertical axis represents events away from the home. Tea leaf signs falling between home and away are said to be leaving. Those that fall between away and home are said to be coming closer.

FOUR TURNS TO THE BOTTOM

When reading the cup, it is customary to proceed clockwise in a downward spiral of four turns — the rim, the center, and the bottom of the cup's wall, followed by a final turn around the floor of the cup. This spiral starts at the handle and finishes at the bottom center of the cup.

Symbols that are found in the first turn of the spiral, along the cup's rim, are timed to occur within a week. The middle turn around the cup's wall is two weeks away. The bottom turn along the base of wall is three weeks away. The fourth turn, spiraling into the bottom center of the cup, represents events about a month away in time.

Events at the bottom of the cup are generally interpreted in their darkest and direst aspects and represent dangerous conditions. Symbols which are fortunate at the top of the cup rapidly become less fortunate as they "fall" to the bottom. For this reason, some makers of astrological and symbol cups place an emblem of safety in the bottom of the cup, to obviate any negative symbol that might fall there. The most common of these protective signs are the ship or the anchor, which represent safety and ward off drowning at sea.

THE STRANGER IN THE CUP

One special tea leaf symbol that stands apart from all the others is when a twig or stick from the tea plant is found among the leaves. This special divinatory mark is called "The Stranger in the Cup" and it foretells a visitor. If the cup is being read for a young woman, the Stranger in the Cup signifies that she will shortly meet her husband-to-be.

A BASIC LIST OF TEA LEAF SYMBOLS

Acorn: At top, slow growth; at bottom, good health.
Airplane: Long journey; a rise in social position.
Anchor: At top, stability and rest; at bottom, safety.
Apple: Achievement; if bitten into, temptation.
Arrow: Point down, bad news; up, good news.
Axe: Difficulties; if at top, overcoming of difficulties.
Baby: Fretting and small worries.
Bag: A trap; if open, escape, from a trap.
Ball: Variable fortune, as ball bounces up and down.
Balloon: A celebration or party soon.
Basket: A treat, award, compliment, recognition.
Bell: Announcement; the nearer the top, the better.
Birds: Good news (see also species of birds).
Boat: A visit from a friend, protection, inheritance.
Book: If open, good news; if closed, hidden secrets.
Bottle: Drunkenness, temptations offered.
Broom: A new home; a thorough house-cleaning.
Bush: A secret friend or secret opportunities.
Butterfly: Fickleness of friends.
Candle: Ask for and receive help from others.
Cat: Gossip, deceit; cat-head, female false friend.
Chain: Engagement, wedding; sequence of events.
Chair: A guest is coming.
Circle: Success, completion; with dots, a baby.
Clock: Better health if medical help is sought soon.
Clouds: Trouble; with dots (rain), many problems.
Coin: Money count the coins to tell how much.
Cross: Death, a funeral, suffering, sacrifice.
Cup: Reward of merit; overturned, justified criticism.
Dagger: Danger from self or others; beware injury.
Dish: Trouble at home; matters require cleaning up.
Dog: Good, true friend; at bottom, friend needs help.
Door: Opportunities arise through an odd event.
Duck: Money, and false gossip about money.
Eagle: Success by soaring over obstacles.
Egg: If unbroken, success; if broken, failure.
Envelope: Good news; with dots, news of money.
Eye: Look sharp; be cautious; you be psychic.
Face: A change is coming, it may be a setback.
Fan: Flirtation, but it comes to nothing in the end.
Feather: Insincerity, undependability, lack of focus.
Fence: Limitations, minor setbacks, easily mended.
Finger: Extra emphasis on whatever it points to.
Fire: At top, achievement; at bottom, danger, haste.
Fish: Increase of wealth or increase in family.
Flag: Danger if you compromise your integrity.
Flower: Compliments, tokens of love and esteem.
Fly: Domestic annoyances require your attention.
Forked Line: You must soon make a decision.
Fruit: Prosperity, a successful outcome to labour.
Gate: Opportunity, future success beckons.

Glass, Water: Integrity and temperance.
Glass, Cocktail: Dissatisfaction with life.
Goat: Beware stubborn people; they may be enemies.
Grapes: Good health, fertility, happiness; inebriation.
Gun: Anger, discord, strife; danger where it points.
Hammer: Hard work is needed; avoid complainers.
Hand: Open, a friendly helper; closed, an argument.
Hat: Improvement, a new role or a new job.
Hawk: Suspicion and jealousy; watch with care.
Heart: Love, pleasure, romance, a thrilling meeting.
Horse: Galloping, good news; head only, a lover.
Horseshoe: Good luck, a winning bet, good fortune.
Hourglass: You must decide something soon.
House: Security and safety; parents.
Insect: Minor problems require immediate attention.
Jewels: Gifts will be offered to you.
Kettle: Minor illness; don't worry; friends will help.
Key: Success, prosperity, understanding.
Kite: Ascent in social position by the help of friends.
Knife: A broken friendship; a justified fear.
Ladder: Job promotion, a rise in life, advancement.
Lamp: At top, a feast; at side, secrets revealed.
Leaf: Change in health: up, better; down, worse.
Letter: News; If cross near, death, if coins, a gift.
Lines: If straight, progress; if wavy, uncertain path.
Lion: An influential friend in a position of authority.
Lock: Obstacles too strong to overcome.
Man: Near handle, a visitor; elsewhere, a pen-pal.
Moon: A change in plans.
Mountain: Great goals beset by difficulties.
Mouse: Someone is stealing from you.
Mushroom: At top, country life; at bottom, growth.
Nail: Injustice, unfairness, unrighteous punishment.
Necklace: Whole, admirers; broken, losing a lover.
Nest: Save your money; take care of your home.
Needle: Recognition, admiration.
Oak Tree: Strength, health, long life; betterment.
Octopus: Danger.
Ostrich: Travel abroad.
Owl: Gossip nearby; a wise person will protect you.
Palm Tree: Success, honour.
Palm Leaf: Victory, martyrdom.
Parasol: A new lover.
Parrot: Foreign journey; people talk about you.
Pig: Greed and carelessness.
Pin: A new job awaits.
Pine Tree: High achievement.
Pipe: Reconciliation of a friendship.
Pistol: Danger is near.
Plough: A struggle ahead; hard going.
Purse: At top, profit; at bottom, loss.
Question Mark: Be cautious; future unsettled.
Rabbit: Bravery to overcome a fear of disaster.
Rainbow: The most difficult time is now over.

Rake: Watch details lest you stumble.
Raven: Bad news; love disaster; death for the aged.
Rider: Good news from afar, especially in finances.
Ring: At top, marriage; at bottom, betrothal.
Ring, Broken: Divorce or broken engagement.
Rose: Popularity, romance.
Scales: Balanced, justice; unbalanced, injustice.
Scissors: Quarrels, possibly separation.
Sheep: Good fortune; a friend does your bidding.
Shell: Good news from over the sea.
Ship: At top, a journey; at bottom, a safe journey.
Shoe: Hard work leads to a change for the better.
Sickle: Illness, sorrow, and pain.
Snake: An enemy, and wisdom to discern who it is.
Spider: Good luck, a reward for industrious work.
Spoon: Generosity.
Squirrel: Save up now for future times of want.
Stairs: Orderly progress leads to eventual success.
Star: Health, happiness, hope; absolute success.
Sun: Joy, success, power, children, well-being.
Sword: Small quarrels turn into serious arguments.
Table: A social gathering at which you'll find favour.
Teardrops: Sorrow and tears.
Tent: Travel for which you are not well prepared.
Thimble: Changes at home; a need for mending.
Tortoise: Criticism, usually beneficial.
Tower: Disappointment and possible ruin.
Triangle: Something unexpected will happen.
Turtle: Slow progress; a sluggard is near to you.
Umbrella: Trouble, but you will be protected.
Vase: A friend needs your help.
Violin: A self-centered person.
Volcano: Harmful and emotional words may erupt.
Wagon: A wedding will ensue.
Wasp: Your romantic problems are due to a rival.
Wheel: If whole, good fortune; if broken, loss.
Wings: Messages from Heaven.
Wolf: Cunning and jealousy.
Zebra: Adventures overseas.

"Tea Leaf Reading, A Brief Introduction," which i taught in 2009, was one of my favourite workshops. I collect and sell antique fortune telling cups, and it was a pleasure to bring out and display the best and the rarest of these, and then to present each participant with a Jane Lyle Cup of Fortune boxed set, complete with a 96-page booklet on tea leaf reading. We brewed and drank tea together and practiced reading each other's grounds, and in addition to this introductory flyer, everyone who attended took home their beautiful tea cups and books. Photos of my own divinatory tea cup collection, as well as my thoughts on women's culture and domestic divination systems, can be found online at my Mystic Tea Room web site, MysticTeaRoom.com.

SANGOMA AND SHAMANIC BONE READING
catherine yronwode

VARIETIES OF BONE DIVINATION

Reading bones as a form of divination is ancient, and can be found almost everywhere in the world. Traditions vary from culture to culture and can be assigned to three major schools of practice:

HEATED AND CRACKED BONE READINGS

This old method is not much practiced at the present time. Turtle shells or large animal scapulars (shoulder blades) are heated in a fire and the patterns of their cracking are interpreted in divination.

MATHEMATICAL SYSTEMS OF BONE READING

The bones used in math-based readings have been marked with spots, lines, or dots, as in African Hakata; carved and given numbered faces, like dice; or are naturally formed in a way that can be read numerically, like the astragalus bones of Mongolian Shaggai. Other math-based divination systems include Obi and Diloggun with Cowrie shells or Coconut pieces; Geomancy, or counting marks made in sand; and the I Ching, which employs cast Yarrow stalks or coins. The outcome of a bone casting that is performed in a mathematical divination system will be based on the number of items thrown and the number of readable faces per item.

SPIRIT-LED INTERPRETIVE BONE READING

In Shamanic bone reading, the symbolism of the animal bones derives from the qualities of each animal species, and also from the qualities of the individual bones. If you are familiar with the botanical "doctrine of signatures," you will have a good start on understanding how the symbolism of the bones developed in various cultures.

Divination by throwing the bones involves the interpretation of patterns, more like teacup or coffee ground reading than like a math-based system, in which "this means that." Zulu Sangoma diviners use the bones as a conduit to carry messages from the Ancestors. This is why you must be "truly gifted" to do the work; it is a form of Spirit contact with your Ancestors and those of the client, who speak through the bones, nuts, and shells.

THE BONES

Some readers only use bones from one animal; in America, this is typically a 'Possum or Chicken. Each bone of the animal has a different meaning. A second dimension of interpretation arises when readers select bones from animals of varied species: The symbolism of each species modifies the symbolism of each bone. Sangoma diviners and Peruvian shamans include seeds, nuts, crystals, and shells with their bones. Each has a meaning based on the spirit of the Animal or Plant tribe from which it came. Sangomas may also make use of game pieces and small fetishes or statuettes to represent human beings, The use of a porcelain doll head carrying the graveyard dirt of a Spirit Guide is a Spiritualist's innovation arising from this ancient tradition. The Ancestors speak through the bones.

As a reader, you will appreciate the reason for having bones of many species. The hand of a Human has a different quality than the paw of a Lion. Some animals are allies, some are harmful or dangerous. There is great value to the diviner in working with unusual bones, due to the powerful associations we feel when we fully respect and spiritually contact wild species that were known to our Ancestors.

In the Sangoma tradition, each diviner's set of bones is different. No two sets are ever the same, and you can't just go out and buy a set of bones the way you can buy a set of rune stones. Even the number of bones is a personal choice. A full set of bones for one diviner may consist of 10 items, while another's bowl may contain 60 or more bones.

BOWL, BASKET, OR BAG

The bones are kept in a container made of gentle materials, neither metal nor stone. Wooden bowls, woven baskets, and Abalone shells are favoured; a cloth, fiber, or leather bag may also be used. Bones are typically stored up high or under the altar near the Earth, but not at eye level. Cover the bones when not in use to respect and protect them. This is not out of necessity to hide the bones, but simply to keep them safe. If you have pets, you may wish to store your covered bowl or bag of bones in a chest or box.

Animal tribes and species, considered without regard to the symbolism of the bones we select from them:

Alligator	Luckiness which also carries some danger
Badger	Bravery, defense, luck, cunning, mischievousness
Bear	Strength, honour, wisdom, greed, slow to anger, twins
Boar	Lust, gluttony, determination, endurance, male vigour
Bull	Potency, wealth, aggression, male sexuality
Camel	Patience, endurance, obstinacy, awkwardness
Cat	Grace, artistry, luck, independence, curiosity
Chicken	Cleaning away sorcery and crossed conditions
Cow	Domesticity, kindness, adoption, nurturance
Coyote	Trickiness, wit, humour, sexual infidelity
Deer	Nature, woodlands, otherworld visitations
Dog	Faithfulness, loyalty, obedience, watchfulness
Fox	Cunning, diplomacy, intelligence, eloquence
Goat	Aspiration to heights, pride, lechery, fecundity
Horse	Success, freedom, mobility, travel, triumph
Human	Ancestral spirits, spirits of the dead, allies, power
Lion	Strength, power, command, nobility, leadership
Owl	Silent power, night journeys, a warning of death
Rabbit	Haste, ability to listen, timidity, sweetness, fertility
Raccoon	Dexterity, cleverness, cleanliness, sexuality
Raven	Message from the dead, procrastination, shape-shifting
Sheep	Humility, conformity, gambling (Astragalus bone)
Sloth	Laziness, slowness, stupor, messiness, sloppiness
Snake	Stealth, renewal, sexuality, poison or strangulation
Walrus	Massive power, defensiveness, territoriality
Weasel	Lies, false friendship, oath-breaking, conspiracy
Wolf	Loyalty, spirit guidance, path-finding, intuition

The symbolism of the bones, considered without regard to the tribe or species of Animal from which they come:

Cranium, Skull	Thought, mind, spirit, essence
Mandible, Jaw	Speech, gossip, discourse
Dens, Tooth	Luck, biting through, attack, defense
Vertebra, Back Bone	Courage, "backbone," resoluteness
Clavicula, Collar Bone	The "key" bone, connectivity
Furcula, Wishbone	Wishes, hopes, dreams that come true
Sternum, Breast Bone	Protection; the "keel" of flight in birds
Costa, Rib Bone	Breathing, suffocation, squeezing
Scapula, Shoulder Blade	Protection (Catholic scapular), divining
Humerus, Upper Arm Bone	Labour, work, lifting, strength
Radius, Arm Bone	Labour, control, precision, cooperation
Ulna, Arm Bone	Labour, work, embraces, war, battle
Carpals, Wrist Bones	Dexterity, acquisition, skill, complexity
Metacarpals, Hand Bones	Dexterity, skill, industriousness
Phalanges, Fingers, Paws	Acquisition, dexterity, reach, touch
Talons, Claws	Attack, defense, gripping, capture
Wing Bones	Travel, flight (arms and fingers of birds)
Pelvis, Pubis, Hips, etc.	Weight-bearing, reproductive areas
Baculum, Penis Bone	Male sexuality, luck in gambling
Femur, Thigh Bone	Journeys, endurance, "trumpet" bone
Patella, Knee Bone	Leverage, assistance, protection
Tibia, Shin, Shank, Leg	Travel, journeys, solitary walks
Fibula, Calf Bone	Travel, companions, journeys
Tarsus, Ankle Bones	Mobility, travel, goals, journeys
Talus, Astragalus	A tarsal; Shaggai divination and dicing
Metatarsals, Foot Bones	Movement, new ventures, travel
Phalanges, Toes, Paws, Hooves	Coming toward or going away

Some items we cast are not bones, but mineral, botanical, zoological, or symbolic objects; among these, some have binary values:

Abalone	Beauty, the sea, wealth, sacred rites, containment
Arrowhead	Enemy attack, attack on an enemy, hunting, "Elf shot"
Bat Nut	Harnessing of dark forces for protection and luck
Bead	Ornament, artistry; if from a grave, it represents that spirit
Bell	Awakening, warning, alertness, music
Buckeye	Health, luck, protection from illness, security
Button	Fastening, connecting; if from a grave: that grave's spirit
Carved Skull	Spirits of Ancestors or the dead, a warning of death
Carving, 3-D	Representative of the image (e.g. Double Carp, Skull, etc.)
Carving, flat	Generally used as coins are; two-sided, yes or no
Cat's Eye	Protection, watchfulness, alertness (or lack thereof)
Coin or Token	Heads wins, tails loses or flees; other imagery per the coin
Cowrie	Female sexuality, reproduction, divination
Crystal	Clarity, directionality, energy flow, a pointer forward
Fossil	Ancient or past form of item if it were not fossilized
Dice	Gambling luck; pay attention to the number on dice
Doll Arm	Pointer, grasper, indicator; interpreted as a human arm
Doll Head	Fixed with graveyard dirt, it holds the spirit of a child
Domino	Gambling luck; if spots up, play; if blank side up, refrain
Double Carp	Extra money, wealth, prosperity at the New Year
Grave Goods	The spirit of the grave from which the item was obtained
John the C.	Strength, power, command, nobility, male sexuality
Key	Opening the way, closing the way; if crossed, a crossroads
Little John	Legal matters, court cases, protection from the law
Magnetic Dogs	If joined, union or reunion; if not, separation
Nut	Fertility and wealth hidden in reserve, savings
Nutmeg	Gambling luck, finances, business success
Queen Eliz.	Womanliness, divination, female sexuality and power
Purba	Demon dagger of Tibetan Buddhism, destroys evil
Religious Item	God's blessings and protections on all your ventures
Ring	Union, wholeness, marriage, remembrance, universality
Seashell	Female mystery (see also Abalone, Cowrie, Cat's Eye)
Y-Twig	Forked road, divided energy, parting, joining, dowsing

A few guidelines and examples that may assist and inform you:

• **The same bone from different tribes may have differing symbolism.** In the Mammal tribe, the clavicula (or "little key" in Latin) turns and articulates; in the Bird tribe, the clavicles are fused, forming the furcula (or "little fork") which we call the wishbone, and to which we assign a different meaning. Likewise the arm, wrist, and finger bones (humerus, radius, ulna, carpals, metacarpals, and phalanges) have different meanings in Mammals than in Birds, for among the latter, they form wings, not arms.

• **The same bone from different species may have differing symbolism.** The Raccoon penis bone is a long-held symbol of domestic and faithful male sexuality; the Coyote penis bone is that of a trickster and a cheater — and even the Dog, known generally for his loyalty, is a synonym for a man who commits fornication or adultery, hence the Dog penis bone is like that of the Coyote, untrustworthy.

• **Some Animals have hands and feet, others only have feet.** A Raccoon's hands differ from its feet; a Goat's four feet are much the same. Therefore the Goat comes and goes, but it does not acquire.

• **If related species have differing powers, choose bones accordingly.** Pythons and Rattlesnakes are in the same tribe, but the Python strangles and the Rattler poisons. Rather than lump all Snake bones together, we select a Python rib to symbolize binding or suffocation and a Rattlesnake vertebra to symbolize courage, "backbone," and the warning associated with the justified ability to strike and to kill ("Don't tread on me!").

• **Occasionally a bone or other item breaks during casting.** No matter how carefully the bones are thrown, it may happen that a bone will break during the casting. First, breathe. This happens. Next, divine the bone as "broken" — the area of life represented by that bone is "broken" for this question or for this client. After the divination, bury the broken bone with respect. A broken bone is not a sign that you must not work with that Animal. It was a message from the Ancestors that was meant for that client.

REMEMBER: We divine by Spirit, not by a set of rules. Always take time to know and feel the Ancestral Spirits in your work.

GOAT HIDE, FIBER OR CLOTH MAT, CIRCLE OF DIRT

Bone reading is conducted on the ground or at floor level. The bones are cast onto a surface that prevents their bouncing or breaking.

A goat skin or grass mat is common in Africa, as is throwing the bones into a circle drawn on soft dirt that has been cleared of vegetation. The skin or mat is rolled up and stored when not in use.

In Southern style African American bone reading, if the reading is held in a circle drawn in the dirt, the circle may be divided by an equal-armed X or cross to create a sacred crossroads or quincunx pattern.

In some traditions, a patterned mat or cloth is used, marked with stylized designs. These patterns are analogous to the designs found in fortune-telling teacups that assist the reader to interpret the images formed by the tea leaves.

BASIC SANGOMA BONE READING

The Ancestors are called and the bones are awakened with elements of air. Incense is used to bring in your Ancestors and the Ancestors of the client. The smoke ascends and the spark of coal guides them in. Go back in time, until your Ancestors and your client's Ancestors are the same. Go farther back, to the era when the Animals have one Ancestor, to when you and the client have one Ancestor with the Animals. Go still farther back, until the Plants have the same Ancestor as the Animals and you. Awaken the bones by breathing on them or fanning them with a horsehair whisk or feathers.

Some readers use all of their bones at each reading; some may wake them up before the reading and then set some bones back, not to be read, according to spirit guidance. As a beginner, you will start with a small set of bones, but if you eventually have many bones and intend to set some back, this does not mean that a "rule" is used for setting some back and selecting some. You must never CHOOSE the bones for the reading – you must ASK them.

Introduce the spirits of the bones to the Ancestors of your client. Ask if they have a message for her. If they say, 'Yes,' then do not question them further, but put those bones in your set, no matter how improbable they seem to you. They will tell you their story when the time comes.

Some Sangomas cast the bones for the client; others let the client cast the bones. Either way is correct, if Spirit tells you it is correct. (Consider how some card readers cut the cards for the client and others have the client cut the cards.) Once cast, the bones may be touched with the fingers or hands, or indicated with a bird's wing or a bundle of feathers.

Bones that fall or bounce outside the circle or off the skin or mat are either not counted or they are said to be moving away, if far from the reader, or not yet having entered the situation, if close to the reader.

Observe the directionality of the bones: Do the teeth attack a certain bone or ignore it? Does a finger bone or doll's arm reach for a financially lucky Nutmeg or turn away from it? You are looking for patterns. The patterns tell the story that your client has come to hear.

Becoming a proficient bone reader can take years, as you learn to communicate with the spirits. Be patient, respectful, and listen closely, and they will relay messages from the Unseen.

THE ANCESTOR ALTAR

Sangomas work with the dead, as Spiritualists do. To truly be a bone reader, you will need to make an Ancestor altar in your home. Do not hide your Ancestor altar in a closet. Create it to be seen, where you can show your pride in your Ancestors. You must have representations of your Ancestors on the altar. These can be photos, figures, or images. If you do not know their names, work as we do in the Spiritual Church with the Black Hawk bucket, calling a lineage of Ancestors into a statuary figure. Offer daily services to your Ancestors. Give them the food, water, whiskey, candies, tobacco, and other things they enjoy most. Never be afraid to request their help. They are devoted to us and assist us because they live within us.

Write a letter to your Ancestors and keep it on the altar, asking them to speak with you through dreams, through trance, and through the bones. Dreams will come easiest; bone reading and trance will develop over time. Eventually everything you see in nature — every flight of birds or bend of a tree limb — will be an omen from the Ancestors that you can divine.

I wrote "Sangoma and Shamanic Bone Reading" as a hand-out for Rev. D. John Michael Hilford's presentation at the 2011 MISC workshops and then incorporated the text into my 2012 book "Throwing the Bones: How to Foretell the Future with Bones, Shells, and Nuts."

HOW TO CREATE YOUR OWN DIVINATION DECK
Michele Jackson

Many cartomancers search for years, buying one deck after another, searching for the perfect deck. No matter how many decks they try there is always something missing — a few cards just don't make sense, or the imagery just doesn't speak to them. However, when you make your own deck, your relationship with every card is intimate. The imagery says exactly what you want it to say. The meaning of every card is engraved in your brain because you personally made every decision about the imagery, from the background colour to the inclusion of a barely noticeable symbol in the upper right hand corner. The size of the cards fits your hands comfortably, or has extra large lettering because you are near-sighted and don't always remember your glasses. This deck is tailor-made for you.

You don't need any special artistic talent to make a collage deck. You have spent a life-time looking at both good and bad design and your eye will usually know instinctively whether something looks good or not. Don't worry about the rules; if you break them in a way that is aesthetically unpleasant, you will know just by looking, and sometimes you will break the rules in such a way that it looks better than it would have looked if you had been trying to follow the rules. Have fun, and don't stress over anything. Nothing is permanent until you glue it down, and even then you can still sometimes make minor adjustments.

MATERIALS

IMAGES

You need as many images as you can find. Don't overlook any potential source. Magazines and old books are logically the first place we look, but don't forget catalogues, family photo albums, greeting cards, and rubber stamps. Now with the internet there are countless sources of online imagery too.

This is as good a place as any to discuss the legal stuff — specifically copyright. You need to decide whether you think you will ever, ever, ever want to share your deck with others, ether by publishing it for commercial sale, or making a few copies for friends or clients. If the answer is yes, be sure to use only images that you own (your own photographs, drawings, etc.) or images that are in the public domain.

Copyright law is beyond the scope of this hand-out, but an excellent source of information for collage artists is FunnyStrange.com/copyright — the site is by collage and tarot artist Sarah Ovenall, creator of the Victoria Regina Tarot Deck.

If the deck you are making is only for personal use and you don't plan to post it anywhere online or share it in any way, it is unlikely that the copyright police will come to your house to arrest you over the use of something you cut out of a magazine or greeting card. However, it is always best to use images that you own or images that are in the public domain.

Don't accumulate magazines or other sources — go through them quickly, cut out what you like or what you think might be useful, and throw the rest away. Keep your card size in mind. If you have a scanner or access to a colour copier, this is less of an issue as you can resize an image within reason. Keep in mind that images that are too small to start with can be difficult to resize very much as they will lose clarity as you blow them up.

A shoebox or plastic storage box should be enough to hold most of your images. You can get as fancy and as organized as you have time, money, and space for, but starting out, it's best to keep everything simple and easily accessible. Your box can hold your images, scissors, and glue stick, all in one place, ready to start working should you find yourself with some free time.

A dining room or kitchen table makes an ideal workspace. Keep one old magazine around for a gluing background, or use paper from your recycle bin. Don't use newspapers or newsprint magazine as the ink tends to bleed when wet with glue.

GLUE

I like Uhu glue sticks, but Avery, Elmer's, or any other name brand works just as well. Do not use rubber cement. While the brush is nice, the glue will dry out and your images will fall off over time. You don't need acrylic gel, or polyvinyl acetate glues. I find them too messy and inconvenient at small sizes. I made my first deck in 1995 and the glue stick glue is still holding strong.

SCISSORS

Any decent pair of office scissors will do for large, simple cuts, such as backgrounds. For detailed cutting I recommend a good pair of cuticle scissors. I like Tweezerman brand. They are guaranteed for life. I have had the same pair for years and they have not needed sharpening. Optionally, you can get an X-Acto knife for cutting inner shapes, but it's not necessary as you can cut an opening in an unobtrusive place and glue it down flush so it doesn't show.

CARDSTOCK

Cardstock is used as a support for your collage. You can buy blank card decks, but for less than a dollar you can buy one hundred 3" x 5" cards. If you like a larger deck, buy them in 4" x 6". Or buy letter-sized cardstock and cut a custom size to fit your hand. You can also use letter-sized card stock to make large originals, and then shrink them down to a smaller size for printing. This is easy if you have a scanner, harder if you have to use a colour copy machine, but still doable. Once you decide on the size cards you want, you can scale your images if you want to work larger.

Those are the must have materials: images, glue, scissors, and cardstock. I made my first deck this way — no scanner, no Photoshop.

BRAYER

This is a "nice to have" item. It is a small handheld roller that you use like a rolling pin to flatten your images. You can purchase it in an art supply store.

VIEWER TEMPLATE

You can make a template with a window the size of your card to get a feel for a layout before you glue it down. Also useful for print on demand decks to make sure that nothing important will be cut off of your card.

AN ACHIEVABLE GOAL

There is a saying: "Eat the elephant one bite at a time." In keeping with this, if a Tarot deck is your goal, I recommend you make a Major Arcana deck to start. It is a less intimidating goal and gives you a useable product when you are done. If 22 cards seems too daunting, try just making the Aces, or just your favourite cards. A Lenormand deck is a bit more of a challenge, but still less intimidating than a 78 card tarot deck. Finally, f you have your own system, you can make whatever number of cards it requires.

PUTTING IT ALL TOGETHER

Once you have your collages completed you are ready to transform them into a useable deck. There are several ways you can go about this.

PRINT ON DEMAND

This is the simplest method, but it requires a bit of planning. Companies that print cards on demand usually have a template available to help you get your cards the right size for printing. If you think you will be going this route, download the template before you start your deck. The safe area is the area you should work within for anything you want to appear in your card. There is usually an area around that called the bleed area. Your image should extend into this area, but bear in mind that it may be cut off. If you don't extend it into this area you may have white showing, which is fine if you want a white border, but not so good for cards on which you want to fill the entire space.

Each of the companies I tried used a different sized card so it helps to know the company you want to use upfront as it is difficult to resize your art in odd increments once it is complete. You can work in multiples of the desired size — for example, if the finished card will be 2.5" x 3.5", you can make your art in 5" x 7" size and reduce it easily. However, images that are easy to identify at 5" x 7" may be difficult to identify at 2.5" x 3.5", so keep this in mind. It is best to work in the size the POD company uses.

LAMINATED

This requires you make colour copies, glue them to cardstock, glue on a back if desired, and laminate them. Please note "make colour copies." Never laminate your originals! If you do, when you want to replace a card or make another whole set, you will not be able to scan the laminated cards without some glare, scratches, distortion, and possibly dirt from the lamination. Mostly glare. Make a colour copy of the originals and then put them away in a photo album or box somewhere until you need them again. If you have a scanner, scanning them at high resolution (300 dpi) would be ideal as you will always be able to print or have a card or set printed. You can buy a laminator, or you can take the cards to Kinko's and get them laminated. You should be able to fit three to five cards in a standard 8.5" x 11" laminating pouch. If you use Kinko's, show the operator how you want it done.

You must cut the cards out before laminating them and you want to leave room between each card so that it seals close to the edge of the card with some sealed space between the cards. When you cut the laminated cards out leave about 1/4 inch or so of this sealed laminate all around the card as this is what holds the card together.

Alternately there are glue machines that will glue the card parts together for you, however, I have never done this so I can't comment on how well they work.

THINGS TO KEEP IN MIND

Relax and enjoy the process. It should be a series of joyful discoveries and happy accidents.

If an image doesn't seem to be coming together, put it aside and do another image instead. Don't force an image or settle for an image that doesn't feel right or doesn't say what you want it to say.

Try moving the image parts around and laying them out several ways before you glue them down. Don't be afraid to make small, light, pencil marks just inside the area of a component in order to remember exactly where you wanted to place it.

Your cutting skills will improve. By the time you finish 22 cards or more you will be able to cut out spider webs.

Don't worry that the styles are different between individual cards — if you use a frame or title, it will pull it all together by giving the deck a point of uniformity.

Don't be afraid to experiment and to push the boundaries by trying complex multilayered designs. But don't look askance at simple designs consisting of a background and only one or two other images, or even just one image, period.

The first card is the hardest — once you see it can be done, the rest are easy.

DIGITAL COLLAGE

If you are familiar with GIMP, Photoshop, Paint Shop Pro, or any other photo manipulation or graphic design programs you can do the entire deck digitally. Even if you use traditional collage, you may find them useful for resizing images, creating frames, adding text, etc. GIMP is a powerful program and it is totally free. Adobe Photoshop Elements is less than $100.00 and is often on sale.

You can use word processing programs like Microsoft Office Word or Open Office, or typesetting programs like InDesign or Quark, to make card labels. Just choose a font, write and print the label, cut it out and use it as the first layer in your collage.

SOURCES

The sources below are just a handy list of things and sites that you may find helpful.

Inspiration Tarot: Gail Fairfield and Patti Provo.
Useful for the blank card templates. The book is out of print but available used. There is also a blank deck by this name, but it is difficult to find. You can also use a graphics program to create templates.

ArtsCow.com
A print on demand company that prints playing cards. Prints unusual shapes like circles and hearts, but no tarot-sized cards as of this writing.

TheGameCrafter.com
A print on demand company that specializes in card decks. Like Lulu.com for cards. Cards are sold to the public, so be careful of copyright.

PrinterStudio.com
Print on demand company. Will print a deck and mail it to you. Does not sell or promote decks. Has tarot sized, smaller and larger decks.

SuperiorPOD.com
Print on demand company. Will print a deck and mail it to you. Does not sell or promote decks. Has tarot sized and smaller decks

LaminationDepot.com
Lamination supply company. A source for pre-cut lamination pouches in various sizes.

Commons.Wikimedia.org/wiki/Main_Page
Wikimedia Commons has 16 million plus public domain and creative commons images

MorgueFile.com
Photos released to the public domain by their photographers. Be aware that not all images of identifiable people at this site are covered by a models release document.

"How to Create Your Own Divination Deck" accompanied Michele Jackson's 2013 workshop on the subject. Michele regularly posts her new card designs at her Facebook.com/michele.jackson.96 outreach site.

THE FORTUNE TELLER'S GUIDE TO SUCCESS
Valentina Burton

ARE YOU READY TO READ IN PUBLIC?

Do you think reading in public sounds like fun?

Do you think you have the personality to handle dealing with the frequently funny but also extremely difficult situations that arise for a public reader?

If so, then here are the steps to follow.

HOW TO FIND A GOOD PUBLIC LOCATION

Of course, it's the public part of reading in public that is the most difficult.

The question of "where to read" really boils down to choosing your clientele and finding a good location: Who do you want to read for and where do they congregate?

The clientele you might find by telling fortunes at a bookstore is different from the clientele you will find in a coffee shop, restaurant, or bar … so choose your clientele according to your own interests and comfort.

Locating a venue will depend on your geographical location, and some readers will definitely find their choices limited by geography. It makes a huge difference if you live in a metropolis, out in the country, or in a tourist area that has a seasonal shifting of population.

If you live in an urban area, finding a venue is fairly easy, because you will have many choices. The basic idea to keep in mind is that your venue contact, who is usually the owner or manager of the venue, will have financial goals for the venue. If you can demonstrate that what you will bring to his venue will add to his profits, you will have his attention.

Do not expect most venues to have any sort of budget for entertainment. Every entertainer I have ever met assumes that David and I are handsomely paid by Hotel Zaza to appear there. Although it is a fancy hotel, bar and restaurant, with a celebrity clientele, there is almost no budget for entertainment!

Do your homework before you present your idea to the venue owner or manager. Visit the space at different times and study the clientele, the architectural layout of the venue (is there a quiet and unused space that would be perfect for a reader?), and the menu price points. We have no trouble currently charging $30.00 for a reading at Hotel Zaza because it is at least $20.00 for a glass of wine.

Another tactic is to spend time in the venue. Get to know some of the staff. Be friendly and fun, and tip them well! Owners and managers are usually very hands-on in restaurants, bars, and small hotels. Become a regular patron and one day spontaneously fall into a conversation with the manager about your fascinating occupation as a card reader, and tell him some hilarious stories about your job. Oh, and, by the way, you have a friend and colleague who reads cards regularly at a bar/restaurant/hotel in another city, and has become a huge draw and attraction for the venue, isn't that interesting? Leave the manager with this idea planted, and the next time you see him he will think he has had a brilliant idea and wants to talk you into reading on Friday nights at his bar.

If you live way out in the woods and don't have anything like a luxury resort or dude ranch nearby, you might wish to focus primarily on doing phone readings, but if you are near to some sort of a tourist attraction, seriously consider altering your presentation and mode of divination to fit the theme and look of that venue.

For example, if you live in a rural area near a dude ranch, especially one where corporate events are held on a regular basis, put away your tarot cards and learn a great system for reading playing cards. Order a set of vintage reproduction playing cards to read with and acquire a Victorian Western costume. (Avoid the Miss Kitty saloon gal look, as this is usually too vulgar for corporate events.) Buy a sweet little Victorian table, make a beautiful cloth to go on it, and create some Victorian-looking business cards. On the cards refer to yourself as something like a "prognosticator" or other such 19th century-type verbiage. Create a web page about your new Western Victorian card reader character. Fun stuff!

Find out who organizes the special events for the dude ranch and arrange a short meeting with that person. Take your laptop, playing cards, and business cards, but don't dress in costume. Try to look normal and businesslike.

When you meet, show the organizer your adorable web page explaining about the lore of divination in the old West and in the Victorian era. Explain how you are ideal for corporate events because your entertainment is so different, and is always loved by the women and young girls at events, just as it was in the 19th century!

Suggest that including you in proposals sent out to corporate clients will show a fresh originality lacking in his competitors.

Do a brief and fun reading for the organizer (and anybody else on site who is interested), and then leave him with some small marketing piece so he will remember you. Remember, his responsibilities and his job rest on his ability to generate a profit for his venue.

Show him how you can be a valuable member of his team and add to his bottom line without costing him a penny, and you'll be in.

Find out what the resort is paying (actually, what the corporate client is paying) for musicians and gunslingers; this will give you some idea how to price yourself.

It is really important to select a venue that gets a fair amount of traffic. I have a colleague who read cards for a couple of years in a beautiful, upscale bar-restaurant, but she finally decided to quit because the clientele dwindled to too few and was too boring.

Carefully choose the place you think you want to read in. You will be spending much time there once you get the ball rolling. Aim for venues you think you will enjoy spending time in, with a clientele that amuses you.

You will end up knowing everything about everybody there, so select your venue well!

HOW TO DESIGN YOUR PRODUCT

Once you have chosen your venue, you must craft your presentation to fit the space. Hopefully, you have already figured out an ideal area in the location to situate yourself.

YOUR TABLE

Find and bring your own reading table. Do not ever use an existing table in a bar or restaurant. Why not? In the first place, a table is valuable moneymaking real estate for the venue and someone will resent you for taking up space there. Second, if you are a female and you are reading cards in a bar, sitting alone for an extended period of time at the bar or at one of the bar tables several nights a week will send the wrong message about your occupation.

Look at the decor in the venue and find, purchase, or make table coverings and props that coordinate with it. This is not the time to be cheap. Make your table look even nicer than the décor. Have a pretty little sign professionally made for your table with your name, what you are offering, and the price.

YOUR CLOTHING

Dress yourself to fit the venue. A brief time spent online researching costume history will enable you to coordinate your costume to the era and the regional style of the architecture and furniture in the venue. Choose things to wear that go well with the look of your table and that will be attractive to the existing clientele in the venue.

If you are a female reader, you have many choices that will complement the decor of your venue. In a very modern space you might choose outfits that are sleek and modern and simple: think Audrey Hepburn. A charming mid-century space might call for something more like Elizabeth Montgomery in "Bewitched." A kooky Bohemian space will allow for lots of fringe and patterns, and you can go completely Stevie Nicks with your wardrobe.

If you are a male reader, avoid looking either sleazy or New Agey, although sleazy is probably preferable to nerdy. Unless the venue is Bohemian, the gypsy dude look doesn't work, and neither does the ponytailed hippie dude look. Leave your Renaissance Faire costume at home, unless your public venue actually is a Ren Faire. For most venues, classic, elegant, and not too casual is the way to go if you are a man. Think of how appealing and intriguing it would be to venture out to an elegant bar or restaurant and come across a male tarot card reader who was well groomed, dressed like Cary Grant, and seemed friendly, interesting, knowledgeable, and fun. Would you choose to get a reading from him? I certainly would! Probably every woman I know would!

STANDING OUT FROM THE CLIENTELE

What does all of this nonsense about tablecloths and clothing have to do with tarot card reading? If the clientele who frequent the venue does not think that you look interesting, charming, and fun, they will not even venture to inquire about your card reading. It won't matter if you are the greatest tarot card reader in the world; if potential clients are not moved to get a reading by what they see of you, all of that greatness is wasted, and another opportunity to show how tarot is amazing and exciting is lost.

OVERCOMING THE RELUCTANCE OF THE CLIENTELE

If you read in public you are an ambassador for all of the divination arts and you need to take that seriously. Many of those you read for will be having their first experience of any kind of reading with you. The general public has two negative assumptions about getting a tarot card reading:

First, they may think that the reading will be a general, cold-reading-cookie-cutter cliché; t,hat it will be stupid, boring, and a waste of time and money.

Second, they are afraid that the reading will freak them out and ruin their whole evening by revealing a terrible, embarrassing secret!

Either of these assumptions can block potential clients from getting a reading at a public venue, so part of your job is to do anything you can to subtly illustrate that the client's experience will not be stupid, boring, a waste of time, scary, or embarrassing. Once you have developed a reputation and a clientele in a public venue most of these problems are solved, because you will have returning clients and plenty of word of mouth business. Until that time, you must deal with this gracefully.

THE AMOUNT OF TIME TO OFFER PER READING

Your actual reading in a public setting should probably not be longer than 20 minutes.It's important not to keep clients away from the bar too long … the manager wants them to keep ordering drinks, and their friends want to visit with them. I usually structure my hotel readings to have two layouts of cards.

The first layout is a quick look at the next six months for the client, briefly touching on everything in their life, and covering the theme and main issues going on.

The second layout answers any question they may have. It sometimes takes a while for the client to choose a question, so I suggest subjects for the question and sometimes will re-word the question.

I go very fast, so I like for the clients to record the session. Almost everybody I see has a smart phone and they record beautifully.

If clients have lots of questions, you can hand them a card and ask them to make an appointment at your private office. You can even write a code word on the back of your business card, tell them to call you for an appointment and give you the code, and you can give them a full-length office visit for $70.00 instead of $100.00 — that is, for the difference between your public reading price and a private session.

HOW TO PRICE YOUR READINGS

Always have a price for your readings. Do not read for tips.

Reading for tips always left me feeling frustrated and unappreciated, but it took me a long time to learn that setting up my public readings so that clients tipped me as payment also made my clients very uncomfortable and left them feeling nervous. This is because people have no idea how much to tip a tarot or palm reader for a reading.

Honestly, most people still have trouble with how much to tip a waiter or cab driver, so how can you expect even the most sophisticated client to have a clue when it comes to how much of a tip will be appropriate for you, the fortune teller? Reading for tips simply doesn't work. Set a price and stick to it. Create readings that are so good that your clients almost always tip on top of the price of the reading.

How should you price your readings? A good rule in bars or restaurants is twice the price of a drink. Our readings at Hotel Zaza are $30.00, and most clients will hand us two twenties. Cocktails at Zaza are $15.00 and a glass of wine is $20.00.

This is just the merest glimpse at the complete 96 page book that Valentina Burton gave to each of the students at her extraordinary 2011 worksop on "The Fortune Teller's Guide to Success." The book also covers reading at parties, in an office, at psychic fairs, and via telephone, plus there are hilarious anecdotes and informative interviews. A member of AIRR, Valentina may be reached at her ValentinaBurton.com web site — and, of course, the full book is available for sale through her site or at Lucky Mojo.

PERFECTING A CAREER AS A PROFITABLE PHONE PROPHET
Marin Graves

POSSIBILITY

- What is a phone psychic? Call and find out!
- How phone psychics differ from in-person psychics
- Training and abilities
    - Different psychic line company requirements
    - EXPERIENCE NECESSARY
    - Host or participate at an event
    - Training through "lesser" venues
- Mental health
- Schedule
- Stigma / Reputation / Family
- Legitimate Business = Taxes
    - Independent Contractor
- Social Security and fixed income recipients

PERKS

- Work from home = Lower Expenses (rent, clothing, travel)
- Business license / Write-offs
- Rainy weather / "PJs Syndrome"
- Set your Hours (single parent, stay at home, last minute expense)
- Agoraphobic / Anti-Social / Not the touchy-feely type? You qualify!
- Multi-tasking

PROFIT

- Wages $10.00 / hr - $300.00 / hr
    - Paid per minute of talk time
    - Investigate payment history of potential employers
    - Incorporating rootwork

PLATFORM

- Must have (and you will) this book: "The Fortune Teller's Guide To Success" by Valentina Burton
- Corporations (Psychic Source, California Psychics, Psychic Friends Network) that maintain a large presence with both print and internet advertising
- Self-promoting web sites (LivePerson)
- Hoodoo Psychics (HoodooPsychics.com)
- Craigslist / eBay / Facebook / Etsy advertising
- Hanging up your shingle, having your own business

PRIVACY

- "People Are Strange"
- Stage names
- P. O. Box address
- Cell phone numbers
- Email addresses
- Facebook identity
- Family

PROFESSIONALISM

- Marketing Basics
- Making yourself known
    - Do it right the first time
    - It is hard to change your identity once you have a client base
- Who is your audience?
- Online bios and names position you in the market
- Browse different sites.
    - What attracts you?
    - Photos (e.g. Realtors)
    - Do they take their work seriously?
    - If not, why should you?
- Not the time to write your autobiography
- Business cards
- Magnets and other novelties
- Inserts in shipping

PHONE LINE BASICS

- The first three minutes
    - Intro
    - Credentials
    - Date of birth
    - Take hold of the reading immediately
- Bringing the reading to a close
- Background noises (dog, parrot, typing, kids)
- Music
- Disable "call waiting" feature
- Salesperson vs. Counselor
- Affirmations / Reading material
- Suggest follow-up reading
    - 1 month, 6 months, 1 year
    - Regular client with scheduled appointments
- Tread lightly on legal and health matters
- When you are wrong
- Dealing with a dissatisfied caller

PRACTICAL ADVICE

- Headset w/ mute
    - Plantronics M175C, $30.00 Staples)
- Cordless phone; have two phones
- Straw for drinking; Throat Coat tea
- Call record (input into database)
- List of suggested books for clients
- Crisis phone numbers
- Statistics of callers
    - Determine what they are for you, e.g. 75% female, 25% male, ages 25-45
- Stay active; this can become a sedentary job
- Hang-ups: Do you, or do you not take it personally?
    - Promotional minutes (5 min)
    - Can't please everyone
    - Telling them what they want to hear (beware of this trap)
- Do not personally become attached to a caller
    - Boundaries like a therapist
    - Do you really know your client?
    - Unhealthy to develop client co-dependency (frequent readings, ten calls a day, midnight calls)
- Birthday and holiday gifts
- Facebook and other forms of visible personal information: Beware: If callers can find you, they will!

PSYCHIC TRICKS

- Turn negative situations into a positives
    - "The cards show this could be a problem but they also show what can be done about it."
- Think about the lasting impression you leave
- Make a friend
    - Compliments
    - Recognize their intuition and help them to develop it
- Relationships, career, and money are the most commonly discussed topics
- Profile your callers
    - Dialect, accent, location
    - Quality of breathing, health
    - Age gradually changes major concerns in life
- Listen, and pay close attention; many callers just want to talk or vent
- Phrasing questions and comments
    - Gender and gender-orientation neutrality
    - Religious and political neutrality
- "Behind the scenes"
    * Notes in your database
    - Internet, Facebook, Google Earth
    - Email photographs

PATIENCE

- Developing your clientele may take time
- Start shifts on time, keep consistent schedules
- Phone "burn-out" and how to avoid it
- Write articles, blogs, and newsletters
- Blog Talk Radio, Youtube: Give sample readings
- Join a mutually supportive membership organization

PROTECTION

- Sacred space
- Protection and cleansing with rootwork

CRISIS COUNSELING NUMBERS

Abused Children	1-800-422-4453
Aids - National Aids Hotline	1-800-232-4636
Alcoholism - Alcohol Helpline	1-800-622-2255
American Cancer Society	1-800-227-2345
Chronic Fatigue Association	1-816-737-1343
Child Counseling, Boys Town	1-800-448-3000
Depression Anonymous	1-855-458 1407
Divorce Anonymous	1-310-998-6538
Domestic Violence Hotline	1-800-799-SAFE
Loss of a Spouse	1-800-342-9647
Missing Children	1-800-USA-KIDS
Planned Parenthood	1-800-230-PLAN
Sexual Assault Hotline	1-800-656-HOPE
Suicide Prevention Lifeline	1-800-273-8255
Veterans	1-800-827-1000

Marin Graves taught an excellent course in how to become a professional telephone psychic reader in 2012. Her flyer, "Perfecting a Career as a Profitable Phone Prophet" outlined the many topics she touched upon during the class. Her students also received a copy of Valentina Burton's "The Fortune Teller's Guide to Success" (which had been presented in 2011). Marin is a member of AIRR and the proprietor of The Psychic Tarot Parlour in Grass Valley, California. She can be reached for readings and rootwork at PsychicTarotParlour.com.

HOW TO SPIRITUALLY CLEAN YOUR HOME OR BUSINESS
catherine yronwode

SIMPLE CLEANSING RITES

Salt, Urine, Ammonia, and Chinese Wash are among the most traditional items used in spiritual cleanings to clear away messes left by enemy rootworkers; open the way for new beginnings; and purify a building in the interests of maintaining a peaceful home, keeping rooms rented, or attracting customers. Dressing oils and perfumed room sprays also have a long history of use in cleansing rites.

SALT

Salt can be added to any floor wash for cleaning. It is customary before using salt to hold a half-handful on the palm of your left hand, draw a cross over it in the air with your right hand and tell it what you want it to do. You can say, "Salt, protect my home in the name of the Father, the Son, and the Holy Ghost, Amen," and it will do so. Salt is a protective mineral.

URINE AND AMMONIA

Urine (and Ammonia, which often substitutes for Urine in rites performed by "nice" people) is added to ritual floor washes, to mark the space as yours and in the belief that it draws in lovers or business customers. It should be your "strong" first Urine of the morning, but don't use too much.

CHINESE WASH

Today, the name Chinese Wash is taken as a sort of generic term, and there are a number of faked-up formulas for it, but the authentic recipe used by the original makers of Young's Chinese Wash was labelled, circa 1920-1945: "A Detergent Preparation with the Delightful Aroma of Oriental Gums and Grasses" and the label was decorated with a smiling Chinese man in a tunic looking down on a group of fleeing devils. The "Oriental Grasses" are the same used for compounding Van Van Oil (e.g. Citronella Grass, Lemon Grass, Ginger Grass, etc.).

The addition of Broom straws to Chinese Wash, although not part of the original Young's formula, was done at home by root workers and hoodoo practitioners. Many contributors to Harry M. Hyatt's 1930s oral histories of hoodoo mention the efficacy of Broom Corn straws for spiritual cleanings.

The use of Broom Corn seems to go back to African usage and to be related to African foot-track magic and thus to the African idea of purification of the doorstep by sweeping and ritual washing down of the path to the home with herbs and liquids.

One 1940s-50s competitor to Young's Chinese Wash was Temple Fragran (no, that is not a typo — it is Fragran) and the makers of that spiritual cleaning product, the Clover Horn Company of Baltimore, Maryland, included the Broom Corn straws right in the bottle, with instructions that when you were finished with the liquid soap, you were to take the Broom Corn straws and scatter them in your yard. This accords with African traditions.

At the Lucky Mojo Curio Co., we too add Broom Corn straws to our bottles of Chinese Wash because many of our younger urban customers are not familiar enough with the tradition to know that they should add them when they first receive the bottle. Thus we try to keep alive the traditional ingredients and usage of Chinese Wash.

Always dilute Chinese Wash in water before use, of course. Use one, two, or three teaspoonful per pail of warm water, depending on the strength of the job you need to do. You may also add a pinch of Lemon Juice and a pinch of Salt to the pail-full, if you like.

BATHE AT SUNRISE AND WORK IN SILENCE

To clear away old conditions and then increase luck or attract people to the building, it is common to rise before dawn and to complete the work before you ever speak a word to anyone.

Start by brewing some Hyssop leaves into a weak tea and washing your body from the neck down to purify yourself. Recite Psalms 51. Dress in clean clothes and collect the cleaning supplies you will need, such as a mop, broom, sponges, dust clothes, candles, incense, The entire cleaning process is performed in silence.

WORK TOP TO BOTTOM, BACK TO FRONT

Wash and cleanse the building from the top floor to the bottom floor, and from the back of each floor to the front, ending at last at the front doorstep.

SEAL EACH ROOM

As you work in each room, light a white candle dressed with Holy Oil and Blessing Oil and burn some incense to purify the room. We recommend a combination of natural Camphor resin (for cleansing), Frankincense resin (for spirituality), and Myrrh resin (for bringing in good things). These should be burned on charcoal, and the Camphor, which comes in a block, should be crumbled up before being burned. You can move the candle and incense from room to room as you work, or you can do as many people do and light a new white candle and burn new incense in each room, leaving each candle to burn out on its own.

SWEEP WITH A NEW BROOM

Some folks follow the scrubbing of the building by thoroughly sweeping it out with a brand new broom that has never been used before, but this is also covered symbolically by the Chinese Wash, which contains broom straws, so it is not absolutely necessary. Yet many find it of help.

PAY ATTENTION TO THE DOORSTEP

The front doorstep, where you will finish the cleansing, is a crucial area and is usually given an extra-thorough scrubbing and it should also be swept while wet and sprinkled with Salt, especially if the intent is to keep away evil visitors.

DISPOSE OF THE SCRUB WATER

When you are all done, throw the left-over wash water out the front door or into the front yard, toward the East, if possible.

SCRUB INWARD WITH OILS FOR BLESSINGS

Once you have finished cleaning the building outwards, it is time to scrub the front doorstep inwards with a mixture of Attraction Oil and Blessing Oil in water, to draw in what is wanted. Dress each window and each door in the building with a drop of Attraction Oil in each corner of the frame. Pay particular attention to the front doorstep. Other oils may be used, according to your situation,

It is an old-fashioned custom (which some people find strange, but many people swear is efficacious) to add a bit of your own Urine to the scrub water that is used to scrub inward. If you cannot or will not do that, then add a dash of Ammonia to the inward scrub water.

The water remaining from the inward scrub is taken through the building and thrown into the back yard, if possible. The inward scrubbing at the doorstep is followed by sweeping inward with a broom. Some people sweep inward along the entire path leading from the sidewalk to the building.

POPULAR VARIATIONS OF THE RITE

JINX KILLING

If you suspect that the place has been dressed negatively by an enemy, you may repeat the entire ritual for 9 days in a row, or do it once on a Friday and thereafter use Chinese Wash mixed with Jinx Killer Oil as a regular cleaning product on a continuing basis.

PROTECTION

For protection of the premises, follow the cleansing with a rite of protection with Salt. Bless the Salt with your prayer for protection, as described above, then sprinkle a small pinch of this dry Salt at each of the four corners of the home and place a fifth pile in the center of the home — under the house or in a little cloth bag taped under a piece of furniture.

DRAWING CUSTOMERS AND MONEY

Add Cinnamon Powder and Sugar to the inward scrub, to draw money and customers. Spray with Hoyt's Cologne. When advertising your place of work, send out flyers that have been lightly dressed with Attraction Sachet and Money-Drawing Sachet.

DRAWING LOVE

To draw love to your home, add Sugar to the inward scrub. Follow the cleaning by writing the one you love a letter that has been dressed with Attraction Sachet and Love Me Sachet.

ESTABLISHING A PEACEFUL HOME

To provide a peaceful home, sprinkle or spray a little bit of Peace Water in the four corners and in the middle of each room after cleansing.

"How to Spiritually Clean Your Home or Business" was Lucky Mojo Shop Hand-Out No. 3, published in 2002 and adapted from my 1995 online book "Hoodoo in Theory and Practice." It has been a favourite with shop customers ever since and has been included in thousands of packages that contain bottles of Lucky Mojo Chinese Wash, Buffalo Ammonia, and Peace Water.

SPIRITUAL FOOT WASHING
Tanisia Mooney-Greer

"I will sprinkle clean water upon you, and you shall be clean from all your uncleannesses, and from all your idols I will cleanse you. A new heart I will give you, and a new spirit I will put within you …"

— Ezekiel 36:25-26
The Holy Bible, New Revised Standard Version

BACKGROUND

Spiritual foot washing is a hands-on purification ritual that is performed on a person or client to rid them of spiritually unclean conditions. It can also be used to confer a blessing or prepare a person for the "next steps" in their spiritual journey.

Spiritual purification by water is an almost-universal ritual. In addition to the well-known rite of Christian baptism, purification by water can observed in many other religions and cultures:

In Jewish tradition, the Mikvah, a full-body bathing ritual, is taken as the final step in a person's conversion to Judaism, once a month for women approximately seven days after their menstrual cycle ends (and a final time after menopause), for men before Yom Kippur, and for both men and women before their wedding ceremony. The Mikvah ritual is so sacred that, in Jewish teachings, it is commanded that the building where the Mikvah takes place be built and secured before any other building is constructed.

In Islamic tradition, Muslims are required to engage in Wudhu, or water purification, before performing each of their five daily prayers. They are not only to wash their feet, but also their hands, face, head, and all bodily orifices, including the mouth, nose, ears, and genitals. Wudhu is described as "The key to prayer, as prayer is the key to paradise."

Since the majority of hoodoo or conjure practitioners are Christian, the practice of spiritual foot washing was adopted from the foot washing ritual as observed in Christian churches. This ritual is a re-enactment of what Jesus had done for his disciples during their attendance at the Last Supper, as described in the Biblical Gospel of John (John 13:1-17).

Some Christian denominations, like the Primitive Baptists, observe foot washing as an integral part of their sacrament, and place it on an equal level with the Eucharist sacrament of unleavened bread and wine.

"The Primitive Baptists, they believe
You can't get to Heaven unless you wash yo' feet"

— Rev. Washington Phillips
Denomination Blues, 1927

Most other Christian denominations use foot washing as an optional ceremony for the Easter holiday season as a lesson in humility and demonstrating Christian service to each other.

In modern times, foot washing has been adapted for use in weddings — either during the actual ceremony or during a bridal shower — as a symbol of promised devotion. Both the groom and the bride bathe each other's feet to signify their intent to serve each other equally in their marriage.

In Hoodoo, the spiritual foot bath is prescribed when the client feels (or the practitioner has identified) that they have stepped on or over some powder, root, or trick that has crossed or "poisoned" them through the feet. It is also prescribed to expel a ghost or spiritual entity from the client's body, or if the client feels spiritually unclean.

MATERIALS FOR THE RITUAL

- **Metal basin or bowl full of clean, warm water:** It should fit the feet. (NO PLASTIC!).
- **Vial or cup of Holy Water or Blessed Water:** You can acquire Holy Water from a priest or pastor, or you can consecrate your own Holy Water by making a sincere prayer over spring water, distilled water, or lightly salted water.
- **Anointing oil:** You can use pre-made spiritual soils, like Lucky Mojo's 7-11 Holy Oil or you can pray over a small bowl of Olive Oil in a manner similar to praying over your own water.
- **Washcloth and towels:** One washcloth and one or two towels is generally sufficient..
- **A new bar of soap:** Use Florida Water soap, Sandalwood soap, or any soap with a cleansing herbal scent, such as Lemon, Lemon Grass, Pine, or Mint.

PROCEDURE: ABOUT 15-20 MINUTES

Have all your materials ready when the client arrives. For convenience and ease of movement, you can use a small stool or folding table to store the holy water, holy oil, bar soap, small bowl, and other items within easy reach.

Have the client take off their shoes and socks. If you are serving a woman and she has panty hose on, give her the chance to go to the bathroom to take off the panty hose. If you schedule the appointment beforehand, you can remind the client to wear shoes and socks, and to forego panty hose, if possible.

When you are ready to begin, say a prayer or invocation, addressing the client's concerns and the purpose of the foot washing ritual. You may hold the client's hands while saying this prayer, or each of you may bow your heads, When the prayer is completed, seat the client in front of you.

Kneel in front of the client with the basin of warm water. Pray out loud as you pour the holy water into the basin. (Optional: You can also pour a couple of drops of the holy oil into the basin.) Have the client place their feet into the water. Pray, either whispering or out loud, while washing the feet and ankles with bar soap, no higher than their upper calf. Don't use too much soap; the cleansing part is spiritual, not literal.

Rinse the feet and legs with the washcloth.

Dry the feet and place them in your lap. Anoint the feet and legs with holy oil and massage it into the skin. Use a light but firm squeezing motion when stroking the calves, especially the back of the calves.

As you rub the feet and legs, be sure to lightly tug on each of the toes. Also, if you know any Reflexology points, you can rub certain spots on the soles of the feet to help stimulate healing and grounding energy for the client. (A particularly good point to stimulate would be the KI-1 or 1st Kidney meridian point on the ball of the foot, below the big toe, as this point is said to filter the body's life force energies and encourages renewal.)

Notice any health indicators you see on the feet or legs, such as varicose veins, sores (which may indicate diabetes), or cold feet (which may indicate poor circulation).

If you are talented in psychometry (psychic reading by touch) or are spirit-led to do so, you can also share any psychic impressions, messages, or intuitive "hits" you receive while handling the client's feet and encouraging any negative energies to leave the person's body.

When you feel as if the energy movement is winding down, lightly stroke the feet and legs three times, then hold the feet. You can say a closing prayer or invocation here, such as a prayer for strength or safety, or just hold the feet silently and breathe with the client to seal the treatment.

At the conclusion of the treatment, stand the client up, look into their eyes, and say a positive closing invocation or affirmation to them. "In the name of the Father, Son, and Holy Spirit, you are healed" or something similar would be appropriate here.

TIPS AND SUGGESTIONS

The spiritual foot washing treatment is an intimate-but-safe ceremony to perform for clients, and can be a moving experience for some people. Clients have been known to cry during the treatment. Feelings of unworthiness and low self-esteem may also surface during the treatment; for some people, it's humbling to have someone do something as intimate — yet platonic — as bathing their feet.

The feet are a part of the body that not many people are used to being handled by others unless they have had pedicures, massage, or reflexology treatments, so be gentle and sensitive to the client's needs and comfort level during the treatment. Tears, laughter, and the healing power of simple touch — along with the concentrated attention and prayers of one individual serving another — are the most powerful and cleansing part of the spiritual foot washing ceremony.

Tanisia Mooney-Greer's "Spiritual Foot Washing" class at the Home of Truth Spiritual Center in 2008 was the most-talked-about workshop that year. Tanisia, garbed in white and radiating an air of confident service, led two dozen people in washing one another's feet. It was awesome. Those who had not attended heard about it and requested the same class in 2009, when the program returned to Forestville. On that occasion AIRR members Lara Rivera and Momma Starr Casas of OldStyleConjure.com led the class, each praying in her own way — Jewish and Catholic, respectively — to teach the technique. In 2010 Lara reprised the class for a third time.

CLEANSING WITH EGGS AND THE ARCHANGEL MICHAEL
Auntie Sindy Todo and Susan Diamond

"A baby visited by you for the first time will have good luck, if you hold a fresh egg in front of it"
– Harry Middleton Hyatt
Folk-Lore from Adams County Illinois

CLEANSING WITH EGGS

One of the best tools to spiritually clean a person is a hen's egg. There is no purer or more natural form representing birth, beginnings, and fresh start than an egg. Folklore about eggs and their uses in cures, remedies, and cleansings can be found in many cultures and magical traditions.

As many conjure workers who do cleansing and protection work know, an egg can help with cleaning up physical sickness, unhappy relationships, mental confusion, and emotional anxiety.

It is also well known (and mentioned in one of our favourite books, "Spiritual Cleansing" by Draja Mickaharic) that you can use eggs in water for bathing purposes or place them in a room to help with nightmares, or negativity. You can cleanse your pets, your house, and your car with eggs.

Eggs are also used in rites of overall protection, including protection of the family by sending away people who exert unwanted negative influences that affect the home.

Absorbing, capturing, containing, cleansing, healing, and even reversing, get-away, and break-up work … an egg is the key!

THE CHAKRAS

Having incorporated what we know from European and American folklore about the use of eggs in cleansing, we next reach farther afield and incorporate ideas that originated in the Hindu traditions of India. In Hindu practice, there are seven points of the body, arrayed up the spine, called chakras ("wheels") which are considered to be symbolic hub-points associated with varied states of consciousness and spiritual development. Utilizing the seven chakras of Hinduism with egg cleansing enables one to accomplish deeper removal of spiritual blocking and negative energy.

This brief description of each chakra is not an attempt to instruct you in the complexities of Hindu yogic practice, but we hope it will help you focus on the specific areas in the body for the present purpose of spiritual cleansing:

- **First chakra — The Root:** For grounding and stability in the material world
- **Second chakra – The Sacral:** For creativity and self devotion
- **Third chakra – The Solar Plexus:** For balance of masculine and feminine power, for manifesting
- **Fourth chakra – The Heart:** For emotional heart and soul consciousness, for expressing and receiving love
- **Fifth chakra – The Throat:** For speech and verbal expression
- **Sixth chakra – The Third Eye:** For clearing the subconscious and channeling intuition
- **Seventh chakra – The Crown:** For oneness with God, for peace and wisdom

In the cleansing ritual below, we don't require an egg from a specific colour of chicken. A white, cream, or brown egg of any breed is your personal choice; it doesn't make a bit of difference, and we encourage you not to be hung up on the visual, but instead to focus on the powerful spirit of this natural instrument.

THE ARCHANGEL MICHAEL

Eggs can be used with various secular conjure oils and candles from the Hoodoo tradition for a specific situation such as Road Opener, Cast Off Evil, Uncrossing, or Healing. However, for intense protection and a sure way to clear off "funk" fast … we recommend using Archangel Michael oils and candles and calling him in for assistance.

Archangel Michael is among the strongest spiritual entities one can call upon for help in works of protection and cleansing. He is acknowledged by people of many diverse faiths and magical traditions, including Jews, Christians, and Muslims. He is possibly the easiest Spirit to feel, see, and receive instant messages and answers from. We recommend always calling him in to help with intense cleansing while utilizing an egg.

THE WORK AND RITUAL

You will need the following:

• An egg
• A pencil
• Archangel Michael Oil
• Cleansing incense, tobacco, or Palo Santo
• A votive candle, tealight, or altar candle
• A container to hold your egg for later disposal

1. Clean your egg under cool water and dry it off. An egg at room temperature is best.

2. Write your name around the egg continuously with your pencil.

3. Make the sign of the cross over your name with the Archangel Michael Oil.

4. Dress your candle with the oil, either by injecting oil into holes in the wax, if the candle is encased, or by hand-drawing the wick towards you with the oil on a free-standing candle.

5. An appropriate prayer to say after you've dressed your candle and egg would be this:

"Archangel Michael, intercede for me with God in all my necessities, and hear my intentions as I perform this cleansing ritual. Obtain for me a favourable outcome in all the areas I send to you. Mighty prince of the heavenly host, and victor over rebellious spirits, remember me, for I am in a weak state and so prone to pride and ambition. Be for me, I pray, my powerful aid in temptation and difficulty; and above all do not forsake me in my last struggle with the powers of negativity, fear and ego. Amen."

6. Holding your egg in one hand, you want to be sitting or reclining comfortably in a chair, on a sofa or bench, or on the floor or ground.

7. Now begin to go into your most comfortable state for meditation. Clear your mind and breathe deeply.

8. Create an image of Archangel Michael in your mind's eye and see him walking towards you. He will hold your hand throughout the cleansing.

9. You will now slowly pass the egg over each chakra point (not touching yourself with the egg). Start at the top of you head and work your way down. At each chakra point you should be concentrating on the focus and purpose of that chakra and asking Michael to help you release the blocks in each area.

Below are some examples of what you may hear from Archangel Michael to release:

• **Seventh chakra:** What is blocking your connection to spirit and your higher self?
• **Sixth chakra:** What are you not seeing or blocking? What do you wish to stop seeing?
• **Fifth chakra:** What is stopping you from speaking your truths?
• **Fourth chakra:** What is binding or closing off your heart?
• **Third chakra:** What do you wish to bring into balance?
• **Second chakra:** What is causing the disconnection with your creative power?
• **First chakra:** What is causing you to be ungrounded?

10. After you have passed the egg over all these areas, say a prayer of completion. The Our Father and the 23rd Psalm are what we recommend.

11. Set your egg in the container for later disposal.

12. Next you will see a golden egg over your head and Michael will slowly bring it down your body, filling you with warm healing energy.

13. After this is complete, come back to your third eye, show gratitude to Michael and say goodbye. Take some deep breaths and come back into your body. Your cleansing and healing is complete!

DISPOSAL OF THE EGG

Dispose of the egg as you feel appropriate. Traditional methods for the disposal of an egg that has been used in a ritual of cleansing are quite varied in different cultures, Disposal methods found among traditional practitioners include throwing the egg at the base of a large tree which has consented to absorb the negative energy, dropping it into the sewer as you walk down the street, tossing it into a crossroads as you walk or drive by, or flushing it down the toilet.

"Cleansing With Eggs and the Archangel Michael" was a 2012 MISC workshop presentation. Susan Diamond is a member of the AIRR and the proprietor of Serpent's Kiss in Santa Cruz, California. She can be reached online at Serpents-Kiss.com. Auntie Sindy Todo is a member of AIRR, a member of the Board of Directors of Missionary Independent Spiritual Church, and the proprietor of Todo Mojo in Seattle, Washington. She can be reached for readings and rootwork at TodoMojo.com.

HANDS-ON CONJURE FOR CLEANSING AND BLESSING
Khi Armand

"For this reason, I am reminding you to fan into flames the gift of God that is within you through the laying on of my hands."

— 2 Timothy 1:6,
Holy Bible, International Standard Version

CONTEXT

Spiritual cleansing, blessing, and healing through a hands-on approach is as old as time, and techniques for various conditions can be found in cultures across the globe. Hands-on spiritual work has significant Biblical precedent in both the Old and New Testaments, and it is employed in the removal of physical illnesses, the ordination of elders, the blessing of the young, and the renewal of the soul.

Although most any rootworker can perform hands-on work, some who specialize in it have a particular charisma or talent for the presentation of these magical practices. Their gestures, when performed smoothly and confidently, can thoroughly enrapture their client within the ritualistic moment as part of work's efficacy.

EGG CLEANSING

The use of a hen or chicken's egg to cleanse a client and remove harmful energies is found in many traditions worldwide, and though popularly known in the western hemisphere through Latin American curanderismo limpia practices, the use of an egg (especially that of a Black Hen) for cleansing and uncrossing can be found in hoodoo as well.

To start, take a clean, raw, room-temperature egg, or one anointed with Uncrossing oil, and ask it to absorb any evil conditions within or around the client. Roll the egg in a downward fashion along your client's body or aura while praying fervently that they be cleansed of any and all things that are not in alignment with their highest good. Visualize darkness entering the egg from the client's body and energy, and continue until the egg feels full.

Dispose of the egg by breaking it at a crossroads, at the base of a strong tree, throwing it into a river, or cracking it into a glass of water to read for signs (and then disposing of it). Dress the client with a blessing, drawing, or attraction oil to finish.

FEATHER WHISKING

Using the feathers of a Black Hen to cleanse and uncross is another time-honoured method found in the hoodoo tradition that can be performed using a number of feathers bound together in a whisk or by using a whole dried Black Hen wing.

Steadying the standing client with your non-dominant hand placed on or near their shoulder, use your dominant hand to sweep their aura with the whisk or wing in a downward fashion across their front in a series of small, swooping "x"s toward their feet. Rotate the client a quarter-turn and do the same on their side, back, opposite side, and return to their front once again, being sure to cleanse the heart and chest area as well. End with a prayer of blessing, or spiritual work toward attracting the client's needs.

FOOT WASHING

Famously performed by Jesus on his apostles, ceremonial foot washing is a powerfully symbolic act of lovingkindness toward one's fellow human being. In conjure, it is a form of cleansing and uncrossing, especially for clients who have been tricked through the feet, or whose fate and life path itself needs untangling and a new direction.

Kneeling in front of your seated client with their legs exposed to the upper calf, place their feet in a basin of blessed and prayed over water. Using a bar of spiritual soap such as Florida Water soap, Sandalwood soap, Lemon Grass soap, or one containing a botanical known for its cleansing properties, wash the client's lower legs and feet while praying intently for their renewal and for new roads to open in their life. Rinse them off and place their legs one at a time on a washcloth folded across your lap and dry them off.

Anoint the feet and legs with a blessing or drawing oil, being sure to stroke lightly but firmly into the calf muscles and to tug lightly on each toe.

You may be led to prophesy or give intuitive messages. Hold both feet while saying a closing prayer and help the client to stand.

RUB-DOWN RITE

The rub-down is a thorough rite of cleansing and protection for a client that is also helpful for easing physical aches and pains.

The client is first administered an herbal tea of mild, ingestible herbs chosen for their magical properties with regard to the client's condition. The best blends contain herbs that are diaphoretic and laxative, but mildness is key. After the client has finished drinking their tea, have them sit or lay down with their legs and arms exposed.

Warm a salve or liniment in the palms of your hands by quickly rubbing them together and apply with full-palm strokes to affected areas if the client is experiencing pain, or simply massage the arms, then legs, using long, pulling and smoothing strokes in a downward (never upward) fashion. Pray aloud all the while that the client's condition be healed and that their needs be met. End with the client's feet, gently pulling on each toe, from little to big, and close with "Amen."

After washing your hands and assisting the client to their feet (and with their donning their outer garments, if necessary), provide them with enough of the herbal tea to last three or seven days along with instructions for how to brew them.

DRESSING THE HEAD

Dressing the head is performed to endow the client with success, blessing, health, clarity, and acuity at tasks requiring mental strength and fortitude. Although there are a number of traditional variations, my favourite is as follows:

Anoint your thumbs with an appropriate oil and place them next to one another at the bridge of the client's nose, applying slight pressure. Slowly spread them apart, tracing the ridge above the eyebrows, saying "May all your works...", before bringing them back to their start and stroking upwards to the crown of the head, adding "be crowned with success."

Interlock your fingers atop the client's head and give their scalp a light squeeze to lock the blessing in. In the case of using King Solomon Wisdom Oil, add, "As King Solomon was wise, so may you be wise, and as his works were crowned with success, so may your works be crowned with success."

HAND BLESSING

A relatively simple, but powerful, gesture, a blessing of the hands can be performed to invoke success and financial blessings into the life of a client seeking employment, gambling luck, increased aptitude as a musician, or greater ability to hold and keep money.

Add a few drops of an alcohol-based cologne of your choice to a bottle of water. Hoyt's Cologne works well, due to its use in prosperity and success work. Consider Rose or Orange Blossom Cologne for a client searching for love or marriage. Cork the bottle with a laundry sprinkler and ask the client to hold out their open hands. Sprinkle the water into their hands and then, using the thumb and forefinger of your dominant hand, gently tug on each of the fingers of the client's hands to pull out negativity.

Fold their palms toward one another within your own and lift them upwards in a posture of prayer. Pray with confidence that they receive the blessings that they seek and, looking them in the eye, grasp their hands tightly, affirm their personal power, and firmly separate their hands toward their sides.

For a client seeking employment, a home, or financial success, a blessed coin may be placed in their hand after the water is sprinkled and before their hands clasped together in prayer within your own. In this instance, do not separate their hands.

CLOSING

Cleansing and blessing clients in-person through the use of hands-on rites and techniques can be thoroughly rewarding for both the practitioner and the client. It is important, however, to ensure that healthy boundaries are maintained both physically and spiritually. Male practitioners may require the presence of a female assistant when performing a rub-down or other intimate, though platonic, hands-on spiritual work for female clients. Practitioners of all genders would do well to ensure that they are spiritually protected before performing hands-on rites of cleansing for others, and should perform at least a minor amount of cleansing on themselves at the end of one or more cleansing sessions.

Khi Armand presented "Hands-On Conjure for Cleansing and Blessing" at the 2013 MISC workshops. He is a member of AIRR and Hoodoo Psychics and can be reached for readings and rootwork at his ConjureInTheCity.com web site.

PROTECTION SPELLS
catherine yronwode

FIERY WALL OF PROTECTION SPELL

To Protect Yourself or the One You Love.

• 7 Purple and 1 black offertory candles
• 1 Black Cat Brand white cross candle
• 1 Bottle Fiery Wall of Protection Oil
• 1 Packet Fiery Wall of Protection Sachet
• 1 Packet Fiery Wall of Protection Incense
• 1 Packet Fiery Wall of Protection Crystals
• 1 Archangel (Saint) Michael holy card
• 1 Packet Graveyard Dirt

PREPARATION

In addition to the items here, you'll need a white handkerchief, a square of tin foil, and a photo of the perpetrator; if no photo is available, write his or her full name nine times on a piece of clean paper; if his or her name is unknown to you, write "The Evil One" nine times on the paper. The spell will not be as powerful without a photo, and even a quick sketch of the person is better than just the name written on paper.

DOING THE JOB

Make the Fiery Wall of Protection Incense Powders into cones on an incense burner. Place the Graveyard Dirt in a china-ware saucer.

Prepare the white cross candle for the Protectee. With a nail, carve the words "Archangel (Saint) Michael Protect Me [or the name of whomever you are working for]." Dress the candle with Fiery Wall of Protection Oil. Dress the Angelica Root with the same oil and place it at the base of the candle. Around it, lay out a circle of Fiery Wall of Protection Sachet Powder. Now dress the seven purple Guardian candles with oil. Place them in a circle right on the circle of Sachet Powder that goes around the cross candle. Sprinkle them with a little of the powder, too. Place the Archangel (Saint) Michael holy card among them.

Finally, prepare the black Perpetrator's candle. With a nail, carve his full name (or the "The Evil One") on it on one side and the words "Keep Away" on the other side. Do not dress this candle. Place it off to one side, outside the circle of candles, on top of his photo or name-paper. Place the saucer of Graveyard Dirt next to his candle.

Light the candles. The purple Guardians are first, then the white Protectee within the circle, then the black Perpetrator's candle far outside the circle.

Light the incense. While it burns, say out loud your prayer or wish for protection and call upon Heaven for aid. Ask for the intercession of Archangel (Saint) Michael, who guards Heaven with a sharp, cutting sword, and enjoin him to protect the one who needs protection with Seven Guardians, whether they be Guardian Angels or Human Guardians (including the Police, if you think this will be necessary).

Let the candles and incense burn until the black candle is half-burned. Then pick that candle up and hold it in your hand. Take the perpetrator's photo or name-paper and lay it on the saucer of Graveyard Dirt. Set it on fire with the Perpetrator's own black candle and say, "Let your evil self be your own undoing!"

When the paper has burned, turn the perpetrator's candle upside down and extinguish it in the Graveyard Dirt and say, "Let your evil works be your ending!"

Allow the rest of the candles to burn out. Gather up the Angelica Root, some sachet powder, and the Archangel (Saint) Michael holy card and wrap them tightly in the tin foil, making a small packet. Tie the packet up in the white handkerchief with four knots. Dress it lightly with Fiery Wall of Protection Oil.

To protect yourself, carry the packet on you; to protect your home, place it by your front door, to protect someone you love, give it to them to carry.

CLEANING UP

Take the left-over materials (melted wax, nail, and so forth) and the saucer of Graveyard Dirt containing the Perpetrator's ashes and his extinguished candle and carry them to a graveyard and throw them against a grave stone, being sure to break the saucer as you throw this mess. Don't say a word; just turn and walk away home and don't look back.

When you get home and everything is all put away and cleaned up, dissolve the Fiery Wall of Protection Crystals in water and wash down your home, while you recite the 37th Psalm ("Fret Not Thyself With Evil-doers …") 37 times.

PROTECTION SPELLS FROM ADAMS COUNTY, ILLINOIS

These spells come *"Folk-Lore From Adams County Illinois"* a 723-page collection gathered by Harry Middleton Hyatt in the 1930s. Hyatt's collection includes accounts of omens and spells for a variety of conditions and purposes, including healing, money, love, and weather prediction, many of them annotated with a brief note on the ethnic or cultural background of the informant. I have kept Hyatt's original entry numbers, but for ease of comparison i have sorted the spells according to the way they are deployed, that is, either for personal protection or home protection. [Comments in brackets are mine — cat].

PROTECTIVE CHARMS WORN ON THE PERSON

9542. "If you keep a silver dime in your mouth, no man can poison you." Negro.

9543. "If you will take a dime and bore a hole in it and wear it all the time on you somewhere, you can't be hoodoo." Negro.

9544. "If you take a dime around each ankle, you can't be hoodooed." Negro.

9545. "If you wear a dime in the heel of your shoe, your enemies cannot put a spell on you." Negro.

9547. "Take a dime and put Red Pepper over the dime, then wrap it up in brown paper and wear it in your shoe, and you will not be hoodoo." Negro.

9562. "Grave dust is what a witch uses to hoodoo you, and you will conquer her if you get some and wear it." Negro.

9591. "Keep a penny in your pocket and you cannot be bewitched." German.

9593. "To keep a person from hoodooing you, keep Red Pepper in your shoe all the time." Negro.

9594. "If you think someone has put something down for you to walk over, you take a piece of brown paper, put some Red Pepper in the brown paper, put it in your shoes, and when you walk over it, it will do you no harm." Negro.

9599. "Wear your pockets inside out to keep the witches off." German.

9619. "Carrying a Rabbit's foot keeps all evil away." Negro.

9620. "Put a piece of Rattlesnake skin in your shoe to keep the witches away." Negro.

9621. "If you wear a piece of Rattlesnake skin in your clothing, you cannot be put under a spell." Negro.

9624. "If you will wear Black Pepper and salt in your shoes, you can walk anywhere and not be hoodoo." Negro.

PROTECTIVE CHARMS AROUND THE HOUSE

506. "If you hang a bottle of bluing down a fireplace, it will keep Satan away." Negro.

9536. "An old woman eighty years old [born before 1855] said she was never bewitched or her people, because her grandfather, then her father, always on the 6th of January, the Three Kings' Day, would put the letters C.M.B. over all outside doors before sunup, so the witches could not get in; and would put the same letters over the stable door so no one could bewitch the cattle." German. [Caspar, Melchior, and Balthazar — C.M.B. —were the names of the three magi or kings who brought gifts to the infant Jesus in the stable on the 12th day of Christmas, January 6th.]

9530. "If you keep Chickens with the feathers turned back the wrong way, you will never be hoodooed." Negro. [These are "Frizzled Fowl" or "Frizzly Chickens" — birds with twisted feathers; they scratch up powders laid around the yard by enemies.]

9550. "To keep the witches out of the house, place a dime under the fireplace." Irish.

9570. "If you put a horseshoe over your door point down, a witch will never come under your door." Irish.

9571. "If a person try to hoodoo you in leap year, put a horseshoe over your door and they can't." Negro.

9589. "I always keep Onions in the house to keep the devils out." Negro.

9592. "I always keep Red Pepper in the house so I will have good luck and not be hoodooed." Negro.

9595. "If you sprinkle Black Pepper and salt around your house, then sweep it up and burn it, it will keep your enemies away." Negro.

9629. "Make a cross on a sack of salt and put it under the front doorstep to keep away evil." Negro.

9646. "If you put a pair of scissors under your pillow, open with the points to the head of the bed, no one can harm you or bewitch you. I was bewitched years ago, and someone told me about putting the scissors under my pillow. I have been doing this every night for years. I have never been bewitched since that time." German.

9663. "Put a piece of silver under your head [while you sleep] and witches will not bother you." German.

9669. "To keep your enemies out of your house, put a tablespoonful of vinegar and a tablespoonful of sulphur in a little can and keep that in the house, and they will never bother you." German.

"Protection Spells" was Lucky Mojo Shop Hand-Out No. 4. The Fiery Wall of Protection spell is drawn from my 1995 "Hoodoo in Theory and Practice" and also appears in my 2013 book "The Art of Hoodoo Candle Magic." The "Adams County" spells were adapted from Harry Hyatt's book for the use of Lucky Mojo shop customers.

A DRESSED LETTER TO ATTRACT LOVE FROM AFAR
catherine yronwode

IS THIS SPELL RIGHT FOR YOU?

This spell employs a paper letter to attract someone for love. It cannot be worked electronically. It is sexual.

First, let me start by saying that in my experience it is easier and more often successful to attract an UNKNOWN lover or mate than it is to get a long-lost lover to return from an unknown place, to turn a casual acquaintance into a lover by long distance, or to attract the attention of a specific far-away person with whom one has no personal link at all.

Second, ask yourself, is your request realistic? (You might be surprised how often people request a spell to sexually attract a celebrity — someone they may have only seen once at an autograph session!)

Third, you must provide the recipient with a means to reply to you. Ask yourself, if you do manage to reach this person through preternatural means, will he or she know how to contact you in return? Does the person you desire have your telephone number, email address, or street address? Do you have friends in common who could pass a message?

If no method of return contact is provided, all you may be doing is inflicting a "dream love" on the object of your affections. He or she may dream or day-dream about you but, not being able to contact you, possibly not even knowing your name or if you are a real person or a figment of the imagination, he or she will chalk the whole attraction experience up to "strange ideas" and the two of you will never meet in person.

I personally have had numerous "love-dreams" in which i met and made love with total strangers. Were they men who had read my books or web pages and were trying to contact me from afar? I'll never know! They seemed to be "real people," but i never have met them in the flesh.

The same goes for people i used to know — i have dreamed quite wonderfully of men i liked years ago in school, renewing our friendships, even becoming lovers in these dreams — but i have no idea where they live now, or how to contact them. If they were working a spell on me, they left out an important factor: i got the "message," but i could not figure out a way to get in touch with them in return.

ASSEMBLING YOUR MATERIALS

Okay, so let us assume that you DO know where the person you desire lives, that he or she knows where you live, that the two of you have some sort of established form of prior communication, and that he or she actually opens and touches his or her personal mail. In that case, it is indeed possible to work a dressed letter spell to attract and draw him or her closer from afar.

Start the process by performing any strong and popular ritual for love-drawing an/or for contact, such as the Lodestone and Candle Spell, the 3-Candle Love Spell, the Pricked Finger Love Spell. The spell you choose for this purpose is entirely your own choice. There is no one "better"or "stronger" love spell.The point is that you will augment its strength and direct its intention by following it immediately with this spell, in which you send the person a dressed letter.

Assemble the following items:

A LOVE-DRAWING SPIRITUAL BATH
Love Herbs Mixture, Follow Me Boy Bath Crystals, Come To Me Bath Crystals, Attraction Bath Crystals, Love Me Bath Crystals, etc.

A LOVE DRAWING FIGURAL CANDLE
Bolivian couple candle, lovers candle, genitalia candle, male or female clothed figure or nude figure candle, etc.

A LOVE-DRAWING OIL FOR THE CANDLE
Follow Me Boy Oil, Attraction Oil, Come To Me Oil, Love Me Oil, Lodestone Oil, Kiss Me Now! Oil, Fast Luck Oil, etc.

A LOVE-DRAWING SPIRITUAL INCENSE
Love Herbs to burn on charcoal, Follow Me Boy Incense, Come To Me Incense, Attraction Incense, Love Me Incense, etc.

WRITING IMPLEMENTS
A pen, a piece of stationery, a matching envelope, and a stamp

A SMALL BASIN OR SAUCER
To contain some of your used bath-water

DRESSING THE LETTER

This spell is best worked in the early morning before dawn, because it finishes at sunrise. Those who take the moon's position into account may wish to perform it as the moon is waxing or growing in size, because it is a spell for increase. Some women may prefer to perform it on the first day of their menstrual cycle, regardless of the moon's position. Those who work by the days of the week may prefer to perform it on a Friday, as that is the day sacred to Venus, the goddess of love. The choice is yours.

Prepare the bath according to its directions or your common sense. Dress the candle, light it, and light the incense. With no other light than that from your love-candle, bathe in the love-drawing bath and save some of the bath-water containing your personal essence in the basin. Place the basin next to the candle.

While still naked from your bath, and still with no other light than that from your oil-dressed love-candle, write the person you desire a sincere letter. Sprinkle the paper with a love-drawing sachet powder, then draw your fingernails down the paper in wavy "snake lines" to mark it. Shake the paper to let the powder fall away and set it aside. Address the envelope, dress it with sachet, mark it with "snake lines," shake it clean, and set it aside too.

Next, formulate your specific desire, by which i mean get it very clear in your mind exactly what you want — for instance, that the person contacts you, falls in love with you, visits you, has sex with you, marries you, raises a family with you, and/or spends his or her life with you. Once you have formulated your specific desire, focus the entirety of your WILL upon achieving the result you wish to accomplish.

Arouse yourself sexually by thinking of the person you want, and at the moment of orgasm, silently voice your COMMAND that the person must come to you and fulfill the conditions that you have willed.

Immediately after, physically relax into a receptive posture and ACCEPT that as you asked, so shall it be done.

After the moment of reverie and acceptance, touch the four corners of the letter with a bit of your sexual fluids. Place the letter in the envelope and touch the four corners of the envelope with your sexual fluids. Seal the envelope with a streak of your bath water and use the bath-water to affix the stamp as well.

MAILING THE LETTER

At dawn, dress in clean clothes. Carry the remaining bath water to a crossroads, throw it over your left shoulder toward the rising sun, and walk back home without looking back. Mail the letter at once — if you can mail it on your way home from the crossroads, so much the better.

If you cannot mail the letter, do not waste your time attempting to perform this spell and do not waste my time (as so many have) by enquiring of me how to adapt it to email or text messaging. It is a spell of physical contact and it replies upon physical contact for its efficacy. If you wish to perform an attraction spell using non-physical means, i suggest a skull candle spell or a picture box spell.

THE MAGICAL ROOTS OF THIS SPELL

The letter-dressing and physical contact aspects of the work are based in old-time African American hoodoo, but the three-part sequence of deploying one's will, command, and acceptance during a cycle of sexual arousal is a method of working taught by the 19th century African American sex-magician Paschal Beverly Randolph (1825-1875), under the names "volantia," "decretism," and "posism,"

Volantia was Randolph's term for using volition or will to silently focus one's full consciousness upon a desired result. By decretism he meant making a decree or command at the moment of orgasm. Posism he described as relaxing into a receptive physical posture or pose after orgasm and gratefully accepting that what you have willed and decreed has come to pass.

Paschal Beverly Randolph was a rootworker who sold love powders and scrying mirrors by mail order, as well as a Spiritualist medium and sex magician. You may read more about him at my Sacred Sex site: LuckyMojo.com/tkpbrandolph.html and also at my Southern Spirits historical archive site: Southern-Spirits.com/randolph-on-hoodoo.html.

"A Dressed Letter to Attract Love From Afar" was published as part of my online outreach to students in 1994. It was uploaded to my Free Love Spells Archive at LuckyMojo.com/lovespells.html#dressedletterlove in 1995, became Lucky Mojo Shop-Hand-Out No. 6 in 2002, and was distributed at Miss Bri's "Love Conjure" workshop in 2010. My related Dressed Letter for Reconciliation spell can be found at LuckyMojo.com/reconciliation.html.

LOVE CONJURE
Miss Bri

LOVE SPELL CLIENTS

Love work may well be the reason that we have magic today. Some of the oldest documented spells are those intended to draw or keep a lover, and love spells are an important part of hoodoo folk-magic. In my professional conjure practice, love work is the most commonly requested type of spell-casting. A solid 85-90% of clients who seek out my love services are heterosexual women. My remaining love clients are heterosexual men, gay men and women, and bisexual partners.

CATEGORIES OF LOVE WORK

I categorize love work into five distinct forms. Understanding which category your work falls into is essential to choosing which oils, herbs, and curios to use, as well as spells that are best suited to the case:

Drawing a New Lover: This is attraction work designed to draw a romantic and/or sexual partner (specified or not) into your or your client's life.

Strengthening a Good Love Relationship: This includes achieving commitment to a monogamous or exclusive relationship, getting a marriage proposal, and intensifying a relationship that is basically in good shape. Requests may be made for heating up the sex or fostering more tenderness and affection.

Repairing a Troubled Relationship: This is not reconciliation, because at this point there has not been an actual break-up, but one or both partners are concerned that there will be a break-up if intimacy, peacefulness, and/or trust are not restored.

Reconciling a Broken Relationship: This is work undertaken after a break-up in an attempt to re-start a relationship. These cases are notoriously tough, with typically low rates of success, especially if much time has passed or if the partner who left has become intimate with another person.

Getting Out of a Relationship: This includes the classic form of break-up work intended to split up relationships and marriages, as well as break-up work when one partner wants to divorce or get out of a relationship.

PROCEDURES FOR LOVE WORK

Divination and/or Consultation: In order to determine which categories of love work you may be involved with, it is customary to have a divination, also sometimes called a consultation, during which the case is spiritually diagnosed by a reputable reader or seer. An outcome, positive or negative, is predicted for the case, and suggestions may be made about work that the client can do for herself or that may be performed by a professional rootworker.

Establishing a Time Limit: In some reparation or reconciliation cases, clients are advised to set a time limit for their work. They are instructed to establish a date by which, if the work has not produced a favourable result, they will let it go, preferably accompanied by a Cut and Clear ritual.

Rootwork: This is hoodoo spell-casting undertaken in cases that have a good chance of a successful outcome. It may be performed by the client, working with a spell kit after receiving training or magical coaching, or it may be performed on the client's behalf by a professional root worker.

THE USE OF PERSONAL CONCERNS

A crucial element in all love work is your target's personal concerns, intimate links to his or her body and soul. Personal concerns are the means by which an effective link is established between the spell-caster and the target, in order to influence the target's thoughts, actions, and feelings. The following hierarchy of personal concerns is listed from most intimate and influential to least intimate and influential; in love conjure, intimacy is a plus.

- Semen, vaginal fluid, sexual fluids
- Pubic hair
- Hair from the head or other areas of the body
- Soiled underwear, nightwear, or socks
- A "measure" of the genitals
- Foot-tracks
- Nail clippings, saliva, skin
- Soiled outer clothing
- Photograph
- Handwriting
- Name

BATHING FOR LOVE

I am astounded at how many clients I encounter who believe that spiritual bathing rituals are good for uncrossing or cleansing only. I consider a bathing ritual a prerequisite for performing good, old-fashioned, down home love work. Herb baths or salt crystal baths for love-drawing and love strengthening are good in most cases, with the exception of Reconciliation and Repairing Troubled Relationships. For these two categories I favour a slightly more complex bathing regimen: Begin with Uncrossing, Chinese Wash, and/or Van Van bath products. Bathe with these products for at least 3 days and then follow with a love drawing or love strengthening blend for another 6 days, so that the total number of days you ritually bathe is 9.

CANDLE SPELLS FOR LOVE

There are about as many candle spells for love work as there are candles! Basically you have 3 categories of candles to work with:

FIGURAL CANDLES

Working with figural candles is similar to working with doll-babies. You may cleanse the candle to remove any mess it might have picked up during handling and sitting on a store shelf. I like cleansing my candles with Rose water prior to using them if I am going to perform love work. Don't wet the wick.

Baptize the candle with the person's name and load it with personal concerns if you have them. Next anoint the candle with appropriate blends of love oils and herbs. Finally, set it up on the altar according to the manner in which you are working.

Human Image Candles: Representing naked or clothed male and female figures, these are often employed in moving candle spells that seek to influence love relationships by moving the two partners in question closer together or moving undesired people out of situations.

Black Divorce Candles: These can be burned on top of a cut-apart petition paper to incite a break-up or divorce, or worked on a break-up jar. You may cleave divorce candles apart before they finish burning out naturally.

7 Knob Candles: For general attraction and love drawing work; burned for 7 days or with 7 wishes,

Genital Figural Candles: These can be worked with to encourage sexual passion and increased physical intimacy. They may also be employed in spells intended to restrict, bind, or harm those areas of the target's body.

Skull Candles: Skulls are employed to influence your target's thoughts, feelings, or perceptions of a situation.

FREE STANDING CANDLES

Free-standing offertory candles in cylinder, pillar, and taper form are worked with in a very similar way to figural candles and in a pinch can be used as stand-ins for them. Offertory and jumbo candles may be loaded with petitions and personal concerns, anointed with oils, rubbed or rolled in herbs and sachet powders, and then employed in altar work. These are also the most popular candles for burning on top of jar and bottle spells.

GLASS ENCASED VIGIL LIGHTS

Sometimes called 7 day candles and Novena candles, these glass encased paraffin candles are dressed and blessed with appropriate oils and herbs and then set on an altar, where they burn for a number of days. Experienced readers and candle ministers can read the candle glass after the wax has burned and send a report to the client.

SWEETENING SPELLS FOR LOVE

Sweetening spells include work in which a jar, bottle, bowl, or box of honey, sugar, molasses, syrup, jam, or similar sweet substance is used to sweeten a person in love. The sweetener may remain in the container or it may be subsequently used in cooking. In addition, a candle or a series of candles may be employed as a focal point of the spell.

One variation on the sweet jar that is also a sneaky trick is the apple in a plant spell — I call it Eve's Apple Spell. In this old school hoodoo work, you take a red Apple or a red Onion, core the fruit, write your petition, roll it up, and place it in the hollowed core. Then you fill the core with honey and a selection of appropriate love drawing herbs, bury the loaded fruit in a flower pot, and place a love drawing plant like a fern above it. Give the fixed plant as a gift to your lover, or as a make-up gift after a fight. If you like, you may bury it in the ground and plant a Rose bush atop it.

MOJO HANDS FOR LOVE

A mojo hand is a variation on one of the oldest spell forms — the container spell. In this case the container is a bag. A popular mojo hand for love is made by taking a mated pair of lodestone grits and separating them, placing one in one bag and the other in a second bag. Give one to your target and keep the other for yourself. The lodestones will draw to one another and draw your target closer to you.

The Nation Sack is a special type of mojo hand worn only by women, to keep their beloved close to them, faithful, true, and cooperative. It is filled with a number of ingredients and is personalized by the woman who wears it in a specific way.

LODESTONES FOR LOVE

Lodestones, also known as magnetic magnetite, are natural magnets found in the earth. Iron within these rocks is naturally magnetized when they are struck by lightening or charged with electricity in a lab. In Conjure we treat lodestones as we would pets, they are considered to be ALIVE and they must be fed with magnetic sand to get them working for you. Lodestone pairs that naturally attract and fit to one another are called matched lodestones.

Matched lodestones are most commonly worked with in love magic, you may work with matched male/female, male/male and female/female pairs. Male lodestones are pointier than females and they may have naturally occurring white spots. Female lodestones tend to be rounder and may have red spots of rust.

Lodestones can be placed on love altars, in bowl spells, honey jars, mojo hands, and doll-babies. Candles may be dusted with lodestone sand, magnetic sand, or rolled in lodestone grit.

Love Pups or Magnetic Scottie Dogs are paired magnets embedded in small plastic figurines. One represents a black Scottish Terrier or Scottie Dog and the other is a West Highland White Terrier (often called a "white Scottie Dog"). The popularity of these novelties was inspired by Black & White Scotch Whiskey and by Franklin and Eleanor Roosevelt's black Scottie Dog, Fala. Magnetic love pups may be worked in the same manner as lodestones and they do not have to be fed magnetic sand. They are especially good for relationships where differences in race, colour, ethnicity, or culture may be an issue.

LOVE TRICKS AROUND THE HOME

The oldest trick that can be incorporated into every day living is one that many ladies are familiar with — feed your guy (or gal) your menstrual blood. This is believed to increase sexual passion and heat, as well as deepen intimacy between lovers. Swish it in coffee, add it to red pasta sauce, or make a full-out tantric ritual of it. You can also freeze or dry menstrual blood so that you have access to it later.

Men may also feed their semen to women (or men), although this is a less common trick.

Another favourite trick is to sew a pubic hair into a hat if your lover wears a hat — that way he will always have you on his mind! Sewing your hair into a man's pants fly keeps him faithful.

A third trick that I like a lot is to add love-increasing oils and waters to everyday personal care products that your partner uses. A little Dixie Love oil in a bottle of shampoo can go a long way.

PRAYERS AND PSALMS FOR LOVE

Song of Songs (The Song of Solomon): The entirety is about love; section 1:2-3 encapsulates this.

23rd Psalm: Recited for general good luck and abundance as well as protection in all area of life.

45th Psalm: Used by a husband on himself to calm an angry wife and encourage a peaceful home.

46th Psalm: Recited by a husband as he anoints his wife with Olive oil when he has done her wrong.

51st Psalm: The Hyssop bath Psalm, used when one has a need of forgiveness.

TIMING FOR LOVE MAGIC

The Waxing Moon (the two week period between the New Moon and the Full Moon) is good for drawing a lover to you, restoring a relationship, building a love relationship, etc. Morning sunrise is also good time to do drawing work, particularly to summon a lover to you.

The Waning Moon (the two week period between the Full Moon and the New Moon) is good for cleansing and banishing. This is a good time to do the Cut and Clear ritual and a good time to do Break Up work. As the sun sets you may do banishing work.

TAROT CARDS IN LOVE READINGS

Some tarot cards seem to have special meanings in love readings and consultations about love spells. What follows is not an exhaustive list and it is not meant to teach you how to read tarot, however, because tarot is the most commonly employed tool in diagnosing love cases, it is important to be familiar with cards that may be significant to love clients. The images described here are found in the Rider-Waite-Smith deck, designed by Arthur Edward Waite and illustrated by Pamela Colman Smith. These are the most popular tarot cards in the world and will be familiar to most card readers.

The Lovers: Says what it means and means what it says.

The Devil: In the imagery, you will notice that the Devil card has the same figures present in the Lovers card but they are in Hell and chained to the Devil. Indicates serious problems in the relationship — qualities like delusional thinking and/or addictions that are destroying the relationship may be present. Can also represent an illicit love affair or a curse on the love life.

The Moon: This card often comes up to indicate that there is a problem with commitment. One partner is not ready to commit to the other because of appetite — sexual or otherwise — and/or due to necessity, such a job, career, or financial concerns that require attention and commitment that would otherwise be going to the relationship. Can also indicate that the relationship or members in it are suffering from a lack of freedom and movement.

The 2 of Cups: This is a card of contradictory meanings. It can indicate deep partnership between a man and woman, man and man, or woman and woman. (Note that despite the evident gender of the figures, this card may come up for those who are considering a same-sex union either openly or not openly.) On the other hand, it can also indicate that while things look good on the surface there is a possible deception underneath; the contemplated exchange of cups may not come to pass.

The 4 of Cups: Another card about commitment and making choices. Here we have a character who is trying to choose — to be committed to one individual or to have the freedom to play the field in pursuit of many. His gesture of denial of the proffered cup may indicate rejection of an offer of love.

The 6 of Cups: This card points to a love relationship from the past or currently happening between two people. There is a friendship here, a psychic bond, and a desire to be remembered, also a level of youthful immaturity. The two may have been childhood sweethearts or may have once thought of each other as brother and sister.

The 10 of Cups: A good, happy card! Coming together with faith and thankfulness, the possibility of family, married life, children (or more children), a new start with much joy, and the purchase of a home.

The 4 of Wands: A solid foundation and a celebration for lovers, sometimes against the odds; a bountiful harvest of happiness.

The 9 of Wands: Suspicion and doubt about one's partner or the relationship. Can indicate a decided lack of sound judgment or clear thinking. Often points to old wounds from past relationships.

The 9 of Pentacles: A woman of grace and power is presented with two choices: a snail at her feet, representing a lover who is slow to come closer or to commit, and a hooded hawk, representing an unknown lover from afar or in her future.

The 10 of Pentacles: Patience will be rewarded with extended family bonds and comfort in old age.

The 2 of Swords: Choices need to be made and boundaries need to be established. The individual may have to make a choice without all the information needed. There may not be a "best" time to make a decision.

The 3 of Swords: The classic sign of a broken heart, tears, and sorrow in love.

The 4 of Swords: Relationship issues from the past are getting brought up in the present and making the future difficult to consider. Arguments and disagreements of the past need to stay there, and both partners should be encouraged to deal with immediate conflicts only.

The 9 of Swords: A card of sleeplessness, it can also literally indicate being left to sleep alone.

The 10 of Swords: A card of deep betrayal, it often can indicate a partner's infidelity.

Miss Bri is a member of AIRR and is available for readings and rootwork through her MilagroRoots.com web site. Her "Love Conjure" workshop was held in 2010.

SWEET SPELLS FOR LOVE AND BEAUTY
Deacon Millett

STARTING SIMPLE

Sachet powders and incense are hoodoo staples, used to perfume the very air with molecules of the herbs and sweeteners used in the work.

A SIMPLE SACHET POWDER
TO ATTRACT POSITIVE ATTENTION

Mix confectioners sugar and powdered Cinnamon to a light tan tone, taking care to sift any lumps until only a fine dust remains. This sachet will attract others to you. Use it on resumes, business cards, love letters, legal papers, official forms, greeting cards — anything you send or give to your target.

To fix something with your sachet powder, sprinkle it over the item, calling out the name of your target. "Customers, I reach out to you and sweeten you toward my goals." Using your three middle fingers, draw downward in a wavy "S" through the powder. Then give it several quick taps to remove the powder. The scent remains, with no powdery traces.

A SIMPLE INCENSE
FOR POSITIVE ENERGY AND INTENT

The hair from a Coconut husk mixed with brown sugar may be burned on a self-lighting charcoal round to enhance any positive work. Light the charcoal first and then add the Coconut and brown sugar mixture. You may then pass any item through the smoke, calling out your petition or desire. Socks are one favourite, whether your own or a loved one's. "Lord Jesus, sweeten my path through life" or "Lord Jesus, keep [name of loved one] coming home to me."

If preparing your home for a "sweet" evening, a smokeless method may be preferred. A bit of sachet powder may be blown into the air or you may use a pot of fixed boiling water on the stove. Add a dash of Vanilla extract and a teaspoon of sugar. To spice it up, go with blended "Pumpkin Pie Spice," a mix of Cinnamon, Ginger, Cloves, Allspice, and Nutmeg.

For more on Powders and Incense, see:

LuckyMojo.com/powders.html
LuckyMojo.com/incense.html

FIXING A SUGAR BOWL

A sugar bowl on the table, used for coffee or tea, can be a center of sweetening for the home. A kitchen sugar canister or cookie jar can also be effective. In these spells we will use petition papers to specify whom we wish to sweeten and to implore both sugar and Spirit to do as we wish.

Rather than a simple flat bottom, the ideal sugar bowl for our use is footed, with a hidden area beneath it which we can fill as we choose. Crafty hoodoos can affix green felt across the bottom, to hide the trick from view. But how many people are going to be looking under the sugar bowl?

A SUGAR BOWL FOR PEACE IN THE HOME

Place a pinch of Lavender flowers, a pinch of Basil, and a whole Clove in the center of a name-paper. Fold it toward yourself, to bring the peace toward you. Then turn it ninety degrees and fold it again. Continue until you have a tight "packet" with the names far inside. Tape your packet underneath the sugar bowl and use it on the table everyday!

A SUGAR BOWL TO BRING TRUE LOVE

Use a single rosebud, a portion of Cinnamon stick, and a piece of Cherry bark. This packet takes more skill to fold, since it is chunkier. You may wish to tie it with red thread like you'd gift wrap a present. This will make it easier to hide beneath your sugar bowl.

A SUGAR BOWL FOR MARRIAGE RENEWAL

If your spouse has left home, place your wedding ring in the sugar bowl overnight to create sweet thoughts of your marriage. This was a favourite spell taught by Susie Bosselmann of the Lucky Mojo Curio Company, whose lady-hearted advice was a help to so many.

A SUGAR BOWL FOR A FAITHFUL MARRIAGE

A petition packet to insure a faithful marriage includes a pinch of Coriander seed, a pinch of Cumin seed, and a single Red Clover flower. Women often add a sprig of Rosemary. Seeds tend to roll during packet folding, so take care!

SWEET BATHS AND SUGAR SCRUBS

The use of ritual cleansing is found in religions the world over, from the Jewish Mikvah to the Hindu Puja. Cleansing baths are often prescribed in hoodoo to help with a variety of conditions, most often the removal of curses, jinxes, and other "messes" put upon one by an enemy, either living or dead. These cleansing baths, with their emphasis on mineral salts, can prove harsh to the skin.

Sweet baths, on the other hand, have a beautiful nature all their own. Many spas now offer sugar as a gentler alternative to the salt scrub for exfoliation. When removing the outer layer of dead skin cells, sugar can replace granular minerals as an abrasive.

When bathing in the conjure tradition, we bring good things up, from the feet to the top of the head, and we push bad things away, from the head down to the feet. This marks hoodoo as an earth-based tradition, rather than one focused on a sky god delivering good from above.

Bathing before dawn, stepping out of the bath between two white candles, air drying while reading the Psalms, and taking an offering of bathwater to the crossroads are all time-honoured traditions in hoodoo.

With these sweet baths and sugar scrubs, I encourage you to rinse thoroughly, until any feeling of "stickiness" has turned to a smooth, silky sensation. Not only does this give a better feeling to the skin, but you'll attract what you most desire — rather than ants and flies!

A SIMPLE SUGAR SCRUB FOR THE HOME

Mix one half ounce hoodoo condition oil (the standard Lucky Mojo size) and one tablespoon of granulated sugar. You may use a little more or a little less sugar to get the right consistency. If this scrub is too powerfully scented, you may add another tablespoon of sugar and a tablespoon of unscented oil. Almond and Olive are favourites, but Coconut oil goes well with many love preparations. You may also add the contents of one herbal teabag. Lavender (for peace), Hyssop (for forgiveness), Rose (for romance), Chamomile (for luck), and Licorice (to force love) are some choices. The best thing about this sugar scrub is that it's perfect for one-time use.

A LIGHT AND DARK SUGAR SCRUB FOR MULTIRACIAL COUPLES

Loosely fill a container with half white and half brown sugar. Put the mix into a bowl and combine well. Begin to slowly Almond oil, enough to moisten the mix. Add Vanilla extract and Rose petals for power. Continue to add oil and mix, add oil and mix, add oil and mix. Return the blended scrub to your container. This bath brings added love to all couples, but especially when cultural differences place added stress on their relationship.

A SUGAR BATH FOR LOVE PROTECTION

Once you've found your love, it's a good idea to work at least weekly to keep it. A tablespoon of epsom salt, a tablespoon of kosher salt, a tablespoon of sugar and three Bay leaves will do the trick. Mix using a clockwise motion in the warm to hot bathwater, and then recite the 23rd Psalm. Try to draw your lover's bath every once in a while — or take a bath together!

A SUGAR BATH TO REVERSE BAD LUCK IN LOVE

For a fresh start in the love department, use this bath once a week for thirteen weeks. Mix together one half pound sugar, one pound rock salt, two ounces Dill leaves, thirteen Star Anise pods, two ounces Lemon Mint, two ounces White Sage, and two cups White Clover flowers. Keep in an air tight container.

A SUGAR BATH TO HELP HEAL A BROKEN RELATIONSHIP

Star Anise, Violet leaf, and Balm of Gilead buds can be added to any of the above baths (or to a tablespoon of sugar) to help reconcile a couple that is arguing, on the outs, or even divorced.

A SUGAR BATH TO BRING GOOD LUCK

To make lucky sugar, add a Vanilla bean and several Cinnamon sticks to an airtight jar of superfine or granulated sugar. Good for the bath or for cooking, it grows in strength the longer you keep it!

A SUGAR BATH TO SWEETEN DREAMS

Hops flowers are said to drive away nightmares, and there are many ways to deploy them effectively. A brown sugar and Hops flower bath will sweeten the dreams of child or adult.

A SUGAR BATH FOR SEDUCTION

Lightly crushed Juniper berries with sugar and a Ginger root will heat up your evening. Gay men, add Safflower petals to the mix!

A SUGARED HERB BATH TO DRAW NEW LOVE

There are several ways to create an herbal bath in hoodoo. One is to boil a tea from the herbs and pour the strained tea into the bath. Another is to place a muslin sack of herbs in the bath; this makes for easy clean up. Loose herbs are also used, and if you like Rose petals floating on the water, I say go for it! To draw new love, I recommend a tablespoon of sugar, a small handful of Rose petals, a small handful of Lavender flowers, a pinch or two of Catnip, a small handful of Red Clover flowers, a Cardamom seed, and a stick of Cinnamon. Bathe by the light of red candles.

CLEOPATRA'S BEAUTY SECRETS

For many, Cleopatra VII is the epitome of feminine strength. She used her power over men as the last pharaoh of Ancient Egypt, outlasting her father and brothers in the role. Glamour, the magic of beauty, is an ancient art, and Cleopatra was certainly an admirable practitioner. The most persistent rumour about Cleopatra's beauty secrets is her use of a daily milk and honey bath. Honey is a humectant, naturally attracting and retaining moisture, and its antibacterial qualities may be helpful in healing cuts, abrasions, scalds, and minor acne. The lactic acid in milk is said to dissolve dirt, oil, and dead skin cells. Together, beyond any practical benefits, milk and honey are an indulgent pleasure for the senses, and it is easy to vary the composition until you come up with something perfect for you.

CLEOPATRA'S LEGENDARY BEAUTY BATH

Three to four cups of raw milk and half to one cup of unfiltered honey were the only two ingredients Cleopatra needed. After a full cleansing in her first tub, Cleopatra was rinsed and ready for her soak. Her second tub had the milk and honey mixture, into which warm water had been run for her bath.

A MODERN TAKE ON HONEY AND MILK

Whole powdered milk (none of this skim business) and pure honey, half a cup of each, are poured into warm running water. Soak for fifteen to twenty minutes, adding more warm water as necessary.

HARRY MIDDLETON HYATT

An Anglican minister and folklore collector, Harry Middleton Hyatt is one reason we have such powerful documentation of hoodoo practices today. His obsession with recording the spiritual and magical beliefs of African-Americans resulted in the five-volume compendium called *Hoodoo - Conjuration - Witchcraft - Rootwork*.

Beginning in 1936, Hyatt used a wax cylinder recording device to capture more than 1,600 interviews with African American conjure practitioners in Alabama, Arkansas, Florida, Georgia, Illinois, Louisiana, Maryland, Mississippi, North Carolina, South Carolina, Tennessee, and Virginia. Hyatt's four year project resulted in close to 5,000 pages of detailed spells and tricks.

The following spell, collected in Memphis Tennessee in 1939 and attributed to Informant 1532, shows the importance of the footprint or foot-track as a personal concern as well as how sugar can be used as an influence over the target.

SUGARING A FOOT-TRACK TO KEEP A MAN YOURS

"Now, listen. If he's leaving the house and you want him to return, you catch that dirt from his toes back to the heel, pull it back. Then you take that dirt and preserve it in some kind of little can and place sugar — you know that sugar is the tamer of the world. The wildest beast, the worst beast, it will tame any of them, the sugar will. Add a little sugar in that and a little salt, and place it in a can somewhere and conceal it in a corner where it will be kept quietly, and as long as you hold that dirt from his feet, you've got him for life.

"There's two things that control an individual, two things, his name and his track."

For more on Harry M. Hyatt see:
LuckyMojo.com/hyatt.html

"Hoodoo Honey and Sugar Spells" is a 96 page book by Deacon Millet, published in 2013 for his workshop of the same name. These sample "Sweet Spells for Love and Beauty" pages are adapted from the book, and the entire volume is available from Lucky Mojo. Deacon Millett is a member of AIRR and Hoodoo Psychics, and the pastor of Four Altars Gospel Sanctuary in the California High Desert. He can be reached for reading and rootwork through his FourAltars.com web site.

THE SUCCESS SIGIL AND DRAWING STEADY CUSTOMERS
catherine yronwode

THE SUCCESS SIGIL

The very simplest spell i know for money-drawing was taught to me in the 1960s by the owner of a store that sold hoodoo spiritual supplies in Oakland, California. All you need to perform it is a ball-point pen and some Money Drawing Sachet Powder and/or Money Drawing Oil or Hoyt's cologne. In a pinch you can use whiskey instead of the oil or Hoyt's cologne. Here's how it goes:

First you need to understand the "SUCCESS sigil." This is a special, cryptic way of writing the word "success." Try it out on paper before you do it on your money. Now write the word

SUCCESS

Then write it again without the vowels, because we are only going to work with the consonants

SCCSS

Next, add another S to the front of the word so that the whole thing is a symmetrical palindrome (reading the same from front to back and back to front)

SSCCSS

Then draw a line through each S to change it to a dollar sign **$** and draw a line through each C to change it to a cent sign **¢**

$$¢¢$$

That is the SUCCESS sigil — **$$¢¢$$**.

Now that you know how to do it, take out every bill in your wallet. Write the SUCCESS sigil diagonally in every corner of each of the bills. Underneath the name of the US Treasurer, write your own full name.

Mark the bills spiritually by sprinkling each one with Money Drawing Sachet Powder and dragging your four fingernails down along it in "wavy snake lines," then shaking the powder off. Dress the four corners of each bill with a drop of Money Drawing Oil, Hoyt's cologne, or whiskey as you say the 23rd Psalm out loud ("The Lord is my shepherd, i shall not want…"). Put the dressed money back in your wallet.

TRAINED HUNTING MONEY

Dressed money made with the SUCCESS sigil or other markings (your name, the words "Return to Me" or the acronym "RTM," a short excerpt from Psalms 23, etc.) is called "trained money" or "trained hunting money" because if you spend it wisely, it will go out into the world and hunt up more money to come your way, just like a good hunting dog.

Coins can also be trained as hunting money. You will need a large Lodestone, Magnetic Sand, a nice-looking shallow bowl, and a bottle of Lodestone Oil or Magnet Oil to do this. Take all of the coins from your pocket and lightly dress them with the oil. The easiest way to do this is to rub the oil on your hands and pass the coins through your hands, Use the bowl to make a little "nest" and line it with the coins. Set the Lodestone in the nest, like a hen setting on her chicks. Every night empty your change out, dress it, and set it into the bowl. Every morning take some change out of the bowl to use in transactions during the day. Feed the Lodestone with Magnetic Sand once a week.

Spend your trained hunting money only on things that are necessary to you or which can bring you more money or success — that is, if you are a student, spend that money on school supplies. If you have a job, spend the money on office supplies, or a uniform, or postage stamps for the business.

The man who taught me this spell said it was especially good if you got a new job that required a uniform and you dressed each bill you would spend your trained hunting money on the uniform rather than writing a check for it.

If you start using trained hunting money like this, in the years to come you will also notice that now and then you will receive money with someone's else's name written on it, or the SUCCESS sigil, or some other cryptic mark, and you'll know that those folks are using similar money-drawing spells.

If you get a piece of paper currency with someone else's name on it, write yours under theirs and say the 23rd Psalm for their success and for your own as you do so. This way you piggy-back your spell on top of theirs and you will both benefit.

DRAWING STEADY CUSTOMERS TO A BUSINESS

When opening a new business, you will want to start by clearing away past conditions in the building through the simple process of washing the premises from back to front with a spiritual cleaning agent such as Chinese Wash or Van Van crystals made up into floor wash. (Both of these are made with Lemon Grass and other herbs.)

After the cleaning, it is time to entice customers. The following spells can be used singly or in combination. I have known shop-keepers who have used all of these spells at various times and in various combinations. I myself use them and they have worked well for me.

MONEY DRAWING WITH A LODESTONE

To get a new business off to a good start or increase the success of an existing business, perform any Money Drawing spell utilizing a large Lodestone and green candles. After the spell is finished, keep the Lodestone in your cash register. Feed it once a week with Magnetic Sand.

MONEY DRAWING AT THE DOORWAY

For steady cash flow, use Money Drawing Oil to dress the doorway of the premises at least once a week. Place Money Drawing Sachet Powder and/or a mixture of Irish Moss (for steady cash flow), Cinnamon Chips or Powder (to draw in both customers and their cash), and Sugar (to sweeten the customers up) at the door or — better yet — under the entrance mat.

Laying either Money Drawing Sachet Powder or the Sachet Powder mixed with the above herbs in the four corners of the room, with a fifth little pile in the center in a quincunx pattern is also traditional. Burning Money-Drawing Incense in the store first thing in the morning is also recommended.

MONEY DRAWING WITH A LAMP

Many people keep a money lamp or money candle burning at their shops during business hours. It can be set in the back room where no one sees it. In the USA, where our currency is green, we use green candles and lamps for money drawing; in other countries, metallic gold candles are the norm, and they are also popular with some workers in the USA.

A money lamp is a regular glass-reservoir kerosene lamp which you have prepared by placing a money-drawing mineral — either a chunk of Pyrite or a Lodestone dressed with Magnetic Sand — and a bunch of coins in the reservoir where they can be seen. The coins can all be silver dimes, or the "lucky" change you took in during your first cash sale, or an assortment of one penny, one nickel, one dime, one quarter, one fifty-cent piece, and one silver dollar — that is, one each of every denomination of coin. You can use green-tinted lamp oil in the lamp.

MONEY DRAWING WITH CANDLES

There are many money candles to choose from: green 7-knob candles, 7-day vigil lights, pyramids, 14-day sanctuary lights, and golden tapers. Whatever you choose, dress it with Money Drawing Oil, place it on a $20.00 bill, and surround it with 4 coins as it burns.

MONEY DRAWING FLOOR WASH

One traditional way to draw customers into a shop or office is to mix up and use your own special Business Success Floor Wash once a week. It must be prepared in complete silence, on a morning during which you have woken up and gone into the store without speaking to anyone, not even family members, and also without going to the bathroom.

When you get to the store, make up and light a cone of Money-Drawing Incense and place it on the floor. Step over it three times, smoking yourself and your clothing well. When that is done, clean up the incense, then get your wash bucket and urinate into it. Add a pinch each of sugar and Cinnamon powder, the ashes left from the incense, and either a few drops of Money Drawing Oil and a half-handful of Van Van crystals, or a half-handful of Money Drawing Bath Crystals. Fill the bucket with hot water and use it to wash the premises from back to front (if there is wall-to-wall carpeting, wash the baseboards only). Sweep the remains of the wash water out the front door onto the sidewalk with a broom. Walk back inside backwards and open the store for business.

"The Success Sigil and Drawing Steady Customers" was Lucky Mojo Shop Hand-Out No. 7 from 2002. Drawing on old spells i learned in Oakland during my teens, it has long been a shop favourite, but was never used as a MISC workshop flyer. More old-time money spells are logged in my online book "Hoodoo in Theory and Practice" at LuckyMojo.com/moneyspells.html.

HOW TO DRAW MONEY AND HOW TO KEEP MONEY
catherine yronwode

14-DAY LODESTONE SPELL TO DRAW MONEY

There are many variations of the old-time Money-Drawing Lodestone Candle Spell. Most are efficacious; here's one i particularly like.

You will need:

- Seven 4" or 6" green candles
- A large magnetic Lodestone,
- A packet of Magnetic Sand
- A bottle of Money Drawing Oil
- A packet of Money Drawing Sachet Powder
- A packet of Irish Moss,
- 7 two-dollar bills
- 7 silver dimes

You can use seven one-dollar bills and seven modern bi-metal dimes, if that's all you have.

Begin this spell at the new moon. During the two weeks that the moon grows, so will your money grow. If you can do it at your place of work, so much the better; otherwise do it at home. Place the Lodestone on a plate on a table or altar. Dress the candles with Money Drawing Oil. Arrange the candles in a moon-shaped crescent around and behind the Lodestone.

Starting from left to right, every morning before 9:00 AM, light one candle and anoint the four corners of one bill with Money Drawing Oil and place the bill under the Lodestone. As you do this, say either the 23rd Psalm or a simple invocation, such as "May my money increase." Then feed the Lodestone with a pinch of Magnetic Sand and say, "Lodestone, as you draw these sands to you, draw money to me by day." Let the candle burn halfway down each day and pinch it out (do not blow it out). At the end of 7 days, all the candles will be half-burned.

Now switch to doing the same spell at night. Everything is the same: you relight one candle each night, anoint one silver dime each night and place it with the Lodestone, say the Psalm or your invocation, and when you feed the Lodestone, you say, "Lodestone, as you draw these sands to you, draw money to me by night." This time you let the candles burn until they are burned out.

The spell ends at the full moon. Clear off the altar or table and bury any left over wax at a crossroads or throw it into running water.

If you worked the spell at your home, take the tray or plate with the Lodestone and the money to your place of work or put it in a bureau drawer in your bedroom where no one will see it. Sprinkle Money Drawing Sachet Powder in the four corners of the room where you do business. Place a pinch of Irish Moss in the center of the room, beneath the carpet or rug. If you have no place of business, do this in your bedroom or living room.

Take the currency and coins off the plate or tray and place them in your cash register or bureau. You can mark them with the $$¢¢$$ sigil as you do so. Place the Lodestone with its Magnetic Sands near the money, out of sight. The Lodestone will draw money to your business or home as long as you feed it once a week with Magnetic Sand and allow it to physically touch incoming money once a week to keep it "trained" to draw money.

Give the anointed money out in change to your customers or use it to buy things that are important and necessary, not frivolous — it will go into the world and bring more money back to your place of business or home to be with the Lodestone.

Renew the Money Drawing powder in the corners and the Irish Moss beneath the center of the rug or carpet after every cleaning of the room that would remove them.

If your specific need is to attract customers to a store, then other techniques, such as placing a Japanese Beckoning Cat statue (Maneki Neko in Japanese) or a Mexican Prepared and Wrapped Horseshoe with a picture of Saint Martin Caballero on it (La Virtuoso Herradura in Spanish) in the store would also be recommended. To learn more about these money-drawing amulets, go to these Lucky W Amulet Archive pages:

Beckoning Cat (Maneki Neko)
LuckyMojo.com/beckoningcat.html

Prepared Horseshoe (La Virtuosa Herradura)
LuckyMojo.com/packageherradura.html

A "MONEY STAY WITH ME" SPELL

Folks work this spell in their place of business, to keep from spending up the profits. Gamblers use it to keep from wasting their winnings. This spell takes seven days, but you can continue for as long as you like, as you will see.

Remember: "It's not how much you get, it's how much you can hold on to!"

You will need:

- A green 7-Knob candle
- A bottle of Money Stay With Me Oil
- A packet of Magnetic Sand
- A packet of Money Stay With Me Incense Powders
- A Large Lodestone
- A packet of Money Stay With Me Sachet Powder
- An incense burner or brazier
- A plate or tray
- A nail
- Four dimes
- A small paper

Write your full name nine times in red ink on the paper. Pin or glue something personal — a photo, hair, or concerns of that nature — to the paper.

If you have no altar, work on a small table or on the top of a bureau drawer. You can store the tray, candle, and dimes in a drawer during the daytime when you are not working the spell, to keep the money out of sight.

Make one-seventh of the Money Stay With Me Incense Powders into cones or place it loose on a brazier. Set the Lodestone on the tray. Place your name-paper under the Lodestone. On each knob of the candle carve the words MONEY STAY WITH ME. Dress the candle with Money Stay With Me Oil. Place the four dimes around the foot of the candle in the form of a cross. Light the incense, then the candle.

Now be honest with yourself. It's not how much you get, it's how much you can hold on to. Dig into your pockets or purse and pull out all your cash. Yes, even the cash hidden in your sock drawer.

Set the change and any bill under $20.00 denomination to one side. Any bill of $20.00 denomination or more, you will use in the spell. Write your name on each bill. (You've seen money like this before, with a person's name on it. Now you know how it got that way and why.)

Dress the four corners of each bill lightly with Money Stay With Me Oil and then dust each bill with Money Stay With Me Sachet Powder.

Place the bills under the Lodestone, neatly stacked and facing them the same way, and laying them East to West on top of your name-paper. Say aloud "Money Stay With Me" and sprinkle a pinch of Magnetic Sand on the Lodestone to feed it.

Let the candle burn one knob's worth and pinch it out (don't blow it out). The next night, do everything as before. Light some incense, re-light the candle, go through your money again, pull out all the bills of $20.00 denomination or more, write your name on them, dress them, dust them, and place them under the Lodestone, only go criss-cross, with the new bills facing North to South atop the first batch. Say "Money Stay With Me" and sprinkle Magnetic Sand on the Lodestone.

Let the candle burn one knob's worth and pinch it out. Do this every night for 7 nights, criss-crossing the bills. Any night when you don't have bills of $20.00 denomination or more, use the bills you have of highest denomination. On the 7th night, after you finish, the bills at the bottom of the stack are yours to spend. Wrap up the four dimes and any left-over wax and incense ashes in a piece of red cloth. Secure it with red thread and tie it up tight. Bury it in your yard, near your front door.

The Lodestone is now "trained" to keep your money. Put it in a drawer, a lock-box, or your cash register. Every night pull all your bills of $20.00 denomination or more, sign them, dress them, and put them under the Lodestone; then take out the 7-day old bills from the bottom of the stack.

Spend the trained money and replace it with new money daily so the Lodestone is always keeping money for you. As time goes by, there are more and more $20.00 bills under the Lodestone. If the stack gets TOO high, you can always start in again with $100.00 bills.

"How to Draw Money and How to Keep Money" was Lucky Mojo Shop Hand-Out No. 8 from 2002. These spells were derived from tricks i learned in Oakland during my teens, and also include an idea from Brother Felix, a rootworker in Georgia. A variant version of the "14-Day Lodestone Spell" can be found in "Hoodoo in Theory and Practice" at LuckyMojo.com/magneticsand.html and a variation of the "Money Stay With Me" spell is online at LuckyMojo.com/moneystaywithme.html.

GAMBLING CHARMS AND LUCKY NUMBERS
catherine yronwode

GAMBLING MAGIC CHARMS

Here is a handy list of some of the most popular lucky gambling charms, amulets, talismans for those who play games of chance. All of them are illustrated at the Lucky W Amulet Archive, a repository of world-wide curios.

Alfalfa: Carried in a mojo hand for money luck.

Alkanet Root Bark: To prevent jealous losers from jinxing you or your winnings.

Alligator Tooth: An old Southern charm; fragile, but powerful to renew money.

Alligator Foot: Its "grasping action" and odd look make it a popular key ring charm.

Allspice Berries: Carried in a mojo hand for money drawing luck.

Anvil Dust: Iron dust collected from a blacksmith's anvil area, used to feed Lodestones.

Aunt Sally's Lucky Dream Spiritual Supplies: Oil, Powder, Incense, and Bath Salts for gaming luck.

Badger Tooth: An old German- American charm; wear it on the left side of the body.

Bat Heart: Wrapped in red silk cloth and worn on the left arm or in the armpit.

Bayberry Root: Carried in a mojo hand for money drawing luck.

Black Cat: The famous Black Cat Bone is used to rule a lover, for invisibility, and for luck.

Buckeye: Carried to prevent rheumatism or fixed with quicksilver for gambling.

Candles: Some burn candles at home while at the casino to "back them up" in luck.

Chamomile Hand Wash: Tea made from golden flowers cleans the hands for money.

Charm Bracelet: One way to wear or carry a multitude of lucky amulets.

Cinnamon Chips: Carried in a mojo for money luck.

Dice Showing Number 7: A Five-Spot plus Snake Eyes makes a Lucky 7 charm.

Fast Luck spiritual supplies: Used for sexual luck and on money for gaming luck.

Five-Finger Grass: A lucky gambler's herb often carried in a Mojo Hand.

Four-Leaf Clover: Pressed flat in the wallet to draw money, health, luck, and love.

Gamblers' Gold Lucky 7 Hand Wash: An herbal wash to cleanse the hands for play.

Good Luck Spiritual Supplies: Oil, Powder, Incense, and Bath Salts for all-around good luck.

Horseshoe: Hung over the door for protection and luck to all who dwell within.

Horseshoe with Horse Head: Much loved by those who play the ponies.

Horseshoe Plastic Key Ring: A lucky talisman from Mexico.

Hoyt's Cologne: Sprinkled on the body or worn as an after-shave while betting or gaming.

Japanese Lucky Seven Spiritual Supplies: An invocation to the seven Japanese deities of luck.

John the Conqueror Root: Carried in the pocket for good luck in money and love.

Lady Luck Spiritual Supplies: A special scent worn by lady bettors and gamblers, not by men.

Lodestone: Magnetic iron ore used to "draw" money, luck, or whatever is desired.

Lucky Buddha Spiritual Supplies: An invocation to Hotei the Lucky Buddha.

Lucky Hand Root: A rare Orchid root shaped like a hand, to bring in the winnings.

Lucky Hand Spiritual Supplies: Made with Lucky Hand Root and used to dress money.

Lucky Mojo Spiritual Supplies: Oil, Powder, Incense, and Bath Salts for gambling luck.

Lucky Number Spiritual Supplies: A formula for conjure goods employed by lottery players.

Lucky 13 Spiritual Supplies: A blend of 13 different money-drawing and luck-bringing essences.

Magnetic Sand: Fine iron dust used to feed Lodestones, including small ones in a mojo.

Mojo Bag: A tied and fixed flannel or leather bag containing lucky roots and curios.

Money Bag Charm: A charm in the shape of a money bag is good luck jewelry.

Money Drawing Spiritual Supplies: Oil, Powder, Incense, and Bath Salts to attract money.

Money Stay With Me Spiritual Supplies: Oil, Powder, Incense, and Bath Salts to keep money.

Number 7: Always a lucky number, and an image of the numeral is worn as a charm.

Number 13: Lucky 13 on a charm bracelet, "Reverse Bad Luck" to those who take risks.

Nutmeg: Carried in the pocket while playing at games of chance.

Playing Cards Charm: Worn as a talisman on an American charm bracelet.

Policy Players' Dream Books: Books of lucky betting numbers for lottery play.

Pyrite: Sparkling golden iron ore that attracts money to it; carried in the pocket.

Rabbit Foot: The ultimate down-home Southern amulet, carried as a key ring charm.

Raccoon Penis Bone (Coon Dong): Wrapped in a $20.00 bill to keep on winning.

Skull Charm: A symbol of daring the odds; a gambler's lucky charm or key chain ornament.

Silver Dime: Protection against conjure and assurance of luck in money matters.

Slot Machine Charm: A gambler's lucky charm or key ring ornament for casino play.

LUCKY NUMBERS FOR GAMES OF CHANCE

Lucky numbers for playing games of chance can be found by various means, including the numerology of names, dreams, hunches, things you see during the day, birth dates, or clairvoyant reading.

The use of lucky numbers is popular among those who play lotteries in which players are allowed to select number-combinations, but lucky numbers are also used by racetrack gamblers to help determine which races to play and which horse to bet on in a given race, and by casino bettors to select which table to sit at when playing games of chance.

LOTTERY NUMBERS FROM DREAMS

Numerological dream books are commonly used by folks to provide lucky betting numbers from what is seen in their dreams. Gamblers who are deeply into number-play may also utilize "run-downs," "work-outs," or "system" numerology books in which new numbers for playing on subsequent days are derived from previous lucky dream numbers or from previously bet numbers that have hit lucky.

There are dozens of numerological dream books and run-down or work-out books available to the public. Some of these dream books include divinatory interpretations for the dream-images alongside the lucky numbers, while others only supply a string of numbers, which allows the authors to fit more dreams into the same number of pages. Work-out and run-down books generally provide the reader with an array of classic and traditional numerological methods to transform today's winning number into tomorrow's preferred pick.

CATCHING NUMBERS TO BET AND PLAY

Dream books specifically designed for lottery play may provide interpretations of dreams, but they also have lucky numbers for you to bet derived from what you dream. Lucky dream numbers are often believed to be the best numbers not only for betting, but also to use as telling "signs" of the kind of luck you will have on certain days, at certain addresses, and in dealing with certain people.

There are many popular dream books in print, undercover classics utilized by folks who like to combine gambling play with signs and significations from hoodoo, conjuration, and rootwork:

- **Aunt Sally's Policy Players Dream Book**
- **Billy Bing's Dream Book**
- **H. P. Dream Book by Prof. Konje (H. G. Parris)**
- **Kansas City Kitty Dream Book**
- **Madam Fu-Fu's Lucky Number Dream Book**
- **Pick 'Em Dream Book by Rajah Rabo**
- **Rajah Rabo's 5 Star Mutuel Dream Book**
- **Rajah's Lucky Number Dream Book**
- **Stella's Lucky Seven Star Dream Book**
- **Stella's Success from Dreams Numbers Book**
- **True Fortune Teller: Dreams and Numbers**

NUMBER SYSTEM BETTING BOOKS

For those who play the numbers regularly, steadily, and often, the numbers themselves acquire symbolism, not merely in terms of dreams, but in terms of odds-busting "runs" or "patterns," whereby old winning numbers can be used to derive new numbers on the verge of catching.

There are many systems by which players work with numerical derivatives, including run-downs (mathematically derived numbers), work-outs (numbers derived from repeated patterns), "relative" (frequently and infrequently winning) numbers, and "following" (subsequent) numbers.

Famous run-down and work-out systems include:

- **Billy Bing's Red Book of Relative Numbers**
- **Billy Bing's Work-Out Book**
- **Billy Bing's Gold Book**
- **Prof. Hitt's Ready Reference Rundowns**
- **Pro-Zo's Authentic Gold Book by Prof. Zonite**
- **Rabo's Rundown and Workout Book**
- **Lucky Three Wisemen Run-Down / Work-Out**

NUMEROLOGY

Numerology refers to any system of correlation between letters and numbers. The numbers may be assigned symbolic meanings and they may be used for character analysis, divination, the making of charms and talismans, and to predict future events.

THE NUMEROLOGY OF NAMES

When working out the numerology of names, all the letters that make up a person's complete name are coded into numbers and added together. In English-alphabet numerology the first name "Tom" is 20 + 6 + 13, for a total of 39. The digits 3 + 9 = 12. The digits 1 + 2 = 3; thus Tom's lucky number is 3.

BIRTH DATE NUMEROLOGY

Reducing dates to numbers is simpler than working with names or words, because each day, month, and year is already assigned a calendar number. For instance, May 12, 1947 is expressed as 5-12-1947 and these numbers, when summed up, equal 11, making this the birth date of a mystically inclined or spiritually gifted person who, by further reduction of 1 + 1 = 2, is also an adaptable and considerate partner and team-member. Combinations of 11 and 2, such as 2-11-22, are recommended for betting.

NUMEROLOGY FROM THE BIBLE

Although many consider it sacrilegious to consult the Bible for lottery numbers, there are some who attest to its efficacy. Pray the 23rd Psalm, open the Bible at random, pick a word at random, derive its total number on the A = 1, B = 2 system, total up the digits, and repeat as many times as necessary to obtain the number of units in the lottery that you play.

LUCKY NUMBERS FROM A READER

Some hoodoo psychics are gifted to pick lucky numbers for clients. In doing so, they may use any of the popular numerology systems to select the numbers, or devise their own unique systems. They may take the client's name-numbers, birth date, address, telephone number, or even social security number into account during computation or they may derive numbers by card cutting, from the client's dreams, or from their own clairvoyant visions.

No reputable hoodoo psychic reader will promise that the lucky numbers he or she selects for a client are guaranteed to hit, but many clients do ask for numbers, and readers who have a gift for this form of work are always glad to give them out, usually as part of a longer reading.

It is the custom that if the numbers a reader gives out are played by the client and they do hit, the client gives a tip to the reader and receives his or her next set of numbers in exchange, without paying a fee.

I wrote this flyer for Ms. Robin York's 2010 "Gambling Charms and Lucky Numbers," workshop, which was an encore of her undocumented 2008 presentation on the same topic. Ms. Robin is a member of the Association of Independent Readers and Rootworkers and can also be contacted for readings or spiritual work at her own RobinsMojo.com web site.

ROSE OF JERICHO: THE RESURRECTION PLANT
Susan Diamond and Auntie Sindy Todo

The Rose of Jericho plant grows in desert environments in North Africa, Egypt, Israel, Iraq, Jordan, Pakistan, Iran and even in some areas of South and North America. It's commonly known as the Resurrection Plant.

When there is no water around, it curls into a tight ball and seems dead. When there is water or it rains, the ball uncurls and turns green again.

LEGENDS AND LORE IN VARIOUS TRADITIONS

According to Christian legend, it is said that the Virgin Mary blessed the eternal plant during her and Joseph's flight to Egypt. In Spain, it is traditionally connected to the Holy Trinity.

It is sought for in the Holy Land by pilgrims as a holy relic. Some are kept in the family and are passed on to the next generation and are brought out at Christmas and Easter time along with other decorations to represent Christ's resurrection.

It is used by those practicing hoodoo, Voodoo, and Santeria for money workings.

In Voodoo it is sometimes used to conjure spirits to induce possession and then bring the person back from possession.

In Santeria and other Yoruba traditions, the plant is said to be sacred to the Orisha Chango and is placed on the altar dedicated to the Orisha. It is used as an ingredient in powders, incense, oils and baths.

Your Resurrection Plant should be treated with respect and honour in your home because according to some traditions, especially in the Middle East, the plant contains a desert spirit which, if not respected, could cause harm to the owner. If the plant is respected, then the spirit will bless the home and be helpful to the owner.

The Resurrection Plant can serve as a living symbol of one's confidence in nature's power to resurrect and bring life to that which seems dead and lifeless.

MAGICAL USAGES

The Rose of Jericho is said to erase negative influences and bring peace, harmony, and abundance. It represents new beginnings, hope, re-birth, happiness, and prosperity in one's life.

If a piece of it is carried on a person it is thought to absorb negative energy and to promote a long and healthy life.

If the plant or a piece of it is kept in the home in a bowl of water, it is said that you will have all the blessings that life can bring.

Another way of working with it is to have it serve as a healing or regenerative "bed" or "cocoon" for a person or pet in need, by placing a representation of them inside. Allow it to dry and restore it again.

The plant can be used as a living altar with various items placed on it, such as coins, crystals, talismans, etc.

It makes a fabulous travel altar by allowing it to close up with your items neatly maintained inside. You simply add water when you get to your destination and voila! insta-altar.

It is also wonderful for blessing and holding petition papers and blends nicely with an outdoor environment for private workings.

CARE OF YOUR RESURRECTION PLANT

You will want to allow Rose of Jericho to dry up from time to time, in order to avoid mould. The length of time would depend on where you live, humidity and temperature being a factor.

A general rule of thumb is to allow to it dry out after one week of being kept open in water.

"Rose of Jericho" was a 2012 workshop flyer. Auntie Sindy Todo is the proprietor of Todo Mojo in Seattle, Washington, and online at TodoMojo.com. Susan Diamond is the proprietor of Serpent's Kiss in Santa Cruz, California, and online at Serpents-Kiss.com.

PROSPERITY CHARMS FOR USE WITH A ROSE OF JERICHO
catherine yronwode

These charms may be set into a Rose of Jericho when it is open and kept in it as it closes.

HORSESHOE CHARM

Originally a protective and apotropaic charm, the horseshoe has, through its association with horse-racing, become a lucky sign of both protection and wealth attained through luck.

MONEY BAG CHARM

The money bag marked with a $ sign (or, in Europe, with a large number such as 1,000 or 10,000) is an amulet of direct simplicity. It represents exactly what it is, plenty of money.

FOUR-LEAF CLOVER CHARM

A four-leaf clover is said to bring luck to the bearer in four different ways, often defined as luck in love, luck in money, luck in health, and luck in the home.

CROWN CHARM

The crown of rulership brings self-assurance, will power, leadership qualities, and recognition in your career search, while you are being evaluated, on the job, in school, or on stage.

KEY CHARM

A key opens the door to new possibilities; it opens doors and symbolizes road opening and the gaining of access to life's great treasure-stores of prosperity and plenty.

DICE AS CHARMS

A pair of dice is always lucky, because it demonstrates the potential for winning; If the pair is set up showing number 7 (either 5 plus 2 or 3 plus 4), it is a form of gambler's luck.

MONEY TREE CHARM

Money growing on trees represents ease of acquisition, as if, instead of labouring by the sweat of our brows, we could reach up and pluck money as one would a ripe fruit.

COINS AS CHARMS

In folk magic, images of money are often used in spells to draw more money and thus a "lucky" coin may be carried, placed on the altar, or added to a mojo to attract financial good fortune. A small Chinese cash coin will fit inside the plant, as will a British West Africa half-penny. The latter bears a protective Star of David and is used to bring in money and to protect it.

LODESTONE GRIT AS A CHARM

Lodestones — naturally magnetic iron ore — are prized for their "drawing" power. They are a vital ingredient in hoodoo practice; in Latin America they are known as "piedra iman."

PYRITE GRAVEL AS A CHARM

Pyrite is a mineral held in high regard as a powerful amulet and luck charm used for the purpose of bringing good fortune in business, money matters, and games of chance.

LUCKY 7 CHARM

Lucky 7 images derive from the dice game of craps, where an initial roll of 7 wins, but there is more to the luck of 7, for it represents the Seven Sacred Planets of ancient religion and magic.

GLASS EYE BEAD AS A CHARM

A small glass bead in the form of an eye (usually blue) is a traditional protective charm whose efficacy is widely attested to in many nations. It guards against jealousy and the evil eye, and in this case, against those who may envy your money-luck or wealth.

To prolong the life of your Rose of Jericho, do not overload it with metal charms, and do not add any bath salts or conjure oils to its water.

"Prosperity Charms for Use With a Rose of Jericho" was my flip-side of the hand-out for Sindy Todo's and Susan Diamond's 2012 Rose of Jericho workshop. The text is from my 1994 online book "The Lucky W Amulet Archive" at LuckyMojo.com/luckyw.html and most of the charms described are available at the Lucky Mojo Curio Co. in Forestville, California, and online at LuckyMojo.com.

HOW TO MAKE AND USE MIRROR BOXES
catherine yronwode

REVERSING TRICKS: THE BASIC ELEMENTS

Reversing tricks are intended to send back to someone whatever was sent to you or your client. They can be performed as a prophylactic, to ward off suspected curses, and if no evil was intended, no evil will befall the target. They can also be used as a form of ethical revenge, whereby a curse is returned to a known enemy. Elements commonly found in reversing spells include:

- **Black Candles:** Solid black or double action.
- **Reversed or Butted Lights:** Candles burned upside down.
- **Oils Stroked Away:** Reversing Oil stroked toward the enemy.
- **Mirrors:** Candle base, tied mirror pairs, mirror box.
- **Mirror-Writing:** Names written backwards.
- **Reversed petitions:** Folded away or upside down.
- **Photos reversed:** Photographs face down or faced toward a mirror.
- **Hot or Spiky Herbs, Toxic Minerals:** Red Pepper, Black Pepper, sulphur.
- **Reversing Animals:** Crab or Crayfish; they "walk backwards."
- **Stern Prayers:** Scriptural justification or reversal.

REVERSING CANDLE SPELL: ONE MIRROR

A simple mirror spell of reversal makes use of a mirror as a base on which to burn a double action candle. The coloured tip is cut off ("butted") and a new tip carved on the black end. The enemy's name is carved backwards (in "mirror writing") on the black portion, from center to end, and the client's name is carved forwards on the coloured portion, from center to end. (The two names are "back to back.")

The candle is dressed from center to each end with Reversing Oil and set upside-down on a mirror. The enemy's photo, if available, is face down on the mirror under the candle. The candle and mirror may be further dressed with Crab shell powder, sprinkled counter-clockwise to undo any evil. The black portion of the candle burns away first, leaving the coloured portion for the restoration of health, love, or luck.

REVERSING SPELL: TWO TIED MIRRORS

Get two small square or round mirrors. Have a photo of the enemy, plus hair, fingernail clippings, or other concerns. Make a small colour copy of the photo and use it as your petition paper, writing the name and your command on the back. Draw arrows in the four corners of the name-paper, pointing outward.

Dress the corners with Reversing Oil, blended with a specific condition oil such as Stop Gossip Oil or Fiery Wall of Protection Oil. In this example, we will add Stop Gossip Oil, and petition accordingly. Place a pinch of Red Pepper in the packet, along with personal concerns, saying, *"May your lying words burn in your mouth if you ever speak ill of me again!"* Fold the paper away from you, photo side out, and turn it and fold it again.

Set the name-paper packet in the middle of one mirror and say, *"May all you say about me reflect your evil back to you!"* Place the other mirror on top and tie the two mirrors together with black thread, as if wrapping a package. Lay the trick where the target will have to walk over it.

REVERSING SPELL: THE MIRROR BOX

A reversing spell burned on a candle can be completely effective, but it will not stop a recurrence of the problem if you are working against a persistent enemy. A tied spell with two mirrors is also extremely potent, but, being a form of foot-track magic, it requires that the trick be laid where the enemy will walk over it. If the enemy is persistent and foot-track tricks cannot be employed, then you can bind your enemy up in a mirror-box spell. This will keep everything evil they do bouncing back to them, hurting them each time they try to hurt someone else.

The mirror box is a form of container spell, in which all the mirror surfaces are turned inward. When a spiritual worker wants to bind the client's enemy into the box and reverse his curses back, a fixed and prepared doll-baby represents the enemy, and it is placed inside a mirror box.

Typically, the doll is laid on a bed of painful and hot herbs, dressed with coercive oils and powders, then enclosed within the box to suffer the reflected consequences of any evil work that is being sent out.

The mirror box is sealed, and it may be kept while it is worked over, but it is common to deploy it burial in a cemetery in the care of a spirit of the dead, and left in place to continue the reversing for as long as the enemy lives. Mirror boxes are usually prepared for clients by experienced hoodoo rootwork practitioners.

THE DOLL

To work this trick you will need a doll-baby to represent your enemy. You can use any kind of doll you like. The doll may be sewn out of the person's clothing, or it may be made of rope, twigs, clay, corn husks, or baked bread, in the form of a human being. If you cannot make or buy a doll, get a black candle in the figure of a person or the Devil, carve the enemy's name on it and use that as an effigy.

Try to obtain something personal of the enemy — hair, a photo, or the like — and incorporate it into the making of the doll. The doll should be baptized and linked to the enemy in the usual way.

THE TYPE OF MIRRORS TO USE

You will need a small box that will just hold the doll-baby or effigy. It need not be large and it can be made of wood, chipboard, or cardboard. It must have a lid.

Go to a store where mirrors are sold and buy one without looking in it yourself. This is difficult; but be sure to not look. If there is a stack of similar mirrors, just take one from behind the front or top one, so you don't look in it. You can glance at the mirrors "squint-eye," but do not gaze or stare into them.

Alternatively, buy tiny mirror tiles of the type sold in craft stores for mosaic work, or buy six 3" or 4" round or square mirror-tile coasters.

The shape of the mirror makes no difference at all. Mirror box spells may be made with neatly cut pieces of mirror, broken shards of mirror, square mirrors, round mirrors, or mirror mosaic pieces. You simply need to have enough mirror glass or as many mirrors or mirror tiles to get at least some mirror on each of the six interior surfaces of the box — the four sides, the bottom, and the top.

SETTING UP FOR THE WORK

You will work by the light of a candle that has been dressed with Reversing oil. If the mirror box is for protection in addition to reversing curses, you may wish to blend Fiery Wall of Protection Oil with the Reversing Oil on the candle. Don't add any "death oils," though. This is a reversing box, not a killing box. Keep your intentions clear.

Jumbo candles are better for shedding light and for dripping wax to use in sealing your work than glass vigil lights, and much preferable for this sort of application. You can use a plain black jumbo, a double action candle that's been butted and stood on its head, or a black-over-red-core reversing candle. You may work within an area marked by four 4" candles dressed with Protection Oil.

You may set your working light on a mirror tile to further protect yourself from the enemy's prying eyes as you work. Observe any unusual changes in the candle as it burns; flaring, smoking, sparking, or other "dangerous" indications will warn you that the enemy is aware of you and is fighting back.

PREPARING THE MIRRORS

If you bought a large mirror, turn it face down, take a hammer and break it into pieces, still without looking into it. If you like, you may write the target's name backwards on the back of the glass (in reverse or "mirror" writing") with a Sharpie marker, then call seven years of bad luck on the enemy as you crack the glass. Since you didn't look into the mirror, the "seven years of bad luck" from breaking it will not be yours, but will go to the person whose name you wrote.

Alternatively, use glass cutters to craft pieces of mirror that will just fit your box as you line it on all six interior surfaces.

If you bought six small square mirror mosaic tiles, you need do nothing with them beyond taking them from their packaging. The same is true if you bought six square mirror tiles or coasters.

CONSTRUCTING THE MIRROR BOX

Glue the broken, or neatly cut, or mosaic pieces of mirror into the bottom, sides, and lid of the box — still without looking. My preferred glue for such work is a brand called Goop; it is sticky, flexible, relatively fast-setting, and makes a very tight bond to a variety of surfaces.

If you bought six 4-inch mirror tiles or coasters, you can use duct tape to join them together to make an open box with all the mirrors facing inward. The sixth mirror is kept to one side to make the lid of the box.

If the mirrors catch your reflection while you work, you may want to clean your reflection out. Sprinkle salt into the mirror box, pray for it to be made clean, and pour the salt out.

THE BED OF PAIN

Having made the box, you will next create within it a bed of pain, using any or all of these items:

- Blackberry leaves and spiny stems
- Nails, needles, and pins, stuck upward through black cloth
- Cactus spines or pads (especially Opuntia spp.)
- Red Pepper pods or flakes; Black Pepper powder
- Spiny Euphorbia or Acacia ("Crown of Thorns") stems

PLACING THE DOLL IN THE BOX

Put the prepared doll-baby in the box upon the bed of pain, face-up. Sprinkle or place any of the following over it, singly or in combination.

- Red Pepper powder
- Vandal Root chunks
- Sulphur powder
- Alum powder (for stopping loose speech)
- Reversing, Crossing, Revenge, Damnation, Destruction, and/or D.U.M.E. Sachet Powders
- Goofer Dust
- Tarantula Spider exoskeleton to hold 'em down

As you work, pray each step of the way. Call on God to protect you or your client by sending every bad thought and bad action back to the enemy, and to bind the enemy in a web of his own deceit and hostility so that he can never harm you or your client again. While sprinkling the doll, say:

"Here you are, [Name], and here you will stay, and from this time forth, all the crossed conditions you try to bring about, and all the jinxes you try to make, all the foul words that you use, and all the evil that you do will come back to you as these mirrors reflect your image back to you — and in this Hell of your own devising you will burn until God releases you in judgement, Amen."

Be specific in your prayer.

TAKING THE BOX TO THE GRAVEYARD

Close the box, tie the lid down with string, finish it with knots, seal the knots with wax from your working candle, and carry the "coffin" to a graveyard. Ask for help to hold your enemy down, and when you find a strong spirit who will help, pay him with dimes. Dig a hole by his right hand and bury the box, saying:

"I bring you the spirit of [Name] in a box. I want you to hold his evil under your strong right hand until i call for him again, or until his body joins his spirit under the ground."

Bury the box, walk away, and don't look back. Go home by a different route than the one you came by.

CLEANING UP

Mirror box work consists of laying a coercive trick, even in a good cause, so when you get home, perform a 13 Herb cleansing bath, Uncrossing bath, or Hyssop herb bath. Recite the 51st Psalm for purification and removal of any sin you have committed.

ALTERNATIVE: THE FLAT MIRROR BURIAL

If you don't have time to make a full-on mirror box and a doll-baby, you can do similar work with two flat mirrors and a full-length photo of the target. Cut out their image to use as a "paper doll." Write the name and birth date on the back, and cross it with your command. Sprinkle it with Agrimony and Reversing powder. Place it between the two mirrors, reflective sides inward. Tie the mirrors together like a package, making a knot every time you cross the starting point. Seal the knots by dripping wax on them from your working candle. The packet is buried in a graveyard.

ALTERNATIVE: THE BOX ON THE ALTAR

If you intend to work with the mirror box on your altar before (or instead of) burying it, you can disguise it a bit. Use a fancy gift box or decorate a plain wood box by gluing a pretty picture and fancy trim to the box lid. No one will see what is inside the box.

"How to Make and Use Mirror Boxes" was adapted from "Hoodoo in Theory and Practice" and distributed at Robin Petersen's "Make a Mirror Box" workshop in 2011. Robin's custom mirror-boxes are beautifully crafted works of hoodoo art and are sold through LuckyMojo.com.

A TRADITIONAL BREAK-UP SPELL IN A BOTTLE
catherine yronwode

IS THIS SPELL RIGHT FOR YOU?

This Break-Up Bottle spell is alleged to cause discord between lovers. It may result in divorce between married people. It is an aggressive, coercive spell. If it succeeds, you may cause people to cry, partners to lose their homes, children to lose contact with their parents. Be sure this is what you wish to do.

There is no one set "Break Up Bottle" spell — so in these instructions you will find several ways of working which are different from one another. All of these variations have been gathered from old-time practitioners in various parts of the South and West.

Some variations may suit your physical situation and location better than others. Some variations may be more overtly harmful than others. This spell is presented in several degrees of severity, allowing you to choose just how much trouble you want to make for the persons upon whom you are working.

INGREDIENTS

- 1 black figural Break Up (Divorce) candle,
- 1 thin black candle
- 1 bottle Break Up Oil
- 1 packet Hot Foot Powder
- 1 packet Inflammatory Confusion Powder
- 1 packet Break Up Sachet Powder
- 1 packet Break Up Incense Powders
- 1 bottle 4 Thieves Vinegar (or Urine, or both)
- 1 Break-Up bottle containing:
     9 Pins, 9 Needles, 9 Nails,
     Black Dog Hair, Black Cat Hair
- 1 packet Break Up Crystal Salts
- 2 White Offertory candles
- 1 packet Hyssop Herb
- 1 packet Devil's Shoe Strings Curio
- 1 packet Devil Pod Curio

PREPARATION:
PERSONAL ITEMS AND PAPER

In addition to the items here, you will need something personal from both parties, and a name paper, which will also function as a petition paper.

PERSONAL CONCERNS

In order to link a magical spell to the person or persons it is intended to affect, we make use of a type of folk-magical element generally known as a magical link. In hoodoo, the magical link is called a personal concern.

Personal concerns comprise items such as hair, footprint-dirt, menstrual blood, semen, fingernail clippings, photos, business card, or the like. The more intimate the better. This spell, like most others that are intended to affect other people, works less often without the personal items. You can try it, anyway, but that's just how it is: If you have their stuff, you've really got them.

NAME PAPER AS PETITION PAPER

Write their full names on two pieces of paper 9 times. Use black ink for the one you want to have get away and red ink for the one you want to stay near you. Use black ink for both, if you want both parties to get away.

Some workers write both names 9 times side-by side in two columns on a single piece of paper, then cut the names apart, creating two pieces of paper, petitioning for their break-up while cutting the paper.

Whatever personal items you use, wrap them up in the name-papers. Fold the paper away for the one you want to have get away and fold the paper toward you for the one you want to stay near you. Fold both away, if you want both to get away. These packets will be referred to as "the couple's personal items."

DOING THE JOB

If you work by the moon, then work during the waning of the moon.

Make the Break Up Incense Powders into cones (use a twist of paper, pack the incense in with your finger, and turn it out of the cone).

On the black divorce candle carve the couple's full names with the words BREAK UP between their names. Dress the candle with Break Up Oil and sprinkle it with Break Up Powder.

For each of the next seven days burn a portion of the incense and one section of the candle. Pinch the candle out between times, never blow it out. During these seven days, you will make and work the bottle.

The bottle contains 9 Pins, 9 Needles, 9 Rusty Nails, the hair of a Black Dog, and the hair of a Black Cat. These are to cause pain, anger, emotional incompatibility, distance, and quarreling between the couple so that they will "fight like cats and dogs" and seek to part from each other.

You have three types of powders. Each is alleged to produce a certain effect. Hot Foot Powder is to drive someone away. Inflammatory Confusion Powder is to cause angry misunderstandings. Break Up Powder is to split two people apart. Choose 1, 2, or all 3 powders; blend them together if you want.

Mix the couple's personal items with the powder(s) you have chosen, then put the mix in the bottle with the other items. You may add Four Thieves Vinegar to the bottle to "sour" the couple's relationship. You may urinate in the jar, symbolically "pissing on them." You may combine Four Thieves Vinegar and urine, if you wish. You may add dog feces (not supplied). You may burn a thin black candle carved with both names (not touching) in the neck of the bottle before stopping it up. Regardless of what you add to the bottle or whether you burn a black candle in it, as you prepare it, pray aloud for the couple's anger and their break-up in your own words or in the name of your God or Saint.

LAYING THE TRICK

This bottle spell may be deployed to lay the trick.

Bury it under the their house or in their path: Like many African spells, this is a form of "foot-track" magic and is activated when it is walked over. If you can't put the bottle under their doorstep or near their home, you may try something that is said to be less effective but to work some of the time:

Hide it in a hollow tree: Pray they can't find it.

Carry it to a graveyard and bury it: Pay the owner of the grave where you bury it with coins or whiskey and pray for the death of their relationship.

Carry it to a crossroads and throw it in: Pray for them to travel apart from each other.

Throw it into running water: Pray to have them both carried out of your life.

SHAKING UP THE BOTTLE

Another way to use a bottle spell to break up a couple is to fill it as above, including vinegar or urine, and when you want to set the couple to quarreling, just stand and shake the bottle, cursing their relationship as you do it. A shaken bottle may never be deployed, or deployment may be long delayed. The bottle is stored in the bathroom upside down behind he toilet when not in use.

Shaking is favoured by root-doctors who work for clients and cannot get close enough to the couple's home to bury the bottle. The worker picks a certain time of day to shake the bottle and curse the couple. This is a slower process, because it is the root-doctor's will-power, not walking over the bottle, that sets it to working, but in the hands of a powerful practitioner, this has been known to bring about a divorce.

CLEANING UP

You don't want to keep any left-overs from work like this in your house. Wrap up any left-over candle wax, incense ashes, and unused materials in a piece of black cloth. Secure it with black thread and tie it. Throw it out at a crossroads or bury it in a graveyard.

PURIFICATION AND PROTECTION

Because breaking folks up is an Enemy Trick, you must cleanse yourself and protect from retribution.

To take off your sin, prepare a bath by steeping the Hyssop Herb in a pot of boiling rain water or spring water. Light the two white candles, stand between them, and pour the Hyssop bath over your head while reciting the 51st Psalm ("Cleanse me with Hyssop; wash me and I shall be whiter than snow").

For protection, drive the 9 Devil's Shoe Strings into the dirt across the path to your door-step to tangle up anyone who may try to retaliate and cross you. Put the Devil Pod outside or behind your door to repel any evil work that may be directed toward you.

"A Traditional Break-Up Spell in a Bottle" was Lucky Mojo Shop Hand-Out No. 9, adapted in 2002 from my 1995 book "Hoodoo in Theory and Practice." It was distributed in 2009 at Lara Rivera's "Container Spells" workshop and in 2010 it was incorporated into a longer and much more detailed hand-out for shop customers titled "How to Make and Use Bottle Spells." Portions of it are found online at LuckyMojo.com/bottlespells.html.

D.U.M.E. SPELL WITH A BLACK CANDLE
catherine yronwode

IS THIS THE RIGHT SPELL FOR YOU?

This spell is alleged to cause trouble, pain, and even death to an enemy. It is not guaranteed to work, and it is recommended that you think every seriously about your needs and desires before undertaking this type of work. It is best to work this spell in justified revenge, not out of anger. The oil that is used to dress the candle is called D.U.M.E. — which is pronounced DOOM and actually stands for Death Unto My Enemies.

INGREDIENTS

- 1 Black figural candle, which can be any of these:
  - Black nude figure (Adam or Eve)
  - Black genitalia (penis or vulva)
  - Black Devil
  - Black skull
  - Black Sabbatic Goat
- 1 bottle D.U.M.E oil

PREPARATION

This candle spell can be used by itself or, if you prefer, it can be used in conjunction with a bottle spell to harm the enemy. A simple bottle spell can be made by putting the enemy's name in Vinegar or War Water (or a mix of the two, which is called War Vinegar), closing up the jar, and standing your candle on top of the jar. You may burn this mess in the bathroom rather than on your altar.

With or without a bottle beneath it, you will now prepare a petition paper for the candle. Write the enemy's full name on the paper nine times. Use black ink. If you don't know the name, use a descriptive phrase, like:

My Enemy
My Woman's Other Man
That Romanian Whore
The God Damned Thief

Write your command nine times criss-cross across the name, such as:

Die A Miserable, Painful Death,
You God Forsaken Mother Fucker

If you have something personal from the enemy, such as their hair, footprint-dirt, menstrual blood, semen, photo, business card, or the like — the more intimate the better — the spell will have stronger links to the person you with to affect. In my experience, andy kind of spell works less often without personal items as a link, and a death spell, which the target will strongly resist, for obvious reasons, is. You can try it, anyway, but that's just how it is: If you have their stuff, you've really got them.

Whatever personal item you use, wrap it up in the name-paper. Fold the paper away for the you want the party named to get away.

Work during the waning of the moon, if you wish to see the enemy wane in strength and sicken or die.

DOING THE JOB

On the black figural candle of your choice, carve the enemy's full name with the word DEATH between the first and last names — like this:

Joe DEATH Brown

Dress the candle with D.U.M.E. Oil. Place the packet beneath the candle. For each of the next 7 days you will be burning a section of the candle. Pinch the candle out between times, never blow it out. Pour more dressing oil on it each day. During these 7 days, you may also work any other revenge or death spell against this particular enemy that you wish.

As the candle burns, you may heat sewing needles or pins red hot in the light of the flame. Hold them with a piece of leather, cloth, or tweezers so that you don't burn your hand. As each pin or needle is heated, stick it into some part of the figural candle's body, starting with the head and working your way down, and as you do this, call out curses of afflicted on each body part. It is traditional to use a total of 13 pins on a human figure and to use many more pins on a skull candle. You may choose to use more or less as it pleases you to do so.

If you use a human figure candle with 13 pins, it is a good idea to and decide in advance which areas to hit, based upon my consideration of the case. Plan and think about this portion of the work.

115

As to the curse you call on the enemy, you may say it in your own way, but i recommend that you follow the form of making it a "justified" curse, and not one performed out of evil spirit or mean heart.

"John Brown, for all the wickedness and for all the evil you have done to me [or to another, whom you should name], i call upon you the curse of sorrow, pain, and death, if my case is justified.

"Lord, you know what evil [Name] has committed. I now demand that he face Divine justice and retribution, if my case is justified.

"May his mind soften and his memory fail, if my case is justified [pin in head].

"May his eyesight become dim and dark, if my case is justified [pins in eyes].

"May his mouth be unable to speak and his lying words burn on his tongue, if my case is justified [pin in mouth].

"May his lungs develop cancer and his breath come hard, if my case is justified [pin in chest].

"May his heart first break and then suffer complete failure, if my case is justified [pin in heart].

"May his stomach pain him and his food bring him no nourishment, if my case is justified [pin in stomach].

"May his guts be tied in knots and stopped up, if my case is justified [pin in abdomen]."

Continue downward, cursing the enemy's genitals, knees, legs, and feet.

Leave the pins in the candle and they will fall one by one as it burns, Leave them where they fall. Before the candle goes out on its own, take the name packet out from under it and burn it in the candle's flame, then put the candle out by tipping it over into a saucer of Goofer Dust or Graveyard Dirt, cursing as you so so,

"May your days be shortened, if it God's will."

CLEANING UP

You don't want to keep any remnants from work like this in your house. Wrap the remnant candle wax in black cloth. Tie up or secure it with black thread. Collect all the pins or needles and put them in a bottle of Vinegar or War Water. Throw the into mess out at a crossroads, a river, or bury it in a graveyard.

PURIFICATION AND PROTECTION

Because harming or killing folks is not very nice, you may wish to cleanse yourself and ask God for forgiveness from sin if you have transgressed. This is optional, but many people find it a good idea to perform this additional spell after the seven days of D.U.M.E. work.

It is also possible that the person whom you have attacked will seek to mount a magical counter-attack. For this reason, it is customary to place protective elements around the home after doing harmful work. Again, it is not necessary to do it, but many people find it helpful to their peace of mind.

INGREDIENTS

• 1 Packet Hyssop Herb
• 2 White Offertory candles
• 1 Packet Devil's Shoe Strings Curio
• 1 Packet Devil Pod Curio
• 1 Packet Red Pepper Powder
• 1 Packet Graveyard Dirt

To take off your sin, prepare a bath by steeping the Hyssop Herb in a pot of boiling rain water or spring water.

Light the two white candles, stand between them, and pour the Hyssop bath over your head while reciting the 51st Psalm ("Cleanse me with Hyssop; wash me and I shall be whiter than snow").

Alternatively, pour the Hyssop over you in the tub or shower and step out of the bathroom between the two white candles, which you should have lit and burning before you begin the bath.

For protection from the enemy, who may try to come back at you with a spell of his or her own, drive the 9 Devil's Shoe Strings into the dirt across the path to your door-step to tangle up anyone who may try to retaliate and cross you. Sprinkle Red Cayenne Pepper powder mixed with Graveyard Dirt across all the paths that lead to your door. Put the Devil Pod outside or behind your front door to repel any evil work that may be directed toward you.

"D.U.M.E. Spell With a Black Candle" was Lucky Mojo Shop Hand-Out No. 10, published in 2002 and adapted from my 1995 book "Hoodoo in Theory and Practice" at LuckyMojo.com/dume.html. It is based on spells i was taught in candle shops in the 1970s.

CURSING AND SPELL-CASTING WITH DOLLS
Robin York

HISTORY

Dolls and poppets, sometimes called Voodoo dolls, can be found in the magic of most people on Earth. They are considered very powerful in many cultures and are used for good purposes as well as evil by tribal witch doctors, root workers, and hoodoo and obeah practitioners in Trinidad, Brazil, Jamaica, Cuba, Haiti, and the United States.

Poppet is a word for a small doll found among Europeans. The term Voodoo comes from Africa and is used in the African diaspora; it means spirits of the God. In the South the term doll-baby is common.

MATERIALS

Dolls can be created from a variety of materials:

• Commercial toy dolls, especially hollow ones
• Cloth; the colour can be appropriate to the work
• Clothing of the target person
• Leather
• Figural candles
• Wax
• Clay
• Twigs
• Rope
• Feathers
• Wood
• Spanish Moss, twisted and tied, or as a stuffing
• An appropriate spiritual incense, used as a stuffing

PERSONAL ITEMS

All dolls are personalized with items either placed inside or affixed to the outside of the figure. The more personal these items are, the stronger will be the link to the person for whom the doll is named.

• Fingernails or toenails
• Hair from any part of the body
• Teeth
• Blood
• Spit
• Sperm
• Personal clothing: socks, underwear, or shirt
• A small copy of a photo of the person's face
• A button from the person's clothes

MAGICAL INGREDIENTS

Dolls may be stuffed with a variety of magically active ingredients selected to have an effect on the person in whose likeness the doll has been made. These include:

• Herbs
• Roots
• Minerals
• Incense Powders
• Goofer Dust
• Graveyard Dirt
• Insects
• Worms
• Snails

The specific items are selected on the basis of how they will affect the doll. For instance, placing Red Pepper in the feet will give the doll a case of "hot foot" and stuffing Poppy Seeds in the head will confuse the person in thought and speech.

The location of the items within the doll will affect the parts with which they come into contact. Pyrite in the hand will bring money. Putting alum in the genitals will result in puckering up those parts so that the person cannot enjoy sex, while alum in the mouth area will silence the person so he cannot testify in court. Likewise, placing Vandal Root in the doll's arm pits will result in bad body odor, but when placed in the mouth area, it will give the person bad breath.

BRINGING THE DOLL TO LIFE

Many people who use dolls for good or evil believe that the spirit of the person is blown into the dolls, and that this can have the influence to make the person's will do whatever the doll maker wants.

Another known technique to link the doll to the target person and bring it to life is to baptize the doll in the target's name.

Whether you give your doll life by blowing breath into the nose or the mouth, by baptizing it, or by cursing it in the target's name, the doll will do the work you bid it to do. It can help or destroy the target, as well as work for you, the practitioner, as you command.

CANDLES AND INCENSE

As you make your doll, you may wish to work by the light of a candle. The candle is also a source of wax which you can drip on the doll or use to seal the doll into a container by drizzling it over knots that are made as you tie the container closed.

Candles available for use come in a array of colours, each appropriate for use on dolls that are made for different conditions and purposes.

Incense is burned on the altar while casting spells in order to set the practitioner's mind on the goals or aims of the work. It can also be used to smoke the doll, as well as to smoke any magical ingredients that will be placed inside the doll.

These are some of the most common combinations of candle colour and incense scent used while working with dolls:

White Candles: These are to be used with doll-babies that are being made for protection, health, and marriage. The incenses used with white candles are Frankincense and Myrrh..

Red Candles: These are used for love. The incense that accompanies these candles is usually one that is formulated for happy loving, such as Come to Me or Love Me, but if it is necessary, you may use a love-domination incense, such as Follow Me Boy, Do As I Say, or Return to Me.

Green Candles: These are used for money, to get jobs, and to win at gambling. Some of the popular incenses that are used with these candles are Fast Luck, Money Drawing, Money Stay With Me, and Prosperity.

Brown Candles: These are used for all court cases and legal matters, including cases where you wish to see true justice done, as well as cases where the target person is guilty but it is your intention to get them to go free, and cases where the party is actually innocent but it is your wish and command that they be convicted anyway. The incenses used with these candles are Court Case, with Law Keep Away added if necessary.

Black Candles: These used for break-ups, to destroy enemies, for evil, and to bring about death. The incense that is used with these candles is Black Arts, Crossing, Damnation, or D.U.M.E. You can mix in Chili Pepper and Black Pepper if you wish.

CURSING THE DOLL

Once the doll has been brought to life with a strong link to the person whom it represents, the true work of commanding and controlling it begins.

It is common to tie the doll's feet and hands together, as a hostage might be tied, in order to limit the target's powers of motion. You may also stick pins or needles into the doll to cause pain. It is traditional to use a total of 13 pins, but the places they are inserted into the doll vary. Typical places to stick them, and the results they are intended to produce:

- **Eyes:** Blindness
- **Mouth:** Silence, bad breath, tooth decay
- **Ears:** Deafness, ringing in the ears
- **Head:** Headaches, cerebral stroke
- **Heart:** Sorrow, heart attack
- **Hands:** Inability to hit anyone
- **Stomach:** Ulcers, vomiting, stomach cancer
- **Intestines:** Gastritis, colon cancer
- **Kidneys:** Kidney stones
- **Womb:** Sterility, miscarriage
- **Genitals:** Painful intercourse, impotence
- **Anus:** Hemorrhoids, piles
- **Hips and Knees:** Arthritis
- **Feet:** Swelling, inability to run away or leave town

While performing this work, you should curse the target thoroughly, stating every reason you are doing so and commanding every result you wish to come to pass. Curse out loud if it is possible for you to do so.

KILLING THE DOLL

It is a common practice, but not necessary, to finish the work of cursing by killing the doll. You may finish off the doll with any of several symbolic deaths:

- **Dismemberment**: Use a razor blade or knife
- **Incineration:** Use lighter fluid and a match
- **Burial at sea:** This represents drowning
- **Hanging:** This gives a shock if the target sees it
- **Running over with a car:** Drench with booze first
- **Placement in a coffin:** Bury it in a graveyard

Performing these simple rituals with a doll can have a powerful effect, so before you begin, be sure that you really want to achieve the results you ask for.

Ms. Robin York wrote this flyer for her 2009 "Cursing With Doll-Babies" workshop. A member of AIRR, she can also be contacted via her own RobinsMojo.com web site.

COURT CASE SPELLS AND LEGAL WORK
catherine yronwode

TIPS FOR THOSE
WHO HAVE BEEN ARRESTED

Here is some tips for those who have been arrested and face court cases, especially those who have been given a court-appointed lawyer. I am not a lawyer and this is not legal advice, just common sense:

1. Do NOT plead guilty at a preliminary hearing. If necessary, you can always plead guilty at a later date. But once you plead guilty it is too late to go back. If you later have to plead guilty, tell the lawyer you only want to plead to a misdemeanour, or what is called "a lesser included offense." THIS IS IMPORTANT! Remember that your lawyer WANTS to do good, but is probably very busy. Tell him you will pray for him and pray that he or she will be able to help you.

2. Make sure that your lawyer understands that there are many people who care about you. If there is anyone you know who could speak about your good character, such as a pastor, coach, teacher, neighbour, employer, or youth group leader, have them write a letter telling the lawyer that they would be glad to testify to your good character. BRING these letters with you to the lawyer. Before you give them, anoint the four corners of each letter with Court Case sachet powders and recite the 35th Psalm over them.

3. If the lawyer refuses to meet with you or breaks appointments often, you may need to write a letter of complaint to the chief public defender. If this does not work, you may need to tell the Judge that you are "not getting adequate representation or effective council." Use these words — but only if all else has failed, because this is risky.

4. Lastly, if the case is going to trial, here are seven practical spiritual techniques that have helped folks in the past:

First, you MUST pray that anyone who has been hurt in any way by this case will forgive you. Pray Psalms 32 aloud once a day. If you are Catholic or work with Saints, pray to El Niño de Atocha.

Second, recite the 35th Psalm aloud at least once a day, for your own good. If you believe that someone is working against you, recite the 37th Psalm.

Third, If any papers are given to you to sign, or you get to hold onto any letters that you or your representatives will send in on your behalf, dress them lightly with Court Case sachet powders, then drag your fingernails through the powder in "wavy snake lines" to mark them, and brush off the excess powder.

Fourth, burn brown candles as you pray (see details below).

Fifth, before going to court, prepare some herbs to carry and a Little John to Chew (also known as Galangal or Court Case Root) to chew while you are in court so that the judge will favour you. (See below for details.)

Sixth, before or on the day of the court appearance, get yourself a beef tongue and slit it open. Get a piece of paper and on it write the name of anyone who will testify against you. Write it nine times. Put the paper inside the tongue with red hot Pepper and pin the tongue with nine pins so it is shut up. (See below for details.)

Seventh, either begin nine days before your court date to recite the 7th Psalm in two portions over a pan of water and wash your face with that water on the day of your court appearance (explained below) or if it is too late for that, then on the day you go to court, bathe early in the morning with Court Case Bath Crystals dissolved in your bath-water or wear clothes (socks at the very least) that have been rinsed in water to which Court Case Bath crystals have been added. You may combine these two bathing and washing rites if you wish.

THE FAMOUS BEEF TONGUE SPELL

To silence a witness, slit a raw beef tongue with a horizontal cut. On a piece of paper write the full name of the witness in red ink, crossing it with the words "SHUT UP!" over the name, nine times in black ink. Cover the paper lightly with Cayenne Pepper powder. Fold the paper away from you and Make similar separate paper for each witness or police officer. insert the papers into the slit tongue. "Stitch" the tongue closed with nine rusty needles or sew it with a needle and thread.

Here are 4 ways to treat the tongue:

1) The Old Southern Way: On the day of the case, boil the tongue with Red Beans, Onions, salt, and Hot Pepper. Have someone at your home to burn brown candles and keep the tongue boiling. If the case is continued, eat the tongue, including the paper. "Eat their name and they can't speak against you."

2) The 20th Century Southern Way: Pack the raw stitched-up tongue in ice blocks and set in a bucket of vinegar just barely covering it. Burn brown candles on the tongue.

3) The Modern Southern Way: Freeze the raw stitched-up tongue in a freezer with alum powder, "freezing the tongue" of the witness; this will last for one year.

4) The Caribbean way: Dress the raw stitched-up tongue with red pepper and put it on the front doorstep of the witness. This will seriously warn them off.

No matter how you handle the tongue, when done with it, bury the needles at a crossroads. Also chew Little John to Chew Root and spit it in the Court-room.

HONEY JAR SPELLS FOR COURT CASE WORK

In addition to shutting up accusers and chewing the root to influence a judge, every court case can use some sweetening — that is, a change of attitude on the part of the judge, the jury, and even the witnesses, so that they come to view you as a nice person and to wish you well and favour your case. The best way to sweeten people in a court case is with a honey jar spell made out in their names.

DRESS YOUR CLOTHES AND CARRY A MOJO IN COURT

In the event that the matter cannot be resolved before it goes to court, bathe or rinse the clothes you will be wearing (or at least your socks) in Court Case Bath Crystals. and carry Deer's Tongue Leaves for your lawyer's eloquence, Calendula Flowers for winning in court, and Little John to Chew Root (also known as Court Case Root) in a mojo bag.

To cause confusion to your enemies, you may add a pinch of Black Mustard Seeds or Black Poppy Seeds to the mojo and a pinch of Confusion Incense Powders.

To protect against slander, gossip, and false accusations, carry a pinch of Slippery Elm Bark in your conjure bag. (Some folks also put a pinch of powdered Slippery Elm Bark into their sewed-tongue stew, too; it is edible and acts as a thickener, like file gumbo.)

Dress the bag with Court Case anointing oil and also wear it on your body as a perfume.

LITTLE JOHN TO CHEW, THE COURT CASE ROOT

In addition to preparing the mojo bag for all the reasons cited above, i find it very helpful to work on the judge's sympathies with a very old spell, utilizing the Little John to Chew Root. To prepare this, simply boil up a piece of Little John to Chew Root in sugar-water until it is quite soft and sweet. The root is spicy, like ginger — to which it is closely related — but it easy enough to chew when prepared in this way. Some people like to keep a brown candle dressed with Court Case Oil burning in the kitchen while they cook the root down.

Take a piece of the prepared root into court with you and chew on it during the hearing or trial, as if you were chewing on gum. Spit a bit of the "cud" on the floor when no one is looking. In the old days, it was said that if you spat this mess where the judge would step in it, he would HAVE to find you "not guilty." This is a form of foot-track magic that would admittedly be difficult to perform in today's high-security courtrooms, but it is worth your time to at least chew the root and discretely get some onto the floor, even if you can't exactly get his foot-print in it. For instance, if you can spit your "cud" in the hall where the judge may walk by, you'd be doing pretty well.

RECITAL OF PSALMS FOR COURT CASES

There are several Psalms that are used in court case work. The most common are Psalms 32 and 35, often recited while setting lights or bathing; Psalms 37, recited if one has accusers whom wants to have brought down; and Psalms 7, which is used in a nine-day rite for the preparation of a face-wash.

"Court Case Spells and Legal Work" was Lucky Mojo Shop Hand-Out No. 16. It was adapted and condensed from the 1995 "Hoodoo in Theory and Practice" web page at LuckyMojo.com/courtcase.html.

BLACK WALNUTS TO FALL OUT OF LOVE WITH AN EX-LOVER
catherine yronwode

A BASIC BLACK WALNUT SPELL

Be sure you want to break the link completely. This is folk-magic, and it works. It is best in Fall, when the Black Walnuts are fresh-harvested. Because it is performed naked, in the dark, it is not suitable for all.

You will need:
- A piece of paper torn from a brown paper bag
- A small pencil with no eraser on it
- Matches
- A black candle — an offertory candle, a taper,or a figural candle of a human being or a devil.
- Black powder incense plus Valerian Root, Red Pepper, and Mullein Leaves, or a black herb-based incense mix such as Black Arts Incense.
- Nine Black Walnuts still in their green husks. or Black Walnuts dried in their husks.
- A silvery metal bowl (stainless steel is okay).

Undress at midnight on a night when the moon is dark. Place the Walnuts in the bowl. Take the supplies into your bathroom. In the dark, with no light, write your ex-lover's name on the paper, and say:

> [Name of Person],
> this is the last time i will write your name!

Light the candle, use the candle to light the incense, look at the name paper and say:

> [Name of Person],
> this is the last time i will see your name!

Fold the paper in half so the name can no longer be seen. Draw a hot bath and throw the nine Black Walnuts into it. The water may turn brownish. Get into the bath with the Walnuts. Pour the dark water over your head nine times and each time you pour it, say:

> [Name of Person],
> i wash you out of my life.

Arise from the bath and pull the plug. As the water runs out, pick up the candle and hold it over the bath water. Take the person's name-paper in your other hand and set it on fire with the candle. As it burns, say:

> [Name of Person],
> i burn you out of my life.

Drop the burning paper into the bath water, wait a brief moment, then plunge the candle upside down into the bath water to extinguish it while you say:

> [Name of Person],
> i extinguish you.

Do not use a towel; let the air dry you. When the water has run out, collect the nine Walnuts (and the husk fragments) and place them back in the bowl. Still naked, walk outside carrying the bowl of Walnuts and throw them away at a crossroads or street intersection or, if that is impossible, throw them against a tree — but be careful to not drop any pieces of them in your own yard. As you throw away the Walnuts, say,

> [Name of Person], you are dead to me
> And dead to me you'll always be
> Wander the world both near and far
> But touch me not, for dead you are!

Carry the empty bowl home without looking back, wash it out, and put it away.

As long as you never write or speak the person's full name again, he or she will remain out of your life and your former love will be broken.

A VARIANT WALNUT SPELL

The same sort of spell can be satisfactorily performed with English or Persian Walnuts (the kind sold in stores), if the Walnuts are prepared first.

Get nine Walnuts and boil them in three quarts of water until the water evaporates down to one quart in volume and turns brown. Then place the Walnuts and their water in the bowl, as described above, and proceed as described except that when it comes time to throw the Black Walnuts into the bath with their husks, throw in the boiled Walnuts with their quart of brown water. The reason that English or Persian Walnuts are boiled first is that without the green husks, and not being Black Walnuts, they are milder, so their essence must be concentrated before use.

"Black Walnuts to Fall Out of Love with an Ex-Lover" was Lucky Mojo Shop Hand-Out No. 11 in 2002.

A SEVEN-STEP CUT-AND-CLEAR SPELL
catherine yronwode

THIS IS FOR THE WOMAN WHO HAS BEEN HURT IN LOVE

1) YES, YOU LOVE HIM.

I know. But that's because YOU are a loving and giving person, not because he is worthy of your love or knows how to return your love in equal measure.

2) YOU WORKED ON HIM AND GOT RESULTS

You got results one time or two times. But the work wears off. The man is still no good, so all you got for that work was the opportunity to waste more of your precious time on a no-good man. Why do i say he's no good? Because the man who is worthy of YOUR love will be your reciprocal equal partner, not some jerk who "isn't in touch with his feelings" or "commitment-phobic" or "irrational" or "can't express himself" or "falls in love too easily" with any Jane Doe he meets. You are making excuses for this guy. Save your energy.

3) HE HAS "STRONG FEELINGS" FOR YOU

Any man so all-fired weak-minded that he will fall in love with a new woman and walk out on you despite his "strong feelings" to the contrary is not worth your energy. If you do a spell to run her off and harness him back this time, he'll do something equally stupid — and maybe worse — later, like walk out on you when you are pregnant or have a little child with him. The man is unreliable and weak-minded. He will break the other woman's heart too, nine chances out of ten, unless she ruins him first.

4) SHE'S WORKING ON HIM

He is not only weak-minded because the other woman is working on him, he also plain doesn't want to grow up. He's strictly after what he wants, and as long as he gets it from one woman after another, he'll play along with each woman for a while. If you challenge him — for instance, when you get to the point where you know that you are worthy of being deeply loved by a man who can give you total satisfaction, then you are asking him to make a real change and transformation in his personality, and he will resist you to the point of leaving you.

5) MEN ARE NOT "JUST LIKE THAT"

There are men in the world who ARE loving, kind, sweet, communicative, and open-hearted. Yes, there are! Sure, we all hear the dumb jokes and see the sitcoms that pit overly-talkative women obsessed with shopping and relationships nit-picking against silent, non-communicative men obsessed with sports and girl-watching. Stereotype humour like that is, of course, based somewhat in the real world. Some of those stereotypes about the differences between men and women are true, in general — but that doesn't mean that they DEFINE the best man for you.

6) MAKE A LIST; NO, MAKE TWO LISTS

Take a piece of lined paper and fold it in half the long way, then unfold it. You now have two columns side by side. In the left-hand column, make a list of the qualities this man had that you really loved and admired, whatever they are — his looks, his friendliness, his humour, his money, his talents, his sweet eyes — WHATEVER it was you liked. Now, in the right-hand column, make a list of everything about him that you did not like, whatever that may have been — his lies, his immaturity, his failure to come through on promises, his fear of commitment, his nasty language, whatever it was that disturbed you or turned your good moods to bad moods when you were around him. Try to make the lists about even in length. Use this list in the following spell:

7) OBTAIN THE FOLLOWING ITEMS

* A black candle
* A bottle of Cut and Clear oil
* A half-handful of salt
* A pinch of Red Pepper powder
* A white candle
* A bottle of Come to Me Oil
* Dried flower petals (Roses are best)
* Clarity, King Solomon Wisdom, or Psychic Vision Incense to clear your thoughts. Frankincense or Copal will do. (Don't get a heavy incense like Myrrh or a sweet one like Benzoin.)
* A packet of Cut and Clear Powder or Van Van Powder or a Lemon
* Scissors (optional) or a knife to cut the Lemon (optional)

Set up your space like this:

```
                    |
                    |
             incense burner
                    |
                    |
white candle        |        black candle
dressed with        |        dressed with
Come to Me Oil      |        Cut and Clear Oil
                    |
                    |
dried or fresh      your        Red Pepper
flower petals    2-column list:   in ring of salt
in a dish       good side | bad side   in a dish
                    |
                    |
```

First, lay down the line of Van Van Powder or Cut and Clear Powder or juice from a Lemon where it says "line" in the layout and then arrange everything else.

Dress the candles. Light the incense first, then the white candle, then the black candle. Center your thoughts and concentrate on clarity and wisdom. Say aloud:

Cut and clear.

Carefully crease the paper and cut or neatly tear it along the original fold, separating the two sides, and holding the "bad" side in your right hand and the "good" side in your left hand as you concentrate on your desire for clarity. When you feel the time is right, put both sides down in front of you and again say:

Cut and clear.

Then pick up the bad side of the list and say:

This is what i cast aside,
cast out, and cannot abide
and i will have no more

Now read the list of his unpleasant qualities aloud, slowly, with great feeling. When you are finished, place a small pinch of the red pepper in the middle of the paper and fold it into a packet. Hold the packet over the black candle and set it on fire. As it burns, drop it down onto the salt. When it is finished burning, grind out the ashes into the salt and red pepper, mixing them all together. Then blow out the back candle. Now pick up the list of good qualities and say:

This is what i desire,
call forth, and require,
and this will come to me

Read the list of good qualities out loud, slowly and with warm feeling. When you are finished, place three of the white flower petals in the middle of the paper and fold it into a packet. Hold the packet above the white candle flame to warm it, but do not set it on fire. Say:

Cut and clear, cut and clear,
i'll keep the things that i hold dear

Touch the packet to your heart, then place it atop the rest of the flower petals, in front of the burning white candle.

Let the white candle burn all the way to the end, then take the packet and put it away someplace among your private things where no one will find it. The next man who loves you will come to you with as many of these good qualities as he can muster and will be an all-around better person than the last one.

When cleaning up after this spell, bury all the left-over incense ashes, white wax, and unused flower petals from the white / good side in your own yard.

Carry the left overs from the black / bad side to a crossroads, or running water and throw them away so that passersby will disperse the energy they hold. The ground-up ashes, pepper, and salt should be thrown over your left shoulder as you walk away from the disposal-ground — and don't look back.

Well, i know this was NOT what you asked for, but you asked for my advice, and this was my best advice, given my understanding of the situation.

Good luck, whether you do this spell or not.

"Seven-Step Cut-and-Clear Spell" was Lucky Mojo Shop Hand-Out No. 12, from 2002. I originally wrote it as a reply to a client's request for a spell to get her man back, and it then became part of my 1995 book "Hoodoo in Theory and Practice," where it can be found on the "Cut and Clear" page at LuckyMojo.com/cutandclear.html. I learned this spell from a Black Puerto Rican worker in Harlem, New York in the 1970s and rewrote it in the style of the then-popular author Anna Riva (hence the rhymed conjuration, a specialty of hers). Once online, it became so popular that in 2009 i was induced to make a spell kit for it, containing "the whole works" — baths, herbs, incenses, oils, and all. It has helped many, myself included.

THE CRYSTAL SILENCE LEAGUE
C. Alexander

THE FOUR BRANCHES OF CRYSTAL GAZING

The crystal ball, the gazing globe, the scrying mirror, the crystal skull are all well known tools of the spiritual worker. If asked *"Why do you use a crystal?"* most psychic readers would answer, *"Why, to see the future, of course."*

Some few among you, who have studied the metaphysical properties of gems and minerals, might also add, *"A crystal can be used for healing."* And so it can be used, either to convey its own essential energies to a person or, much as a hen's egg is used, to collect negative spiritual energy and remove it from the body.

But there is much more to the crystal than divination or healing. There are, in fact, FOUR branches of crystal gazing.

1) **The Visionary Branch**
    also called Crystallomancy or Seership

2) **The Projective Branch**
    also called Silent Influence or Sending

3) **The Receptive Branch**
    also called Induction or Receiving

4) **The Transformative Branch**
    also called Crystal Magic or Healing

Let us examine these four branches in detail:

THE VISIONARY BRANCH: CRYSTALLOMANCY OR SEERSHIP

When we think of a spangled Gypsy Lady or a Mage in robe and turban gazing into a crystal ball, we are envisioning the crystal's use as a tool of divination, a tool not dissimilar to the fortune-teller's cards, bones, pendulum, or spirit board. The seer who looks deep into the crystal ball, the crystal point, the crystal skull — who sees, as if upon a stage, the enactment of things hidden deep in the past, things not of this world, and things yet to come —whose gifts of Clairvoyant Crystal Vision provide answers to all questions asked — is a gifted individual whose services will be much in demand.

THE PROJECTIVE BRANCH: SILENT INFLUENCE OR SENDING

There is a form of spiritual work which many attempt, but at which relatively few succeed. This is called Sending — the projection of silent thoughts intended to influence another's mind. In the practices of magic and religion, every spell that is cast, every prayer-light lit, every doll tied and bound, and every fervent incantation has the potential to influence another. Some concentrate on a candle's flame, some seek to enter the dreams of others, and some, who know the secret of the Crystal, employ it as a tool to focus and direct their thoughts, to heal or harm, to arouse or subdue — in short, to create an impression in the mind of someone else. Those who succeed with the use of the Sending-crystal within The Crystal Silence League may develop a singular dedication to the task of sending messages of help, strength, and healing to those who sought our aid.

THE RECEPTIVE BRANCH: INDUCTION OR RECEIVING

For every Sender, there is also a Receiver, and what has been discovered is that as we sent messages of courage, power, health, and joy to others, they do indeed receive them. Using affirmations as "codes of instruction," we induce positive change in the lives of others. We charge nothing for this service — prayer is free — and all we ask is that the receiving subjects possess and focus on a small crystal ball. With that spiritual link, we Send— and they Receive!

THE TRANSFORMATIVE BRANCH: CRYSTAL MAGIC AND HEALING

Crystals themselves have intrinsic power encoded in their lattices — and just as practitioners of Herb Magic work with the spiritual, medical, and culinary properties of herbs and roots, so do practitioners of Crystal Magic employ the innate qualities of minerals and crystals to transform or change the energetic vibrations of those who come in contact with them. It is from these premises, including the use of crystals as spiritual allies, that we develop the work of Crystal Healing and Crystal Magic.

THE RETURN OF
THE CRYSTAL SILENCE LEAGUE

The Crystal Silence League was one man's vision, and when he passed from life in the 1950s, the League too passed and was seen no more. Many years have elapsed, and now a group of metaphysical adepts who admire C. Alexander's work have revived The Crystal Silence League, not only for a new generation, but in a new way. Instead of relying on one supremely gifted sender who arose at the crack of dawn and sent his prayers to all who requested them, we choose the modern method of distributed or networked prayer: I pray for you — you pray for me. Thus we create a spiritual world wide web of prayer.

To start, you need a small crystal ball. A simple 2-inch clear glass palm ball is good to begin the work, and, if you find the gift for it, you might try other spheres — deep red to send and receive messages of love and sexuality, rich green for the codes of prosperity, aqua or blue for healing, amber or purple for stability and success, or midnight black to work by night among the dreaming millions.

We affirm messages of affirmation and hope that speak to your current issues. We in the Crystal Silence League send these messages to YOU every day, and you in turn may pray for others, increasing the circle of prayer. Log on to our web site — **CrystalSilenceLeague.org** — to leave a prayer request. Then, once a day, go into what is called "The Silence," and receive your blessings!

THE METHOD

We work together for the good of all. Dedicants of the Crystal Silence League send thoughts and prayers of joy, health, strength, love, success, and protection to all, and, in turn, receive the fruits of mutually supported prayer.

If you are able, join our world wide band when your view of the Sun is morning-fresh and again as night-time falls. As the Earth speeds and spins around the Sun, so do the hours succeed one another around this busy globe. As one mind finishes the prayer, another takes it up, always moving Westward, steadily Westward, a torch of Mind passed in a relay-race of Love and Purpose and Will. Catch the thoughts arising from your East each morning, send your thoughts to those abiding West of you each night.

Now Is the Hour: Let us work for results NOW.

MORNING

Each morning as you awaken, begin to think that you are free, strong, masterful, victorious, supreme. Clarify your brain and prepare your mind to receive messages by mental induction through the Crystal. Go into The Silence, if only briefly. The messages of affirmation will come from the East. Look where the Sun will rise, is rising, or has risen. From thence cometh hope! Receive it and believe it! Then send out your own first Mental Induction thoughts to clear your way, and to influence others throughout the day.

MID-DAY

Watch your chances on all sides throughout your day. Be alert mentally as well as bodily. Keep your business under your own hat. Keep your plans close. Be self-sufficient. If a change is suggested, make sure it means advance, then act to realize it. Do not act impulsively, but act firmly and quickly. Keep out of vain discussions, think and push your thoughts into action. Drop the deterrents of yesterday, and let go of all their tension. Stop revisiting with your thoughts the cemeteries of the past. NOW — Mid Day — holds the biggest hour of your life. Your plans and thoughts are supported by the prayers of all The Crystal Silence League!

EVENING

At night, drop all negatives, hold the positives, and see your day complete. Open a window before retiring, stand before it and take five deep breaths. As you breathe, BELIEVE that what you desire HAS COME TRUE. Think it. Summon your FAITH in it. Now spend a sacred moment in The Silence with the Crystal. Send power to the West. Support the prayers of those who need your aid in this, THEIR waking day.

Prepare yourself for sleep. Think as you go to sleep the thoughts you began when you first awoke. Unseen forces will create, produce, adjust, and reveal possibilities for you while you sleep. This is as absolute as Day and Night.

"The Crystal Silence League" was the subject of a 2011 MISC workshop at which a 32 page book and a crystal ball were given to each attendee. We have reprinted here a few opening paragraphs from the book, which is available in its entirety from Missionary Independent Spiritual Church. Be sure to visit our free prayer chain site at CrystalSilenceLeague.org.

PATRON SAINTS FOR OCCUPATIONS AND CONDITIONS
catherine yronwode

Accountants	St. Matthew	Childbirth	St. Anne
Actors	St. Genesius		St. Gerard
Adopted Children	St. Thomas More		St. Ramon
Air Travel	St. Joseph Cupertino	Children	St. Nicholas
Amputees	St. Anthony		Infant of Prague
Animals	St. Francis of Assisi	Chivalry	St. George
Architects	St. Barbara	Churches	St. Joseph
Arthritis	St. James	Civil Servants	St. Thomas More
Artillery	St. Barbara	Clergy	St. Charles
Artists	St. Luke	Comedians	St. Genesius
Astronomers	St. Dominic		St. Vitus
Athletes	St. Sebastian	Composers	St. Cecilia
Aviators	O. L. of Loreto	Cooks	St. Lawrence
	St. Joseph Cupertino		St. Martha
Bachelors	St. Christopher	Court Workers	St. Thomas More
Bail Bondsmen	St. Raymond	Cranky Children	St. Sebastian
Bakers	St. Honoratus	Dancers	St. Vitus
	St. Nicholas	Desperation	St. Jude
Bankers	St. Matthew	Dieticians	St. Martha
Barren Women	St. Anthony	Difficult Marriages	
Battle	St. Michael Archangel		St. Thomas More
Birds	St. Francis of Assisi	Dog Bite	St. Hubert
Blacksmiths	St. James	Dog Lovers	St. Roch
	St. Dunstan	Domestic Workers	St. Martha
Blindness	St. Lucy	Doubters	St. Joseph
	St. Raphael Archangel	Druggists	
Bodily Ills	O. L. of Lourdes		St. Raphael Archangel
Bookkeepers	St. Matthew	Dying	St. Barbara
Boy Scouts	St. George		St. Joseph
Breast Cancer	St. Agnes	Editors	St. John Bosco
Brewers	St. Luke	Environmentalists	
	St. Nicholas		St. Francis of Assisi
Bricklayers	St. Stephen	EMTs	St. Luke
Brides	St. Nicholas	Enemies of Religion	St. Sebastian
Broken Heart		Engineers	St. Joseph
	O. L. Maria Dolorosa	Epilepsy	St. Vitus
Builders	St. Barbara	Eye Diseases	
Businesses	St. Martin Caballero		St. Raphael Archangel
Butchers	St. Luke	Eyes	St. Lucy
	St. Anthony	Faith	St. Anthony
Cab Drivers	St. Fiacre	Falsely Accused	St. Gerard
Cabinetmakers	St. Anne		St. Raymond
Cancer Patients	St. Peregrine	Families	St. Joseph
Candlemakers	St. Ambrose	Family Harmony	St. Dymphna
Carpenters	St. Joseph	Farmers	St. Isidore
Cavalry	St. George		St. George
	St. Martin Caballero	Fathers	St. Joseph
Charitable Societies		Fever	St. Peter
	St. Vincent de Paul	Fire	St. Lawrence

Firefighters	St. Florian
Fireworks	St. Barbara
Fishermen	St. Andrew
Florists	St. Theresa
Foot Trouble	St. Peter
Gardeners	St. Sebastian
	St. Fiacre
Glass Industry	St. Luke
Glaziers	St. Mark
Goldsmiths	St. Luke
Gout Sufferers	St. Andrew
Grandmothers	St. Anne
Gravediggers	St. Anthony
Greetings	St. Valentine
Grocers	St. Michael Archangel
Hairdressers	
	St. Martin de Porres
Happy Death	St. Joseph
Hardware	St. Sebastian
Healing of Wounds	St. Rita
Hesitation	St. Joseph
HIV-AIDS	St. Lazarus of Dives
Home Builders	O. L. of Loreto
Home Sellers	St. Joseph
Homosexuals	St. Sebastian
Horsemen	St. Anne
	St. Martin Caballero
Hospital Staff	
	St. Martin de Porres
Hostages	St. Raymond
Housekeepers	St. Anne
Housewives	St. Anne
Hunters	St. Hubert
Impossible Causes	St. Jude
Incest Victims	St. Dymphna
Infertility	St. Anthony
Insanity	St. Dymphna
Invalids	St. Roch
Jewelers	St. Luke
Jurists	St. Juan Capistrano
Kidnap Victims	Niño de Atocha
Labourers	St. James
Lamp Makers	O. L. of Loreto
Lawyers	St. Genesius
	St. Thomas More
Leather Workers	
	Sts. Crispin and Crispinian
Librarians	St. Jerome
Lightning	St. Barbara

126

Locksmiths	St. Dunstan	
Loneliness	St. Rita	
Long Life	St. Peter	
Lost Articles	St. Anthony	
Lovers	St. Valentine	
	St. Raphael Archangel	
Lumbago	St. Lawrence	
Machinists	St. Hubert	
Masons	The Two Sts. John	
	St. Clement	
Medical Students		
	Dr. Hernandez	
Mental Illness	St. Dymphna	
Merchants	St. Francis of Assisi	
Messengers		
	St. Gabriel Archangel	
Midwives	St. Raymond	
Milliners	St. Catherine	
Miners	St. Barbara	
Missing Persons	St. Anthony	
	Niño de Atocha	
Missions	St. Theresa	
Monastics	St. Benedict	
Monks	St. Benedict	
Motorcyclists	O. L. Miraculous	
Musicians	St. Cecilia	
Navigators	O. L. Star of the Sea	
Needle Workers		
	St. Francis of Assisi	
Nerves	St. Dymphna	
Notaries	St. Luke	
	St. Mark	
Nurses	St. Agatha	
	St. Camillus	
Occultists	St. Cyprian	
	St. Albertus Magnus	
Organ Makers	St. Genesius	
Painters	St. Luke	
Paramedics	St. Luke	
Paratroopers		
	St. Michael Archangel	
Pawnbrokers	St. Nicholas	
Peddlers	St. Lucy	
Peril At Sea		
	St. Michael Archangel	
Pharmacists		
	Sts. Cosmos and Damian	
Philosophers		
	St. Catherine Alexandria	
Physicians	St. Luke	
	St. Raphael Archangel	
Pioneers	St. Joseph	
Plague	St. Roch	
Plasterers	St. Bartholomew	

Poets	St. David
Poison Sufferers	St. Benedict
Police Officers	
	St. Michael Archangel
Poor	St. Anthony
	St. Lawrence
Porters	St. Christopher
Postal Workers	
	St. Gabriel Archangel
Potters	St. Sebastian
Pregnant Women	St. Gerard
	St. Raymond
Printers	St. Augustine
Prisoners	St. Barbara
	St. Ramon
	Niño de Atocha
Prisoners of War	St. Leonard
Procrastinators	St. Expeditus
Public Relations	St. Paul
Radio	St. Gabriel Archangel
Race Relations	
	St. Martin de Porres
Radiologists	St. Michael Archangel
Realtors	St. Joseph
Rheumatism	St. James
Sailors	St. Brendan
	St. Christopher
	St. Nicholas
	O. L. Star of the Sea
	O. L. Caridad d. Cobre
Salesmen	St. Lucy
Shoemakers	
	Sts. Crispin & Crispinian
Scholars & Schools	
	St. Thomas Aquinas
Scientists	St. Albertus Magnus
Sculptors	St. Claude
Secretaries	St. Genesius
Seminarians	St. Charles
Servants	St. Martha
Service Women	St. Joan of Arc
Ship Builders	St. Peter
Sick	St. Camillus
	St. Michael Archangel
Sick Poor	St. Martin de Porres
Singers	St. Gregory
	St. Cecilia
Skin Disease	St. Peregrine
	St. Lazarus of Dives
Snake Bite	St. Patrick
Social Justice	St. Joseph
Soldiers	St. George
	St. Joan of Arc
	St. Sebastian

Solitary Death	
	St. Francis of Assisi
Souls in Purgatory	
	Anima Sola
	O. L. of Mt. Carmel
Speedy Results	St. Expedite
	Infant of Prague
Stationers	St. Peter
Steel Workers	St. Sebastia
Stenographers	
	St. Cassian Tangiers
Stock Brokers	St. Matthew
Stomach Trouble	St. Charles
Storms	St. Barbara
Students	St. Thomas Aquinas
Surgeons	
	Sts. Cosmos and Damian
Surgery Patients	
	Infant of Prague
Tanners	St. James
Tax Collectors	St. Matthew
Teachers	St. Gregory
Television	St. Clara
Temptation	St. Michael Archangel
Theologians	
	St. Thomas Aquinas
Throat Trouble	St. Cecilia
Tile Setters	
	The Two Sts. John
Tongue Trouble	St. Catherine
Toothache	St. Patrick
Travel Safety	St. Christopher
Truck Drivers	St. Christopher
Tuberculosis	St. Theresa
Tumor	St. Rita
Ulcers	St. Charles
Undertakers	St. Sebastian
Veterinarians	St. James
Vocalists	St. Cecilia
Watchmakers	St. Joseph
	St. Peter
Widows	St. Paula
Wisdom	St. Sophia
Women in Childbirth	St. Raymond
Workingmen	St. Joseph
Writers	St. Lucy
	St. Catherine Sienna

"Patron Saints for Occupations and Conditions" was Lucky Mojo Shop Hand-Out No. 13 in 2002. It is adapted from my 1995 book *"Hoodoo in Theory and Practice,"* online at *LuckyMojo.com/patronsaints.html.*

SANTISIMA MUERTE, MOTHER OF THE MOST HOLY DEATH
Lou Florez

VENERATIONS AND TRADITIONS OF THE DEAD IN MEXICAN CURANDISMO AND BRUJERIA

"The Mexican … is familiar with death, jokes about it, caresses it, sleeps with it, celebrates it. True, there is as much fear in his attitude as in that of others, but at least death is not hidden away: he looks at it face to face, with impatience, disdain or irony."

—Octavo Paz

The following Novena, or nine-night ritual prayer cycle, is a unique twist on Santisima Muerte's traditional ceremonies, and is used specifically to imbue a lover with desire. This ceremony centers around an offering to La Muertera (Santisima Muerte) in the form of a sugar skull which is used as a figural representation of the target. During the ritual, Santisima Muerte and the Dead are evoked as allies to the petitioner and asked to sway the heart of the lover with benediction, mercy, and desire.

It is thought that since the Dead know what it is to be alive, and specifically the need to be loved, they can stand on behalf of the living, and act as divine intercessors. Santisima Muerte, as The Mother of the Dead, is not only Death, herself, but their guardian and protector. She stands as the link between the petitioner and their named and unnamed ancestors, and when called in this form, manifests an inseparable longing.

"The living pray for the Dead, and the Dead pray for the living"

— Mexican Proverb

MEXICAN SUGAR SKULL

THE SUGAR SKULL RECIPE

- Large bowl
- Medium sugar skull mould (purchase online by searching for "Mexican Sugar Skull Mould")
- 1 1/2 teaspoons meringue powder
- 1 3/4 cup of sugar
- 1 pinch powdered red food colouring
- 1 teaspoon water
- 1 4" red candle

Thoroughly mix ingredients together, either with your hands or spoon, making sure that the colouring is evenly distributed. Next, gently sprinkle the teaspoon of water throughout the bowl, and mix everything together until the contents have the consistency of wet beach sand. You will know when the mixture is ready to mould when you leave fingerprints after squeezing the sugar in your hand.

ROYAL ICING RECIPE

- 2 lbs. powdered sugar
- 1/2 cup meringue powder
- 2/3 cup water
- Powdered food colouring

Beat with an electric mixer until icing peaks (about 9 minutes). Mix the icing with the colourant in disposable cups, then fill a pastry bag, or a makeshift pastry bag with the mixture, and you are ready to decorate. (To make a pastry bag, use a sandwich bag with a corner cut off.) If this is your first time using royal icing, you ought to know that it is a cement type icing used for making ginger bread houses. It is not known for its taste, but it dries strong and hard.

THE MOULD

Mound sugar into the mould and pack the mixture firmly, making sure every inch of the mould is filled. Using a butter knife, straight edge, or cardboard square, scrape off the sugar until the back is completely flat. Place a stiff cardboard square (6" x 4") over the mould and invert immediately. Lift the mould off carefully, making sure that the mould does not scrape the sides. (Tip: If sugar mixture sticks to the sides or does not fall out completely, it is too wet. If this happens, re-mix with a tablespoon of sugar.) Hand wash and dry your mould after every fifth skull to avoid sticking or clumping.

Let the sugar skull sit for five minutes, and in the meantime prepare your candle with a thick coating of red, royal icing at the base. When you are ready, gently insert the base of the candle approximately two inches into the very center of the skull's forehead. You will notice that some of the features might have shifted, and depending on your aesthetics, you may correct these as you see fit.

The moulded sugar skulls need to air-dry on their cardboard squares for approximately one day. Do not make sugar skulls on a rainy or high humidity day, because they will not turn out. When your skull is completely dry, you should be able to pick it up in your hand without it crumbling. While it may seem fragile, it is actually pretty sturdy and should be ready to scoop out and load.

INGREDIENTS: LOAD

- Melon baller or small scoop
- Personal concern of target
- Hibiscus flowers, dried
- Myrrh resin, crumbled
- Catnip herb, dried
- Fennel seeds, dried
- 1 Abrus Precatorius "Red Bean"
- Santisima Muerte, Rose, and Chuparrosa Oils,
- Red Royal Icing

SCOOPING AND LOADING

With your melon baller, gently scoop out a hole the diameter of a quarter. Load your skull with the personal concern of the target individual. If you do not have an individual in mind, write a petition to Santisima Muerte listing the five qualities you are looking for in a lover. One at a time, take each of the "load" ingredients listed above and load the skull while praying:

"Spirit, Body and Soul of [Name], come to me [Your Name or Client's Name] because I summon you, I dominate you, I seduce you, [Name]. Let your thoughts be only of me alone until you surrender and humiliate yourself at my feet."

As each ingredient is loaded, sprinkle three drops of the oil mix while reciting the Ejaculatory Prayer:

"Death, dear to my heart, don't abandon me, protect me, and don't let [Name] have one moment of peace; keep him restless and bothered with the thought of me always."

Apply a layer of red royal icing evenly across the bottom of the skull. Turn the skull upside down over a coffee cup or mason jar and let dry for 15 minutes.

DECORATION

There are many ways to decorate your skull, so use your intuition. You can use coloured feathers, beads, sequins, glitter, coloured royal icing, and coloured foils to bring your offering skull to life!

NOVENA TO LA SANTISIMA MUERTE

The Novena starts on a Sunday at Midnight and lasts for about one hour. You will need the following:

- An incense burner
- Charcoal
- Marigold flowers, dried
- Myrrh resin, crumbled
- Rose petals, dried
- The fixed and loaded sugar skull
- The 3-oil mixture used above
- A depiction of Santisima Muerte
- Any offerings you want to present
- Eight 4" red candles (these are held in reserve and are to be anointed with the Santisima Muerte, Rose, and Chuparrosa Oil mixture and burned on the skull from nights 2-9, after the first candle goes out on night 1)

As each night begins, burn Marigold, Myrrh, and Rose on the charcoal while passing the sugar skull through the smoke, saying:

"Spirit, Body and Soul of [Name], come to me [Your Name or Client's Name], because I summon you, I dominate you, I seduce you, [Name], Let your thoughts be only of me alone until you surrender and humiliate at my feet."

Place the skull on top of a plate or burning container in front of the depiction of Santisima Muerte, and use the oil to anoint the candle from base to the wick, reciting the Ejaculatory Prayer

"Death, dear to my heart, don't abandon me, protect me, and don't let [Name] have one moment of peace; keep him restless and bothered with the thought of me always."

Next anoint the eyes while saying:

"Great Mother of Death, let [Name]'s eyes see only and want only me."

Then anoint the ears while saying:

"Most Holy Death, make [Name]'s ears hear only my voice;" and finally anoint the mouth saying, *"Sainted Death, Mother of Us All, make [Name]'s tongue want for my taste."*

Now the Novena officially begins with the presentation of any offerings given to the depiction of La Muertera.

Light the candle on the skull, and recite the prayer for the night. On nights 2-9, use a fresh candle on the skull each night,

FIRST DAY: "Most Holy Death, The favours that you have to grant me: Make me overcome all difficulties so that for me nothing is impossible, no obstacles, barriers,no enemies, that no one does me any harm, that everyone is my friend and that I am victorious in all my dealings and things I do; May my house be filled with all the good virtues of your protection." (Three Our Fathers)

SECOND DAY: "Death Saint, my great treasure, never go away from me at any time: You ate bread and gave me bread, and as you are the powerful owner of the dark mansion of life and Empress of darkness, I want you to grant me the favour that [Name] is at my feet humiliated and repentant and that he never leaves my side when I need him, and that you make me get what was promised to me." (Three Our Fathers)

THIRD DAY: "Jesus Christ Conqueror who on the cross was conquered, conquer [Name] that he is overcome by me. In the name of God, you are a ferocious animal; you will come back to me as a tame sheep, mild as the Rosemary flower. Adored Death, I implore you earnestly that with this titanic force that God gave you, instill in [Name]'s heart that he has eyes for no one but me, and that I am his everything, that you grant me this which I ask, having great faith in this Novena, and I light a candle every Tuesday of every week at twelve midnight." (Three Our Fathers)

FOURTH DAY: "Dear Death: I ask you with all my heart, that as God made you Immortal, and the powerful owner and Queen of the Darkness Unknown hereafter, that with your great powers, which you have over all mortals, make [Name] unable to eat at any table or sit in any chair and grant that he has no peace; I wish that he becomes obliged to be humble and devoted at my feet and that he never again goes away from me." (Three Our Fathers)

FIFTH DAY: "Glorious and Powerful Death, taking advantage of your kindness, as my protector and owner, I ask this favour: As the invincible madam that you are, I beg that you make [Name] so that he can't enjoy strolling around, so that he can't walk or eat with other women, or sleep unless he's at my side. Grant that his thoughts are about me only, by his own choice, and that he gives me the happiness of having all of his love. " (Three Our Fathers)

SIXTH DAY: Oh Sovereign Lady! In that the Holy Trinity in our Eternal Father has blinded the life of all mortals to the fact that you will come to everyone sooner or later, whether rich or poor or in youth, who does to us all the same, old, young, child; we enter your domain of death when God decrees. I implore you that [Name] is much in love with me, not just for physical beauty, but also for my soul, and that he comes to me faithful, submissive, kneeling at my feet." (Three Our Fathers)

SEVENTH DAY: "Liberate me from all evil, and with the titanic power with which God endowed you, make it so that we enjoy eternal heavenly nightless days. Protector and owner: I beg you to grant me the favours I request in these prayers. I have made this petition." (Three Our Fathers)

EIGHTH DAY: "Miraculous and Majestic Death: I ask that with your immense power you return my beloved, [Name]. Don't let him for one minute be sociable or tranquil with anyone he comes across; neither with friends nor with women may he be at ease. Grant that while sleeping, he thinks of me, and that he listens to the words I say to you in his sleep, and that he does what I ask." (Three Our Fathers)

NINTH DAY: "Blessed Protector Death: By the virtues that God gave you I ask that you free me from all evil, danger, and sickness and that instead you give me LUCK, HEALTH, HAPPINESS AND MONEY, that you give me friends and freedom from my enemies, also making [Name] come before me, humbled to ask my forgiveness, humble as a sheep, keeping his promises and always loving and submissive." (Three Our Fathers)

These prayers to Santa Muerte are quoted from LuckyMojo.com/santisimamuerte.html. They match the copies given to me from my elders, and the Mexican Novena booklet to Santisima Muerte.

DEPLOYMENT OF THE SKULL

Once the Novena is complete, you can deploy the skull by either hiding it in a gift that is given to the target or by burying it on their premises. Following the initial prayer cycle, an offertory candle to Santisima Muerte is given "every Tuesday of every week at twelve midnight" in order to continually feed the spell, and to give light to the Dead so they can act on your behalf.

"Santisima Muerte" was distributed at Lou Florez's 2012 workshop. A member of both AIRR and Hoodoo Psychics, Lou can also be contacted via LouFlorez.com.

WALKING THE LABYRINTH
Elvyra Curcuruto-Love

WHAT IS A LABYRINTH?

A labyrinth is a unicursal design drawn within a bounded space. A single route leads in to the center and back out again. A labyrinth is not a maze — that is, it is not a figure with more than one entrance, with branching paths, or with a confusing design.

The oldest and most universal labyrinth is a spiral, a pattern seen in all cultures and on most continents, and one designed to work actively with the life force. More complex labyrinths come in different shapes and with different numbers of circuits. These are some of the meanings ascribed to labyrinths, according to the number of circuits they have:

- 3 Circuits: Celestial, universal consciousness
- 4 Circuits: Temporal, earth-based
- 7 Circuits: Rites of passage as well as healing
- 11 Circuits: Mysticism and psychism
- 12 Circuits: Magical, masculine consciousness
- 13 Circuits: Intuitive, feminine consciousness

THE CLASSICAL LABYRINTH

The Classical labyrinth, also known as the 7-Circuit or Cretan labyrinth, is found all over Europe and India in in ancient as well as modern settings. Ancient labyrinths were constructed near shorelines, over running water, and on ley lines, and were used for various rites and spells. This is the type of labyrinth we will be walking today.

THE MEDIEVAL LABYRINTH

During the Medieval period, when pilgrimages to the Holy Land became dangerous, a decision was made to create an alternative, which brought forth the placement of labyrinths in the floors of European cathedrals. Walking these labyrinths was intended to convey the benefits of an actual, physical pilgrimage.

Most of the Medieval cathedral labyrinth designs have four sections of turns within a formal circular or square enclosing boundary. The use of this quadratic layout is said to relate to the cross of crucifixion, the four parts of the Mass, the four elements, the four cardinal directions, the four seasons, and the four parts of the brain.

WALKING THE LABYRINTH AS A RITUAL

The creation of the Medieval labyrinth as a form of pilgrimage has led to the contemporary use of labyrinths of varied designs, including Classical labyrinths, for spiritual journeying.

Energetically the Classical labyrinth can be seen as a tool of balance as well as challenge. It balances the right and left hemispheres of the brain but challenges our abilities to stay focused on the path and not lose our way.

The 7-circuit labyrinth can be likened to the seven bodily chakras of Hindu philosophy, out of which comes healing of the mind, body, and spirit. It also connects to our use of the seven notes of the musical scale and thus it is said to create the music of the spheres. The circuits are numbered 3, 2, 1, 4 (going into the center) and 7, 6, 5, 8 (going back out). The notes, in the key of C, would be as follows: 3 (E), 2 (D),1 (C), 4 (F) and 7 (B), 6 (A), 5 (G), 8 (C).

Ritual tools, such as drums, rattles, and flutes assist to create the sacred space. A drumbeat is the heartbeat of the Earth Mother and works to synchronize our heartbeat to Hers.

The labyrinth's turns symbolize changes and evolution. The journey to the center is a journey to selfhood, a quest of the soul to meet the Divine Mother / Father / All There Is. It is a mystical experience; walked, traversed, and explored for centuries. Many have written about it in personal as well as historical terms and still more have experienced it. It is a pilgrimage.

As you prepare to enter the labyrinth, remove watches, cell phones, and any other electronic devices, excluding any internal or necessary medical or health devices. Quiet your mind and listen to the drumbeat. In all ritual there is a focus, an intent, so internally state the focus of your intention or purpose for entering the labyrinth. Enter the labyrinth trusting your instincts as you move inward, physically and internally. Releasing negativity, "letting go and letting God/dess" — this is the cleansing process.

Be fully present as you walk the labyrinth. If you feel yourself wander mentally or emotionally, listen to the drumbeat to come back to yourself and the present moment.

Walk at your own pace and if anxiety comes up, possibly as you make the turns, breath deeply, still your mind, and focus once again on your breathing, the drumbeat, and the Now. This may be a point where you are grappling with having lost your way spiritually, physically, mentally, or emotionally.

Just before you step into the center of the labyrinth, the energies (electrically) will drop, challenging you to take the last step to walk over the threshold into the realm of Spirit. This is the point in the ritual where an initiation occurs.

When you reach the center, you reach the Divine. In ancient times, a female priestess acted as the conduit from the Divine Mother / Father / All There Is to the initiates or ritual participants, bestowing a gift upon each of them, possibly a word, a phrase, a physical item, or a healing touch.

You will receive a gift, and upon accepting it, your journey into the deep culminates. After resting for a moment, you start the journey back out, retracing your steps.

As you meet others along the path, there is an unspoken acknowledgement that we are all on this journey of selfhood. Watch how you move past others, as this too is an example of how you move out in the external world.

Some labyrinth rituals are designed to lead deep into your fears and shadow side and you will meet the Dark Mother. Other rituals, like the one we are experiencing today, open the way to the Bright Mother.

A LABYRINTH SPELL TO CLEANSE OR CHARGE AN ITEM

The labyrinth is a multi-faceted tool. In addition to landscape labyrinths, which are large enough to walk, it can be made in a smaller version, called a finger labyrinth, which is worked by tracing your finger over the paths for meditation and for the enactment of magical spells, both light and dark.

Create a finger labyrinth by copying a labyrinth onto an 8 ½ x 11 piece of paper. Put an item in the center and leave over night. This will cleanse the item. To charge the item with spiritual energy, leave it in the center for another night. Working in this way by the phases of the Moon is also very powerful.

"Walking the Labyrinth" was distributed at Elvyra Curcuruto-Love's and Dr. Johannes Gårdbäck's 2013 workshop, during which participants walked The Red Brick Labyrinth at Lucky Mojo. Elvyra is a member of AIRR and can also be contacted via her own Elvyra.com web site.

The Red Brick Labyrinth was inaugurated on May 4, 2013 — World Labyrinth Day — and was built under the direction of Dr. Lea Goode-Harris of the Santa Rosa Labyrinth Foundation, at SRLabyrinthFoundation.com, who also kindly suppled the illustrations.

THE LABYRINTH IN OLD SWEDISH TROLLDOM
Dr. Johannes Gårdbäck

SCANDINAVIAN LABYRINTHS

The oldest known labyrinths are found in Greece and Italy, dating back to around 1200 BCE. They are found, often carved in stone, along the north and westward migration routes of the ancient Celts, especially in areas along the Mediterranean and North Atlantic seas. A common name for them is "Cretan" labyrinths, after the island of Crete, but although some are prehistoric and some are modern, current scholars prefer to call them Classical labyrinths, which places them within the period known as Classical antiquity.

Those who identify Classical labyrinths as "Cretan," and envision them as a Mediterranean landscape feature are often surprised to learn that the far-Northern Scandinavian nation of Sweden has approximately 280 landscape labyrinths along its far stretched coastline, and that similar labyrinths are also found in Finland, Iceland, and various other European coastal countries. As with the labyrinths of Greece and Italy, these ancient Scandinavian labyrinths are most common along the shoreline, where they can be found erected as features in the landscape, engraved onto furniture and working tools, carved in churches, and stamped onto medals.

In Scandinavian folklore and in the folk magic practice called Trolldom, the coastal positioning of labyrinths is related to their employment in community-benefitting rites or spells to ensure good weather for fishermen and for fish-catching magic. However, in addition to this primary magical use, the labyrinth has been, and still is, employed to give strength to various spells and to facilitate other kinds of magical work.

LANDSCAPE LABYRINTHS

THE CASTLE OF TROY

In Sweden the labyrinth is also known as the Trojeborg — "Castle of Troy" — and during the Middle Ages it was associated with various games, all relating to reaching the maiden in the middle of the labyrinth. It may seem odd to some, but the myth of Troy is a founding pillar in many European folkloric legends, not only those of Greek mythology.

LABYRINTHS AND THE FESTIVALS OF SPRING

For the common people, labyrinths have been associated with yearly feasts and celebrations, especially those festivals which are held after Easter and before Midsummer.

In Sweden, these celebrations include:

The Feast of the Holy Trinity: Also known as Trinity Sunday, this Christian holiday is celebrated on the Sunday after Pentecost (which itself falls fifty days after Easter), meaning that it is an annual moveable feast that occurs approximately eight weeks after Easter.

The Feast of Valborg: Also known as Walpurgis Night, this annual Spring festival of wild revelry is celebrated with the lighting of bonfires on the night of April 30. Its name derives from Saint Walpurga, an 8th century English Christian missionary to the Frankish Empire, but despite her sanctity, the festival is Pagan.

May Day: Also known as Beltane, this day-time festival takes place on May 1, immediately following the night-time Feast of Valborg. It is an ancient annual celebration with European Pagan roots that is very deeply associated with the fertility of both the land and its inhabitants.

Historically, the use of the landscape labyrinth at these important Spring festivals coincided with similar landscape-oriented ritual practices, such as well-drinking (journeying to sacred wells to drink the conferred blessings of the water), grove visiting (walking through sacred wooded groves and forested areas), and bonfire lighting (lighting, dancing, and running through or around large bonfires).

The walking or running of the labyrinth in the Spring of the year indicates that it has long been associated with sexual rituals and rites of fertility. The varied Medieval games of the Castle of Troy, in which a maiden stands in the center of the labyrinth, and the goal is to reach and win her hand, also demonstrate a continuation of these ancient sex-magical practices, one that extended well past the prehistoric and Classical eras and into Christian times, albeit in modified form.

LABYRINTHS AS SPIRIT TRAPS

LANDSCAPE LABYRINTH SPIRIT TRAPS

As noted above, the building of landscape labyrinths along the coastal shores in Scandinavia relates to their use in rituals or spells to ensure good weather for fishermen and for fish-catching magic. When a landscape labyrinth is used in this manner, it is almost always for the purpose of catching the spirit of the winds, binding fish near to the shore, or in order to attract spirits into the labyrinth to give power to one's spells.

TRAPPING THE WIND OF THE NORTH-WEST

"Catching the spirit of the winds" is a literal term describing the entrapment of spiritual entities. It is not the same as the modern Christian and New Age concept of the labyrinth as a tool that supports "spirit journeying" or "spirit pilgrimages." In this ancient Scandinavian practice, the labyrinth functions like a Jewish demon bowl, Arabic djinn-bowl, or English witch-bottle; the spirit enters and is bound within. When a landscape labyrinth is used to entrap the wind, the spirit that is most often talked about is the wind of the North-West — the most dangerous wind for any traveler of the seas. This concept can be extended to conjure any North-Western oriented malady, considering the labyrinth as a yearly wheel or using astrological magical concepts of position.

CROSSING THE LINES

The most common way to catch the spirits of bad weather, or to bind fish or anything else, is to walk into the labyrinth, focusing on the purpose and intent at hand and taking great care not to step outside the lines. Upon reaching the center. the practitioner walks straight out, crossing all the lines of the labyrinth. This cannot be done by the spirits and thus they are captured inside the labyrinth. The procedure is usually repeated a specific number of times in a row: If the labyrinth is built with seven circuits, it is walked and exited seven times; if it is built with eleven circuits, it is walked and exited eleven times.

LABYRINTHS AS AMULETS OR ON TOOLS

When the labyrinth is carved on a tool or worn around the neck as an amulet, it is almost always for protective reasons. The idea is that spirits can be caught and the power of spells can be cached within in the labyrinth.

CHALK FINGER-LABYRINTH SPIRIT TRAPS

In modern practice hand-size finger labyrinths are occasionally found. They may be made out of clay or on a round wooden surface painted black. On the surface a labyrinth is drawn with chalk to create a binding spell or spirit trap. The finger is drawn along the path of the labyrinth while ordering the spirit to enter and to be bound within it. The finger is lifted, leaving the spirit within, and the labyrinth is then wiped off the black disk, using a wet cloth. The cloth, or the water that can be squeezed from the cloth, is disposed of at a nearby three-way or Y crossroad or in a cemetery by tossing it over the left shoulder and taking care not to look back when going home.

LABYRINTHS AND THE SUN-CULT

In recent years, European Pagans have incorporated the use of the landscape labyrinth in a form of Sun cult. In this mythos, it is said that the Sun has been captured by Winter inside the labyrinth and it is to be ceremonially found and released in Spring, thus restoring the power of the Sun and the life giving, nurturing powers of fertility.

This idea combines two pre-existing Scandinavian labyrinth concepts: the labyrinth as an adjunct to the fertility rites of Spring (with a substitution of the life-giving Sun for the maiden in the Castle of Troy) and the use of labyrinths as spirit-traps (with the false imprisonment of the Sun substituted for the intentional imprisonment of the evil spirit of the North-West wind).

FORTUNE TELLING IN LABYRINTHS

The art of magical fortune telling or "spaedom," in which the practitioner declares and directs the future and fortune of his intended target, has also commonly taken place in the center of a labyrinth, especially among the Laplanders and the Sami people of Sweden, Norway, Finland, and Russia. Like so many other things in magic, it was usually said that such a labyrinth loses its powers if it becomes known to others. So keeping your labyrinth a secret may well be a good idea.

"The Labyrinth in Old Swedish Trolldom" was distributed at Dr. Johannes Gårdbäck's and Elvyra Curcuruto-Love's 2013 workshop, inaugurating The Red Brick Labyrinth. Dr. Johannes is a member of AIRR and Hoodoo Psychics and he can be contacted for readings and spell-casting services at his web site, TheRootDoctor.se.

HIGH-TECH HOODOO
Kast Excelsior

SYMPATHETIC MAGIC IN CONJURE

The fundamental principles of sympathetic magic are present throughout the workings of conjure. By taking a closer look at foundational aspects of sympathetic magic, we can see the tried and true spiritual techniques that conjure has inherited from ancient practices and, thereby, extrapolate a forecast of how those methods can and will be authentically applied in both modern and futuristic environments.

These basic principles reveal the underlying mechanics that allow information, effects, and conditions to be received and sent remotely through divination, conjuration, and spell-work. Take a special note of how the laws of sympathetic magic are supported by the current, mainstream sciences of quantum mechanics theory.

THE LAW OF LIKENESS

This law or principle of magic is the belief that any two things that share a likeness (even if only through symbolic representation) are intimately connected and that, furthermore, they will become existential reflections of each other, so that effects produced upon one can be mirrored in the other. The law of likeness is the principle upon which hoodoo doll-baby magic is founded, with conditions imposed upon the doll being expected to produce similar conditions in the life of the person whom the doll resembles. This principle is also at the foundation of the herbal "Doctrine of Signatures," a concept whereby plants that resemble certain body-parts may be called upon to medically, spiritually, or magically affect those body parts.

THE LAW OF CONTAGION

This law of magic is defined as the belief that any two things that have had contact with each other will retain a subtle energetic "bridge" or link, regardless of current physical distance and intentionally conceived conditions can be sent from one end of the link to manifest at the other end. It is this principle of "contagion" that has empowered the development and refinement of the use of bodily personal concerns in hoodoo, including foot-tracks, blood, hair, sweat, saliva, soiled clothing, and nail clippings.

SOME ELEMENTS OF MODERN QUANTUM MECHANICS THEORY

Quantum Superposition and Complementarity state that all possible outcomes of a particular manifestation exist simultaneously; it is measurement and observation that will actually steer a distinct manifestation to move into our experience. Non-locality states that any two particles that have ever been in contact with each other will continue to be able to instantaneously effect one another at a distance, regardless of proximity in space-time.

INTEGRATING NEW DEVELOPMENTS OF MODERN LIFESTYLES

Although hoodoo bears ancient traces and it developed in rural areas of the country, it has historically made very practical use of new tools and technologies as they have emerged into our day-to-day lives. Many of the items we take for granted as common to the practice of conjure were, at one time, considered to be new developments, and hoodoo practitioners have always been forward-thinking and practical in the adoption of new technologies.

From the 19th century advent of photography, cheap colour printing, and household freezers to the 20th century mass manufacture and distribution of packaged grocery goods and cosmetics, the practice of conjure has seamlessly woven the elements of modern living into practical magical tools without ever abandoning its pre-industrial roots in herb usage and hand-crafted tools.

THE CYBER ELEMENT AND ALPHANUMERIC DIGITAL CONCERNS

From the 1980s to the 2000s, modern global culture made a monumental shift of focus into computer-related realms. Cyber-space has evolved into a complex, interactive environment and a full-blown element of modern life. Two strong themes in this environment are digitization and personalization. This generates a plethora of personal concerns to be extracted from the alphanumeric and digital environments that represent individual people, places, businesses, groups, and institutions.

SOURCES OF DIGITAL PERSONAL CONCERNS

Sources of personal cyber-concerns include digital Images (photos, scanned/saved images, online screen shots), social media avatars and photos, URLs and screen savers, company logos, voicemails and sound memos, Google satellite and street-view location shots, drivers license and identification card numbers, vehicle license plate numbers, bank account and routing numbers, IP addresses, emails, circular astrological natal charts (as petition papers), custom sound-byte jewelry.

METHODS OF MAGICAL TRANSMISSION

Modern tools and devices, both digital-electronic and non-digital, can be used to transmit conditions through the subtle application of the traditional ingredients of conjure, such as herbs, roots, incense, oils, powders, and washes. Examples include cellular phones and smart phones, desktop and laptop computers and tablets, toy dolls and posable human figures, and home decor items such as lamps, picture frames, sculpture, and statuary.

PROGRAMMER CONJURE AND MULTI-MEDIA SPELL-WORK

More advanced techniques of high-tech hoodoo are available at the level of programming through the language of computer code or with multi-media editing applications. But it isn't mandatory that you become a master programmer or software editor. There are many products and services that are free or of little cost that will give you the basic abilities to manipulate typesetting, artwork, still photography, audio files, and video recording, and if you choose not to develop your personal skills with these programs, you can commission someone to assist you in the creation of multi-media spells. For example, several members of the Association of Independent Readers and Rootworkers are also professionally skilled in typography, graphic design, and audio-video editing and have the knowledge and power to help construct your digitally edited conjurations.

During this workshop, you will receive a disc collection of images that can be used in your personal conjure work. Some are of suitable size for creating labels for glass-encased candles, others incorporate scriptural prayers, and some consist of graphics that can be composited with your selected photographs of target individuals to craft personalized images for use in mojo hands, petition packets, or container spells.

SIGILS AND HYPER-SIGILS

In hoodoo, we are familiar with the magical use of sigils. From the success sigil ($$¢¢$$) and the Solomonic seals to simple icons of hearts, dice, eyes, four-leaf clovers, and horseshoes, American conjure practitioners have always worked with visual symbols.

The British occultist and artist Austin Osman Spare (1886-1956) is credited with the development of another method of sigilization that condenses the letters of a written spell or petition sentence into a symbol which can then be used in a magical work. For example, it may be placed in a photo-image, written on a paper, inscribed into a wax candle, drawn on a glass-encased vigil candle, or flashed in a video spell.

A hyper-sigil expands the idea of a sigil into more complex forms of multi-media expression. The term "hyper-sigil" is said to have been coined by the Scottish occultist and comic book writer Grant Morrison, although the concept has been utilized in previous generations. The idea is to create an artistic expression through a narrative (a comic, a book or short story, a painting, a play, a song, a movie or video) as a condensed and encoded spell. Members of AIRR have already produced hyper-sigilized video spells, uploaded them to Youtube, posted the links on their Facebook profile pages, and thus enticed the targets of the spells (and other passers-by) to click and view.

REMEMBERING YOUR ROOTS

It's a positive and empowering thing to come full-circle. As we've seen, the living essence within hoodoo has always actively kept up with the times, while never losing its roots, both literal and figurative. With the new tools and approaches now at your fingertips through high-tech hoodoo, you can extend the reach of your conjure practice into the cyber realms of multi-media manipulation, while continuing to support your work on a foundation of traditional folkloric methods that incorporate the tried and true powers of the spirits of our Ancestors, Animals, Herbs, and Roots.

"High-Tech Hoodoo" was distributed with "Hoodoo Jukebox," a two-CD set of audio and graphic files, at the 2013 MISC workshops. The CD set, edited by Kast Excelsior and Professor Ames, with contributions from members of AIRR, is available for separate purchase through Lucky Mojo. Kast Excelsior is a member of AIRR and can also be contacted via ConjureHaus.com; Professor Ames is a member of AIRR and is also available at Skullbone-Emporium.com.